IT HAPPENED IN MIAMI

WORKS OF ORAL HISTORY BY THE FROMMERS

It Happened in the Catskills

It Happened in Brooklyn

Growing Up Jewish in America

It Happened on Broadway

It Happened in Manhattan

It Happened in Miami, the Magic City

IT HAPPENED IN MIAMI

THE MAGIC CITY

AN ORAL HISTORY

MYRNA KATZ FROMMER AND HARVEY FROMMER

TAYLOR TRADE PUBLISHING
Lanham • New York • Boulder • London

Published by Taylor Trade Publishing
An imprint of The Rowman & Littlefield Publishing Group, Inc.
4501 Forbes Boulevard, Suite 200, Lanham, Maryland 20706
www.rowman.com

Unit A, Whitacre Mews, 26-34 Stannary Street, London SE11 4AB, United Kingdom

Distributed by NATIONAL BOOK NETWORK

British Library Cataloguing in Publication Information Available

Library of Congress Cataloging-in-Publication Data

Frommer, Myrna.
It happened in Miami, the Magic City : an oral history / Myrna Katz Frommer and Harvey Frommer.
pages cm
Includes index.
ISBN 978-1-58979-950-9 (hardcover : alk. paper) — ISBN 978-1-58979-951-6 (electronic)
1. Miami (Fla.)—Social life and customs—20th century. 2. Miami (Fla.)—Biography. 3. Interviews—Florida—Miami. 4. Oral history. I. Frommer, Harvey. II. Title.
F319.M6F75 2015
975.9'381—dc23
2015024678

∞™ The paper used in this publication meets the minimum requirements of American National Standard for Information Sciences—Permanence of Paper for Printed Library Materials, ANSI/NISO Z39.48-1992.

Printed in the United States of America

For our family

I started out to go to Cuba
Soon I was in Miami Beach
That's not so very far from Cuba
But oh what a rumba they teach
—"The Miami Beach Rumba," Irving Fields

Contents

Introduction ix

Voices xi

Prologue 1

1 Preservation of Art Deco: An Overnight Twenty-Five-Year Success 3

2 Everything Started Happening in the Eighties 16

3 Along Ocean Drive: The News Café, the Versace Story, and the Return of the Models 27

4 Dancing Up a Storm at Mango's 34

5 It's Not All about Ocean Drive: What Happened on Lincoln Road 42

6 Postwar Glamour 49

7 Morris Lapidus: Architect of Joy 60

8 Early Days 67

9 Still the Segregated South 81

10 A Little beyond the Law 97

11 Ali and the Fifth Street Gym 101

12 Looking through a Lens of Culture 112

CONTENTS

13 A Beautiful Friendship: Jeff Lehman and The Betsy Hotel 135

14 The Jewish Presence 145

15 The Cuban Impact 157

16 Mini Memoirs 171

Michael Aller 171
Marvin Rey Baumel 172
Kimberly Falconer 176
Roberson de Franc 178
Roberto Juarez 179
Helen Kaplan 181
Joe Kaplan 183
Mitchell Kaplan 184
Joseph Krutel 186
Sue Levenberg 191
Diego Lowenstein 193
Luisita Pacheco 196
Harold Rosen 198
Philip Smith 200
John Turchin 206
Robert Zuckerman 209
David Wallack 212

Epilogue 215

Acknowledgments 224

Index 225

About the Authors 238

Introduction

One of the ways in which oral history works best is in preserving a world that soon may be no more. A sense of immediacy, of urgency, propels the preservation of stories that will disappear with the generation that has lived and experienced them.

This much was realized in our first work in the genre, *It Happened in the Catskills* (Harcourt Brace, 1991). By capturing the memories of a hundred Borscht Belt participants and observers, we were able to produce an affectionate, poignant, and socially significant record of a fabulous world that has since ceased to exist.

Now, as we move into our second quarter century of writing oral histories, *It Happened in Miami, the Magic City* continues in this vein. At the same time it comes up to a dynamic present, for the story of Miami can hardly be said to be over. Built on a confluence of events occurring over the course of the twentieth century and into the twenty-first, the City of Miami and Miami Beach—collectively Greater Miami—claim an internationally recognizable identity from having become a burgeoning neo-metropolis, a brilliant center of finance and culture, and host to Art Basel, the international extravaganza of modern art.

Problems of depressed real estate values, racial tensions, drugs, and crime seem to belong to a forgotten past as new skyscrapers create ever-changing skylines. Properties on the order of the Mandarin Inn, the Four Seasons, the Viceroy Icon complex, and the Epic Hotel welcome high-end companies and leisure travelers while the world's largest collection of cruise ships docks at the Port of Miami.

All of this will, of necessity, be part of the story *It Happened in Miami, the Magic City* will tell. But at its heart will be recollections of a flamboyant past centering largely around three historic themes.

First, the era when Miami Beach became a popular destination for New York Jews who, already half in love with the Latin beat they ingested along with the borscht in Catskill hotels, stamped their presence on what until recently had been a highly restricted millionaires' enclave and not too long before that, a swampy island in the bay.

Second, the massive influx of Cubans in the wake of Castro's takeover of their island home who made of Miami a "Little Havana" and Spanish its preeminent language.

Third, the revival of South Beach and its deteriorating and abandoned Art Deco hotels spurring the transformation of decaying blocks of "old folks' homes" into a resort locale evocative of St. Tropez.

How this came to be over the course of roughly three-quarters of a century is recalled, reimagined, and re-created in these pages through the reminiscences of nearly seventy individuals—some well known, others not so well known—their memories forming the content of this narrative, their accounts enhanced by stunning visuals, both vintage and contemporary, from Art Deco palaces to postwar mid-century modern (MiMo) fantasies to reimagined turn-of-this-century eclectic combinations—in short, the oft-imitated but still singular Miami style.

Having gone through the process of learning what happened in Miami from the post–World War II period well into the second decade of the twenty-first century from those who have lived it, we are reminded of the architect Le Corbusier's comment when he concluded his work on the United Nations complex. "New York is not a completed city," he said. "It is a city in the process of becoming. Today it belongs to the world."

It seems Miami can make the same claim. From the beach to downtown, from Coral Gables to Coconut Grove, from the causeways to the keys, a multitude of impressions merges into a collective image while the rhythm and the beat of Irving Fields's Miami Beach rumba go on.

Voices

MICHAEL ALLER, aka Mr. Miami Beach and the Sultan of Smooze, is the tourism and convention coordinator for Miami Beach.

JO ANN ARNOWITZ is executive director and chief curator of the Jewish Museum of Florida-FIU with more than thirty-five years of experience in the museum field.

GEORGIANA AYERS is a community activist in the Miami area known to one and all as Spitfire.

MARVIN REY BAUMEL is a longtime Miami resident. A Latin bandleader in the 1950s and 1960s, he has also been a successful conference speaker for nearly half a century.

SETH H. BRAMSON, adjunct professor of history and historian in residence at Barry University, has earned the reputation as the country's leading Greater Miami historian.

HOWARD BRAYER, a docent for the Jewish Museum of Florida and volunteer tour guide, conducts a popular Jewish food walking tour.

VOICES

DEBORAH BRIGGS is vice president for marketing, philanthropy, and programs at The Betsy Hotel in South Beach. Since 2008, she has been executive director of the PG Family Foundation.

SUE BRUSTMAN in 1985 created her public relations firm, which specializes in things culinary. Ahead of the curve, she saw the direction Miami Beach was heading and wound up representing some of the top restaurants and chefs as well as key figures such as Tony Goldman.

ANN BROAD BUSSELL has lived in Miami since 1940. A former teacher in the Miami-Dade County system and at Barry University, she is the daughter of the late Shepard Broad, a leading developer and attorney and founder of the American Savings and Loan Association of Florida.

DIANE WOOLFE CAMBER became director/chief curator of the Bass Museum of Art in 1980. For the next twenty-seven years she worked to propel the institution into its role as a major Miami cultural institution and was active in historic preservation work including the renovation of the Art Deco District.

CHARLIE CINNAMON is the owner of a public relations firm in Miami that he founded in the 1950s. He specializes in the arts, music, theater, and special events.

LISA COLE was the Fontainebleau Hotel's director of public relations for more than a quarter century. She is now Hilton's southeast director of communications in the United States.

MARLO COURTNEY has been senior managing director of Tony Goldman Properties for more than thirty years. Formerly the chairman of the Miami Beach Planning Board, he works on the continued development of South Beach and Wynwood and serves as the chairman of the Ocean Drive Association.

SILVIA KARMAN CUBINA, executive director and chief curator of the Bass Museum, was a director of The Moore Space in Miami from 2002 to 2008.

SUSAN T. DANIS is the general director and CEO of the Florida Grand Opera, Doral Center. Her more than twenty-five years of arts administration include a dozen-year stint as executive director of the Sarasota Opera.

ROBERTO DESSOMMES is a longtime manager of the News Café on Miami Beach's Ocean Drive.

CLARENCE DICKSON was the City of Miami's first black police chief. When he retired in 1988, he was lauded for serving the department for twenty-eight years with grace and dignity.

ERIC DOMEGE, together with his partner, Christian Roth, heads the famed designer sunglass collection headquartered in Miami.

KIMBERLY FALCONER is the owner and tour director of Ocean Force Adventures in Miami Beach.

ALICE ARSLANIAN FIFELSKI is theater manager at the Adrienne Arsht Center for the Performing Arts.

ROBERSON de FRANC is originally from Haiti. He works as a valet and room attendant at the Viceroy Tower in Brickell.

LILIA GARCIA is an arts educator and the director/art curator at Dynamo Art CocoWalk and at the Hunter/CGAF Galleries.

IRA GILLER is a developer, architect, and past president of the Miami Beach Chamber of Commerce. One of his major projects involved the fusing of two historic buildings forming the Jewish Museum of Florida in Miami Beach.

MARGARET GRIFFIS O'BRIEN is a longtime Miami Beach resident. Her mother came to the United States from Cuba.

IRVING "RED" HELLER is retired assistant director for the Miami-Dade Police Department and a cofounder of the South Florida Shomrim Society.

He was the first Jew to attain the rank of assistant director of the Miami-Dade Police Department.

JUNE HENDERSON is executive and personal assistant to David Wallack, owner of Mango's Tropical Café in South Beach and Orlando.

MARTIN JEAN is an Art Deco tour guide with the Miami Design Preservation League. Originally from New Hampshire, he developed an avid interest in Miami Beach architecture when he moved to the area in 2009.

JACK JOHNSON is a member of the City of Miami Beach Planning Board, chair emeritus of the MB Community Development Corporation, and executive board member of the Miami Design Preservation League.

ROBERTO JUAREZ is an award-winning artist whose work has been exhibited in top-flight museums and galleries. His public work is on display in such places as the Miami International Airport and the Miami Children's Courthouse.

HELEN KAPLAN has lived in Miami Beach since she was a young child. She attended the University of Florida and worked as a bookseller at her son's bookstore, Books & Books, when it first began.

JOE KAPLAN is originally from Chicago and has lived in Miami Beach since 1953. He has been a labor lawyer for nearly fifty years representing unions all over Florida.

MITCHELL KAPLAN is the owner of Books & Books and cofounder of the Miami Book Fair International. A two-term president of the American Booksellers Association (ABA), he remains actively involved with the organization. In 2011, the National Book Foundation presented him with the Literarian Award for Outstanding Service to the American Literary Community.

FANNY KERBEL is the wife of Marcos Kerbel. A CPA, she is now a retired senior audit manager at MBAF, CPAs in Miami.

MARCOS KERBEL is a CPA and CFP banker who spent twenty-two years heading the Miami branch of the Israel Discount Bank. He is a professor at Florida International University and Barry University and leader in Miami's Cuban Jewish community.

JOSEPH KRUTEL is a real estate broker and a film producer. His most recent project is the HBO show *Ballers*, alongside executive producers and creators Mark Wahlberg and Steve Levinson and starring Dwayne "The Rock" Johnson. The show was shot on location in Miami, and a lead character, Joe Krutel, is named after him.

JIM LAWRENCE has spent many years working at the Coral Gables Museum and as a building manager at the Bass Museum in Miami Beach.

JEFF LEHMAN is managing director of The Betsy-South Beach. In his 20+ years in Miami Beach, he led the restorations and was general manager of both The National Hotel and The Palms Hotel & Spa, and has served or been the chairperson for twelve years of the Miami Beach Visitor and Convention Authority. He also has held leadership positions in other civic areas.

SUE LEVENBERG first arrived in Miami in 1948. She owned a famous juice bar named Lee's and the restaurant Inside.

NEIL LOOMIS is a businessman who lives in the Boston area. He has been a visitor to the Miami area through the decades.

DIEGO LOWENSTEIN is CEO of Lionstone Development, which initiates, owns, and develops world-class hospitality and residential ventures in the United States and international markets. He is a third-generation leader of the fifty-year-old firm.

FLOYD MAC McSWANE lays claim to being a longtime bellhop at the Fontainebleau Hotel where he has met and worked for a who's who of personalities in his decades on the job.

VOICES

ALAN MANDEL is of Cuban origin and a longtime Miami resident.

JUSTIN MOSS is director of Broward operations and outreach, Florida Grand Opera.

GEORGE T. NEARY has been since 1998 associate vice president of cultural tourism for the Greater Miami Convention & Visitors Bureau. The former executive director of the Miami Design Preservation League, Neary had a major role in helping to preserve the Art Deco District.

ALAN NIVEN came from Cuba to Miami in 1961.

JOHN NIVEN is a well-known dermatologist. He came from Cuba to Miami and is the husband of Mary Niven.

MARY NIVEN, the wife of John Niven, came to Miami from Cuba.

FERDIE PACHECO was the personal physician and cornerman for Muhammad Ali and other boxing champions. Formerly a celebrated TV boxing analyst for several television networks, he is also a highly prolific author and painter.

LUISITA PACHECO is the wife of Ferdie Pacheco and president of the Pacheco Gallery. She was a well-known flamenco dancer and ran a dancing school.

JONATHAN PLUTZIK is the chairman and principal owner of The Betsy Hotel on Ocean Drive in South Beach. He is an art aficionado and philanthropist.

ED PONDER is the director of guest services at The Betsy Hotel.

DAVE ROGERS, a whirlwind personality, fixture, and a treasure on the Miami scene for decades, has excelled in the world of insurance and knows his way around a good story.

BERNIE ROSEN was sports director at WTVJ in Miami for thirty-five years. He developed an exclusive relationship with Muhammad Ali, hired the nation's first female sportscaster in 1967, and covered virtually every major Miami sports event in his time.

HAROLD ROSEN, two-time mayor of Miami Beach, is an attorney and longtime observer of the political and civic scene.

CHRISTIAN ROTH, together with his partner, Eric Domege, heads the famed designer sunglass collection headquartered in Miami.

AL SCHLAZER has been senior sports manager at Disney Sport Attractions in the Orlando area. He has coached six national tennis championships and thirty academic all-Americans at Miami Dade College where he was a dean and athletic director.

BASHA SCHLAZER is a graduate of Florida International University with a degree in parks and recreation. She worked for the City of Miami Department of Parks & Recreation for twenty-eight years and retired as its events coordinator.

LANEY SHELDON was a dancer and dance instructor in Miami Beach at the Fontainebleau Hotel.

PHILIP SMITH is an artist whose work is in the collections of the Whitney, Boston's Museum of Fine Arts, and the Pérez Art Museum in Miami, among others. A former managing editor of *GQ*, he is the author of *Walking Through Walls.*

MARC SOYKA is one of Miami's best-known innovators and restaurateurs. His eateries include the News Café and Soyka Restaurant.

RAMÓN TEBAR is the music director of the Florida Grand Opera. He is also artistic and music director for the Palm Beach Symphony and has conducted major orchestras in a range of venues.

JOHN TURCHIN is a master builder who, together with his family, has developed many of South Florida's most majestic real estate projects.

DAVID WALLACK is the owner of Mango's Tropical Café in South Beach, a world-famous landmark that attracts more than a million patrons annually. A sister operation of Mango's opened in Orlando, Florida, in 2015.

CLAIRE WARREN is a retired school administrator in the Miami-Dade system and a longtime active area resident.

ROBERT ZUCKERMAN is a renowned Hollywood photographer who created advertising and publicity imagery for famous films and whose portrait portfolio includes many celebrities. In 2014, Zuckerman was appointed Dean's Distinguished Fellow at FIU's College of Architecture and the Arts.

Courtesy of Frommer Archives

Prologue

Come with me. I want to show you something.

—Tony Goldman

MARLO COURTNEY: Tony Goldman and I met at the Empire Roller Dome in Brooklyn, where we went roller-skating on Wednesday nights. It was very, very Brooklyn. I had been involved in the garment center around that time, and my friend Marc Soyka was into a specialty store on the Upper West Side when we decided we would find a way to open up our own personal roller disco in Manhattan. It was a lot of pounding the pavement, a lot of walking up and down to see what we could find. During this time I met Tony Goldman one night at the Empire Roller Dome, and from then on, Tony and I became best buddies. It became this great friendship.

One night Tony said to me, "Come with me. I want to show you something." He takes me for a ride down Greene Street in SoHo where garbage trucks were going in and out of this building and pointed out how garbage was being transferred from one truck to another. That was right in the middle of SoHo, where today you have all these very, very high-end luxury retailers. "I'm going to build the greatest nightclub you've ever seen right here," he said.

This was 1977, when Tony was just discovering SoHo. He was building the Greene Street Café while Marc and I were building the Metropolis Roller Disco.

We would send him our guys; he would send us his guys. But before long, we realized Tony was becoming very successful with the Greene Street Café while the life of Metropolis was no more. So we closed that business, and Marc and I began working for Tony. We created a new entertainment room, a nightclub/comedy room. We called it Upstairs at Greene Street.

Tony was very, very generous, one of the most generous people I've ever known: a true visionary. With Tony, it was never a handshake; it was always a hug and a kiss. We were best friends. Tony was single at this time. I was single; Marc Soyka was single. We traveled a lot together. There was a lot of carrying on. By the early eighties, SoHo was starting to emerge, and Tony was very entrenched in the neighborhood. He had developed a passion for the cast-iron architecture and historic preservation.

By the middle of 1984, Tony was diversifying some of his interests. He invested in a property in Coconut Grove, but it didn't really turn him on. Then, a local real estate broker who was very active in Miami and Miami Beach said, "I want to show you something."

He puts Tony in the car; they drive across the MacArthur Causeway, and he makes the left turn onto Ocean Drive. Tony says, "Stop the car." He gets out of the car, walks over to a pay phone, and calls me. "Get on a plane, and get down here now," he says.

1

Preservation of Art Deco

An Overnight Twenty-Five-Year Success

To me, historical meant at least one hundred years old.

—Harold Rosen

GEORGE NEARY: In America we live in a movie star culture. We're always waiting for our comeback. Look at Brooklyn—who would have believed it?

Europe is on a horizontal plane; it got to a place five hundred years ago, and it never changed. In the United States, you knock down a building, you put something else up, and it's a new place.

The transformation of Miami Beach started in the Art Deco District with the appearance of Barbara Capitman, a writer and interior designer from New York. She came down to Miami in 1974, saw the buildings that lined Ocean Drive, and couldn't believe it—Art Deco buildings everywhere. It was Barbara who started the movement to restore them. Her efforts led to an astonishing change, a reinvention of the community.

She formed the Miami Design Preservation League and the Art Deco Preservation League. She also had the Miami Beach Art Deco District listed with the Department of the Interior as a National Register Historic District in 1979, although it wasn't until 1992 that it was finally declared a local historic district by the City of Miami Beach in order to preserve it from demolition. That's how long it took.

HAROLD ROSEN: In the 1960s, '70s, into the '80s, most of our Jewish people lived in the hotels along Ocean Drive, apparently sent down by their children. They had a room. They had hot plates in their rooms. They would sit on the front porches of the hotels looking out to the sea, rocking, waiting to die.

DAVE ROGERS: You'd look at the porches of the Avalon Hotel, the Beacon, places I later insured, and you'd see these old ladies in rocking chairs. It cost them maybe $150 a month to live like they were on the French Riviera, only it was Miami Beach.

CHARLIE CINNAMON: For the last eighteen years of her life, I had my mother come down to Miami Beach, so it all worked out in a kind of nice way. There were the old bubbies on the rocking chairs and the theaters that had Yiddish shows and vaudeville. At that time, I was handling a theater called the Cameo: "*Yader voch a nier show*" ("Each week a new show"). I could get my mother in for free with a good seat. It was a big deal.

DIANE WOOLFE CAMBER: Barbara Capitman wanted to find a way to accommodate these elderly Jewish people who lived in the hotels, not have them pushed out by gentrification. They could live very cheaply in these places; the rooms were small, but it was comfortable enough for them. Barbara identified them as retired garment workers who were brought there by the garment workers' union. She had come out of this socialist ethos.

MICHAEL ALLER: Ocean Drive, once the most glamorous part of Miami Beach, had really deteriorated. A lot of people had moved north to Boca, Palm Beach, West Palm Beach, Delray. Those who stayed were mainly Jewish people on fixed incomes who'd go to the dances at the Tenth Street Auditorium.

NEIL LOOMIS: My grandmother, Sarah Cohen, was one of them. She stayed at The Betsy Ross Hotel on Ocean Drive for about twenty years, ten months every year, from September to Memorial Day. I don't know why she picked this place. It wasn't anything like what it is now. It was more like a rooming house, very nondescript: a bedroom, a bathroom with a sink, a hot plate. But it was right on

The front desk of The Betsy Ross Hotel in the 1950s. Courtesy of The Betsy Hotel

Ocean Drive, right across the street from the beach. How much better than that can you get?

She had some fifty thousand things wrong with her and would never have lived to be ninety-four if she hadn't been down there where she had a lot of friends. She was born in some part of Russia and wasn't an educated woman. Her husband had been killed; she raised my mother and her sister and brother very well. She was an excellent seamstress, could sew like nobody's business, could knit and crochet. Beyond that, I don't know that much about her life on Ocean Drive except that she loved it.

The time I'm remembering now is a day in the mid-eighties. I've been in Miami Beach since then with other people, but now, looking over my life, I am brought back to that time. I was with my wife and our two children; one was four or five, the other one or two. We were in Orlando, had gone to Disney World. This day was rainy and cold, so I thought we could shoot down the Florida Turnpike, go to Miami Beach and see if it's warm down there, and while we were there, we could see my grandmother.

We made it down in about two and a half hours and got a vacation rental on Meridian and Seventeenth Street, where we planned to stay for three days. And being there, in the neighborhood, I remembered the place. Walking down to the beach from Seventeenth Street, I said to myself, "Yeah, this is the area." All the bubbies were still coming down from up north to this stretch—right here.

We didn't call my grandmother ahead of time or anything. We just showed up. I asked at the desk if Sarah Cohen was around. "She's out on the beach," we were told. So we went down to the beach. It wasn't a particularly good beach day, but there she was, just kind of standing there.

She had never seen my children before. She loved seeing them now. We walked along the promenade and took her out to dinner in the restaurant next door. I remember that we missed the early-bird special and people said to us, "What are you doing coming here now? You missed the early-bird discount."

I can't begin to tell you how great that day was. She had been here for a long time, and something of her was in this building. Even now I can sense her presence, feel her love radiating up through the floor. And I will always remember the day I came here, unplanned and unexpected, to see my grandmother and let her see her great-grandchildren.

Courtesy of David Wallack

DAVID WALLACK: My father pioneered renovation co-ops in the South Beach area. He bought various buildings, got that formula growing, and was selling a room for $5,000. Now it's $80,000, but he did fine selling it at $5,000.

The summer was largely for Cuban families. They loved the beach and would take an apartment on Ocean Drive for the season. But there were also the year-round people that my father rented to monthly, the weekly people, and the daily people. It was like a motel apartment.

He had bought the Renaissance Hotel in the mid-seventies, and that was where I created my care facility, the Eastern Sun. I was very much into eastern philosophy then. At the same time, I was clerking for a law firm that represented hospitals, and while I was doing legal research, I came upon a law that was passed in 1976 that dealt with these small houses in residential areas where five or six elderly people were boarded. The state found that many of them were very

The Eastern Sun van back in the day, doing its thing. Courtesy of David Wallack

substandard and passed a law that required the owners of what were called adult congregate living facilities to be licensed and to abide by certain standards for the care they were dispensing.

I took a look at the law and said, "Number one: this is as minimal as it gets. And number two: you're looking at it this way. Why not take it this way?"

Our family had committed to converting two adjoining residential buildings at 900 Ocean Drive that they had owned since 1955 into an ACLF. It was the first commercially based personal care residence for elderly people, the first facility of its kind in the state of Florida. I had grown up there. I folded the towels. I knew all the customers. It was part of my world.

From my position, I could see how the customer base in Miami Beach had fallen. Partly it was because the northeast Jewish clientele had died off, but even more so it was because the entertainment had left. Where Miami Beach hotels had been paying $10,000 a week to Frank Sinatra, Sammy Davis Jr., Dean Martin and

Jerry Lewis, Las Vegas hotels were now paying them $50,000. The entertainment leaving, coupled with the age of the clientele base, turbocharged the dropping out and sinking of Miami Beach.

It had become desolation row. The buildings were painted white like death, because white is the cheapest paint and lasts the longest. The further south you went on Ocean Drive, the seamier the part of town. Joe's Stone Crab was thriving as ever, but it was an island unto itself, a destination. There were these little bars and the First Street jetty that people were fishing off of. Some surf shops had opened up along First and Ocean Drive when surfing hit with the Beach Boys in the sixties, but there was nothing else. The dog track had closed. The whole area was a wasteland.

That left the old people who lived along and around Ocean Drive the victims. I would not let the people at my place go to their parked car alone. Police went in four-car convoys; none were on the streets. That's how militant they were.

When criminals and crazy people started coming into my ACLF, I got mace and a baseball bat. One night I caught a guy and hit him with the bat. He flew right over the rail on the second floor and never came back.

But that led me to put up gates. They were meant to keep people out, but they also kept people in. I thought it looked like a jail. I called everyone together on the front patio where we had all our parties. "Listen," I said, "this is your home; these are your gates. You can vote to tear them down." They voted to keep the gates.

GEORGE NEARY: Miami Beach had become a complete dump. No one would buy a building there, invest in a building, renovate a building, believe someone would stay in a building. And then Barbara Capitman invited a man named Tony Goldman to a conference she was hosting. It would be about rehab development, not knock down. Tony, who was from New York and a real estate man, fell in love with the idea. He would wind up buying a building a month for twenty-four months.

Courtesy of Ira Giller

IRA GILLER: Barbara Capitman played a unique role in the Art Deco movement that was beginning to take shape. She brought together people like Tony Goldman with people in the arts community who understood what she was about. She was very demanding, able to see in buildings what the locals didn't, and she was able to articulate it.

Norman Giller with son Ira. The two would go on to work together. Courtesy of Ira Giller

Time and again, my father had said the people who came to Miami and made money were not the locals. They came from out of town and saw what the locals couldn't see. It's a cycle that repeats itself.

The Art Deco movement started in 1979. The notion was that we had this beautiful architecture—let's not tear it down; let's revel in what we have. But it didn't get real traction until the mid-eighties. It was difficult to get people to come to grips with the idea. They'd walk into a building, look around, and say, "This had its day; let's replace it with a high-rise."

People in the business community were afraid that those who favored renovating Art Deco hotels would stifle business. The business model had been, "Tear down the small building; build a three-story building. Tear down a three-story building; build a ten-story building." They didn't understand how the small buildings could be economic engines. It was Tony Goldman who realized we could regenerate communities and market them in a way that would capture the charm of what had been and capitalize on it.

My father used to say, "Buildings don't live forever. They have their time, and then it's time to move on." But the magic of the Art Deco District is that instead of tearing down a hotel and building a three-, four-story building and making the money there, buyers began to figure out the economics. They put restaurants into the hotels, and suddenly they were making money because of the restaurants. And as they made more money, their rents went up.

DAVE WALLACK: By the 1990s condos were in, but there was still an overall depression. When I first created the Eastern Sun, there was no law to regulate it, no zoning. No mortgages were being given by the banks at that time. I put my business plan together and brought it to Bart Goldberg of Jefferson National Bank. He looked at it and said, "I like this; I'm going to give you a mortgage." That allowed me to renovate two adjoining buildings, Park C and Surf C, so they were part of the Eastern Sun. I put the elevator right in the middle to make it easier for people to walk to it all the way from the back.

That was how my care facility began. It was my ashram, my home, my business. It opened in 1978 and closed in 1990. During this time, people were asking, "What's he doing? He's the only one making money here." In retrospect, it seemed no matter what I would do, I would be successful because I'm an innovator.

The Eastern Sun was flourishing with New Age holistic philosophy: a cleaner diet, stimulating activities, music, and massage. It involved my own family, as well as the families of the residents, in a celebration of life. It was the first in Florida to pioneer hospice and hurricane evacuation of the elderly.

The Art Deco movement began when the Roney Plaza was knocked down and replaced with a box. That was like tearing the heart out of Miami Beach. The Roney had been the elite of Miami Beach architecture, the castle of Miami Beach. It turned my head.

Just around that time Barbara Capitman found out about me and came to see me in my office. She was a matriarchal-type person, very emotional about Art Deco because she was an outsider. At City Hall, she was regarded as a threat. But I found her to be a great woman, a leader with conviction, intelligence, and wisdom. She would come into my office, and I'd have to give her a box of tissues—she was so emotional.

DIANE WOOLFE CAMBER: I worked closely with Barbara Capitman during the preservation era. She recruited people—I was one among them—who quickly got involved in the Art Deco movement.

Barbara had a scratchy voice and wasn't an effective speaker. I became a spokesperson for her, in part, because of that. But she was an effective writer and galvanizer in her own right. She brought together a ragtag bunch: gays who were in the design world, architects and interior designers, people whom she needed for the history and connections with the past—I fit into that last role. Also with my background in architectural history, I was able to write about it in a meaningful way.

Courtesy of Jack Johnson

JACK JOHNSON: In 1969, my partner and I moved to Wilton Manors, a suburb of Fort Lauderdale where we were to live for fifteen months. Today it's one of the gayest communities in America, but in 1969 it was not booming. One day, we went down to Miami Beach. We drove along Ocean Drive where all these elderly people were sitting in rockers on the front porch of hotels. We weren't interested in the hotels, however; we were interested in the beach.

Years later when I was working for the United States Department of Housing and Urban Development in New York City, I was offered a promotion that required relocation to Miami. By now, I knew a little bit about Art Deco architecture, and working for HUD, I had developed a great interest in housing. I took up residence in a building on Tenth Street and Jefferson. The two blocks were in bad shape, but there were no old folks on rocking chairs any longer. At the same time, there were some beautiful Art Deco buildings at the bottom of Ocean Drive.

Richard Hoberman and I had been friends in the New York HUD office. Now, we met again in Miami Beach where he was executive director of the Miami Design Preservation League working with Barbara Capitman. Through Richard and Barbara, I got involved in the MDPL. I became a board member and a tour guide—a job I hold to this day.

I learned that most of the Art Deco buildings were built between 1935 and 1941. They were influenced by Art Moderne and were called Modern until the 1960s when the term Art Deco was applied. There are still some stunning Art Deco buildings left at the bottom of Ocean Drive such as the Century and the Balfour, my favorite being the Crescent, which is unusual because it's asymmetrical. There's also the Essex House on Tenth and Washington, a nautical Art Deco building, only two stories high, with an extraordinary lounge. About half a dozen architects were the principal figures of the Art Deco movement; their hotels could be found all over the Miami Beach area. But it was on Ocean Drive that they stood in a row in a splendid oceanfront setting.

After I retired from HUD, I joined the Miami Beach Community Development Corporation, also founded by Barbara. The organization worked with developers to buy and restore old buildings on Lincoln Road, Washington Avenue, and Ocean Drive. Tony Goldman was very instrumental here. He developed the Park Central Hotel, the building on Eighth Street and Ocean Drive, which also houses the News Café, The Hotel (originally the Tiffany) on Collins Avenue and Eighth Street, and a relatively new development across the street that was sympathetic to the existing architecture, with retail on the ground floor and offices above.

Later on, Tony would be involved in the revival of Wynwood, a neighborhood south of the Design District in the City of Miami that has lots of galleries and street art.

MARLO COURTNEY: Tony had this great devotion to architecture, to making sure the story was told over and over, to its becoming a worldwide story. He could articulate and get people to become part of a movement knowing that there were people in Miami Beach who wanted to knock down all this stuff and build canals.

DIANE WOOLFE CAMBER: There were some Miami Beach commissioners and people in the Chamber of Commerce who were dead against what Barbara and her group wanted to do. Their plan was to knock down. Our plan was to restore and redevelop the entire area.

GEORGE NEARY: The problem with Americans is we have no history; we have no interest in the past, and until recently we haven't valued the arts, culture, and preservation. Since 1974, the Art Deco Preservation League has been on the front lines, fighting for preservation. Abe Resnick, one of the commissioners, was on the other side.

Born in one of the lost cities in Lithuania (there's a section in Yad Vashem devoted to lost cities), Abe fought the Germans, was taken prisoner by the Russians, escaped to Cuba, and from Cuba came here. He had this interesting background, but he lacked the appreciation. All Abe wanted to do was put up high-rises. He knocked down some of the best buildings in Miami Beach—the New Yorker, for example.

His line was, "I couldn't see the invisible, so I couldn't do the impossible." But I have to admit, he's a wonderful guy.

The Netherland Hotel—classic Art Deco. Courtesy of The Netherland Hotel

HAROLD ROSEN: I was against all the preservation business. Historic nonsense, I thought. To me, historical meant at least one hundred years old. Still I gave Barbara Capitman the first ten Gs she got from a mayor.

Courtesy of John Turchin

JOHN TURCHIN: Many of the preservationists in the Art Deco movement were not from the Beach. "We're gonna save your history," they'd say. "You don't know any better."

We've always had a debate with them over whether a building should be saved or knocked down. If a building has no steel, is crumbling, falling apart, how do you save it? What's good architecture? What's taste?

The Art Deco buildings were not of the best materials; they had minimal steel. In the interests of historic preservation, the owners would put a hardship on a building just to save its façade when they could just as well reproduce the building with the same design and architecture.

I'm not in agreement that everything should be saved. I think the character and size of a building should be preserved, but with good architecture you can build anything.

IRA GILLER: I was president of the Chamber of Commerce during this period. We began looking into how we could re-create what we are all about. We realized we had hundreds of hotels, very few of which were competitive in the current market. Maybe we needed to revisit what we were doing in the city and serve more as a residential community in downtown Miami. Maybe we should try to get older hotels to become apartment houses for younger families, working people. We were groping for another formula to make things work other than the bubbies sitting on the porch.

No style comes from nothing. Art Deco is related to Art Nouveau, which dates from the late nineteenth century. It emphasizes curves and elaborate design. Art Deco is more geometric, simpler, although it can be elaborate. The largest Art Deco collection in the world is in Miami Beach at the Wolfsonian Museum of Miami Beach. The owner, Mickey Wolfson, has donated the museum and all its collections to Florida International University.

JEFF LEHMAN: The revival didn't really take off until the late eighties when Art Deco had already become part of a designated historic area. Today the Art Deco influence is a theme that we're all required to adhere to.

GEORGE NEARY: When I first came down here, my office was in the Hotel Leslie on Ocean Drive. You could park right in front of the hotel—there were no parking meters. If you got married in 1945, you can still go into the building where you got your marriage license. In Hartford—where I come from—that didn't happen because they knocked down all the buildings. In Miami Beach, more than eight hundred buildings were saved from demolition by the Miami Design Preservation League.

We say the Art Deco movement is a twenty-five-year overnight success. As it grew, so did the engine of South Florida. Barbara had aligned with the Haitian community in a neighborhood in the City of Miami. When they subsequently moved to another neighborhood, Barbara aligned herself with another group of people who lived in the same area. They were into style and design and ended up creating the Design District.

Barbara formed the National Society of Art Deco. Today these societies are all over the world—in Cleveland; Boston; Ethiopia; South Africa; Brazil; Tulsa, Oklahoma—all formed by her. The Miami City Ballet, the New World Symphony concert hall, so many other cultural institutions are part of her legacy. All of them and all the rest go back to the Art Deco movement.

Everything comes from that.

2

Everything Started Happening in the Eighties

Like in *The Wizard of Oz*, colors were coming out, pastel-shaded paintings.

—David Wallack

SUE BRUSTMAN: In 1978, I came to Miami from New York where I'd done music PR. I was now freelancing for a gallery. One day the woman there said, "Why don't you go to Hank Meyer? You could sharpen some of your writing and make some money." Hank was the dean of PR in south Florida at the time. I took her advice and got hired.

I was part of a media junket that the managing editor of *GQ* had signed onto, and driving back from the airport, I was bemoaning the fact that Miami Beach was not hipper or more energized. There was no place to eat, very few cafés. I used to fly back to New York for a decent meal.

He said to me, "You know, Susan, all you need is one hip restaurateur who knows how to create café society to come down to South Beach, and the whole place will turn around."

I had a plan to start my own business the next year. Now I said, "Please, send him to me." He sent me Gary Farmer, the manager of Indochine in lower Manhattan. Gary had a cocktail column in *GQ*, was a very knowledgeable guy, and was tired of the rat race in New York. He wanted to move to Miami.

I picked him up at the airport, connected him to all the right people, and as a result of that encounter, the mission that would turn South Beach around began with a restaurant on Washington Avenue between Sixth and Seventh Streets that he named the Strand.

At this time, South Beach was populated largely by the elderly who lived in tiny Art Deco apartments. The architecture was there, but the inside of these places was pretty seedy and very inexpensive. Barbara Capitman and, later on, her son Andrew were working with a lot of architects to preserve the Art Deco color and architecture. We got behind them—150 people who saw the potential of the Beach and were fighting the plans to raze it and put up big resorts that would have ruined the pedestrian quality of life in the neighborhood.

PHILIP SMITH: In the early seventies when I was twenty-one, twenty-two, I left Miami for New York. I was a painter, and there was no art scene in Miami. My paintings have very odd narratives, although I think Miami itself was a very odd narrative back then, and I think that strangeness came from living in Miami.

I am a Miamian no matter where I exhibit, and I've exhibited all over the country, all over the world. But I get very antsy if I don't come home. Now, I was missing Miami so much, I would have the *Miami Herald* delivered to me in my New York brownstone. Finally, I decided to move back. That was when I met Barbara Capitman and saw this fantasyland that was basically all boarded up.

I convinced Gary Farmer, who had planned to move from New York to LA, to change his destination to Miami. "I need a place to eat," I told him.

"Miami?" He thought I was crazy. But he came down for a weekend, and I took him around. It was so deserted we were able to get into any building on Ocean Drive, on Washington Avenue. Then we went into a building on a lonely stretch of Washington Avenue. Gary looked around and decided this would be the place for his new venture, a restaurant he'd name the Strand.

The Strand was on the site of the former Famous restaurant, which featured old-fashioned Jewish cuisine with the bottle of seltzer on the table, a platter of lox, a plate of kreplach. They were losing market share, and the Strand took over the lease.

Immediately, it created a buzz. *Interview* magazine sponsored the opening. Celebrities such as Mickey Rourke, Lauren Hutton, and Julian Schnabel came in.

Philip Smith. Courtesy of Philip Smith

Edward Albee was there along with investors from the art world. There was press from all over the country.

A restaurant is the heartbeat of a community, and the success of this restaurant for the three years it was in existence really helped spark the turnaround of South Beach. You would walk into the Strand, and everybody you knew would be there.

There was no other restaurant to go to unless you wanted to spend $100 at a place like Joe's Stone Crab. The food was modern American with affordable things such as hamburgers and soup with homemade bread. The décor was very chic, seafoam green, an L-shaped dark wood bar and 150 to 175 original Art Deco chairs gotten from a cruise line that had put its furnishings into an auction house.

I learned the restaurant business as a result of being around the Strand. I was there when they chose the glasses. I helped put up mosaics in the restrooms, watched the ordering processes, and, as a publicist, saw where the stories could go.

Sometimes I'd go to the Strand at seven, seven-thirty in the evening, start out with soup and bread and a glass of wine and stay until one in the morning. The place would host cutting-edge acts such as a local theater group performance or a rock performer or a Latin crossover person who did poetry and music. The art world was there. There were celebrity items, business stories, events. It was a salon, and, at the same time, the only bistro around.

Miami at twilight. Courtesy of Frommer Archives

Still, they weren't making much money, and it was exhausting. The people who started the place were getting tired of working so hard and not making much. So, after three years of existence, it closed, although not before it had left its mark on the area. As for me, a public-relations professional, the Strand was an accelerator that enabled me to make contacts all over.

Gary put this place on the map with the Strand. One time we saw a girl with hair bleached white walking out of the Versace mansion, which I think was a rental at that time. "I want someone like that working for my restaurant," he said. There was no group factor down here; no one was hip.

I took pictures of the scene and sent them to everybody in New York saying, "Please buy these buildings and save them." They were so cheap. At the time you could buy any building in the Art Deco district; they were like $250,000.

I started a building called the Helen Mar. I told a friend, "You should buy this." He bought it, renovated it, and started selling apartments to New Yorkers for $28,000. I bought the penthouse that had previously been owned by Lilly Pulitzer and lived there for a couple of years.

SUE BRUSTMAN: Suddenly, all the *Condé Nast* people wanted to hear what was happening on South Beach. I would interface with stuff that was going on with the Convention & Visitors Bureau—they had these wonderful media junkets. Not everyone knew about South Beach; it was still forming. Later on, they would be big boosters. But for the moment, I would call and say, "Let me share something with you about a neighborhood about to happen."

Everything started happening in the eighties. There was no end to exciting things for a reporter to write about. Every time a coffee shop or a new pizza place opened, there was something national about it. So many celebrities were coming down. There were so many parties and so many models. It was very much like the Lower East Side was before it became *chicky-cuckoo*. Art galleries started to pop up along with places where you could get fantastic fashion. The bridges on the weekend would be packed all the way into Miami.

Suddenly, there were nightclubs, both gay and straight. During Miami Beach's turnaround, when it became known as South Beach and the Deco District, the gays and the models were what gave it national acclaim.

The gay community was so chic; they were such tastemakers in terms of the opening of boutiques and galleries. The models started to do all these shoots on South Beach that ended up in the pages of *Vanity Fair* and *Condé Nast*. And these gorgeous six-foot-tall fourteen-year-olds were seen Rollerblading up and down Ocean Drive.

Worked out, plugged in, and enjoying a walk along Washington Avenue.

DAVID WALLACK: Like in *The Wizard of Oz*, colors were coming out, pastel-shaded paintings. Now you go into City Hall, and all my colors are on the chart, but then it was, "Oh, how garish!" Alex Daoud was the mayor then as well as a boxer; the renaissance turned around mainly because of his efforts. He would just take all of these criminals behind the convention hall, beat the crap out of them, then drive them to Miami where he'd drop them off and say, "You come back to the beach, and you'll be going to the hospital."

That had an effect. All of a sudden women could walk alone on the streets. Photographers from Europe arrived because the prices were so low, and their historical perspective allowed them to appreciate the buildings. Models started coming; gays started coming; clubs popped up. All of a sudden there was nightlife. I was going to all the openings; I played in some of the clubs. There were beautiful women in droves: models, models, models.

Tony Goldman was the leader of leaders. He walked Ocean Drive, and then he led us in walking that street and turning around, not just seeing the ocean but the buildings once again. From that came color and music, entertainment and food, and all the wonderful things that we enjoy as our prosperity. That is what Tony brought: prosperity.

Even in this early period, people started buying buildings. Some came too early; they bought and lost their buildings. It was like a Ponzi scheme, except they weren't cash flowing.

But these Deco buildings were there.

JOSEPH KRUTEL: Tony was definitely the spur for South Beach, a major player for resurrecting the Art Deco area. He owned the building that News Café was in, and it was when the News Café opened that the evolution of the neighborhood began.

SUE BRUSTMAN: When I first came to Miami in the 1970s, I would go back to Manhattan to eat and for the cultural buzz. Back then there was very little going on down here. Now the scene had become very exciting. The pinks and pastels, the light, the waterways, the natural beauty of Miami Beach was attracting everybody.

By the late 1980s, supermodels such as Naomi Campbell were a common sight. Soon, boutiques and trendy restaurants opened; some were owned by popular entertainers such as Sean Penn and Prince. The area became a magnet for chic young hipsters from the United States, Europe, and Latin America, and the annual Art Deco Weekend began drawing hundreds of thousands of visitors.

PHILIP SMITH: In 1980 and 1981, when I was managing editor at *GQ*, people on the staff would go to distant shores for their spring and summer shoots. In the winter, they'd often go to the Caribbean. "Why don't you go to Miami?" I'd ask them. They'd never heard of it.

On one of my trips to Miami, I scouted locations and took back pictures. "Here's where you can shoot the resort wear," I told them.

They were going to Mexico to shoot for Calvin Klein when the clothes got caught in customs. They didn't have a choice. So I found this beautiful mansion on Bayshore Drive. Bruce Weber and Calvin Klein had come down with me, and we did a shoot. Unfortunately, however, all the clothes got stolen.

MARLO COURTNEY: What brought us a great deal of excitement in the 1980s was *Miami Vice*, of course, but also the catalog companies and magazines such as *Der Spiegel* from Germany. In the fashion world, it was all about catalogs back then because there was no Internet.

All the modeling agencies were my tenants; I had Ford, Zoelle, Le Jeune, all of the more fashionable ones. You'd go out at seven o'clock in the morning and see the trailers and models outside all of these buildings painted in pastel shades, which was the backdrop they were looking for.

What could work better than to have pictures of these buildings in fashion catalogs? Meanwhile, we were developing hotel products and marketing our products around the world.

GEORGE NEARY: Miami Beach is a very small town that was settled and saved not only by Barbara Capitman and those who took up the Art Deco movement's cause, but by a whole cadre of gays and lesbians. They could see what other people couldn't see. They loved the style, the design, the color, the whole Art Deco thing. Who wouldn't want to live on a beach with nobody on it? Those who could joined together. One guy was a colorist; he began to paint the buildings in different colors. A lot of *Miami Vice* shots were in buildings he painted.

Sadly, he died of AIDS. So did others who were here in the early days. The gay community had been a small community then. But there was acceptance that comes from being on the beach, where you find people with a very tolerant attitude. Miami Beach had become much freer. Gay people from all over were coming here.

MICHAEL ALLER: Anita Bryant, a runner-up Miss America and a spokesperson for Florida Citrus, had come out against gays in 1977, saying such things as, "Homosexuals cannot biologically reproduce children; therefore, they must recruit our children."

We came out to protest. We boycotted orange juice. People picketed in front of Anita Bryant's house in Miami. She was quickly put in her place, and the Miami gay community was pulled together like never before.

That was the impetus for the gay movement. The power of the issue united us as we marched down Biscayne Boulevard. It was a pivotal moment for Miami Beach. I felt a lot of pride in being gay, in being a citizen of Miami Beach.

SUE BRUSTMAN: Before the Strand, no one paid attention to Miami Beach's food except for Joe's Stone Crab. But now we had a group of chefs known as the Mango Gang who started using local ingredients and tropical fruits and doing beautiful things with them. These chefs were in Coral Gables for a while and then moved to South Beach. Douglas Rodriguez had a place on Lincoln Road that, when he first started out, he called Wet Paint Café (which would later become the location for Books & Books). He did the Latin-fusion cuisine, and it was spectacular.

A real community is born when chefs are associated with very distinct neighborhoods; and Tony Goldman, who was just the most joyous, visionary soul, a realtor with a passion for history and neighborhoods, realized how much bridges were needed between communities.

When Tony wanted to see a community evolve, he would seek out the people he felt would be right for the community and give them great rates on leases. He didn't promote it or tell anyone about it, but he'd bring in the right mix of people. He could see something and envision what it would look like in ten years.

Tony's vision for South Beach encompassed both the artistic and the real estate levels. He bought eighteen properties, couldn't afford to renovate all of them all at once, so he did one or two a year. In New York, he had bought a lot of the fashion leases in SoHo, which helped bring in art galleries. Now, he did something similar in Wynwood, a neighborhood near the Design District, which he called The Museum of the Streets. In New York, he had helped build bridges where he was pretty well known. Now he was doing it in Miami.

DAVID WALLACK: In those days, Jamaica was my home away from home, and that home was in Negril. I lived in a very small town where I had to walk three and a half miles to get to a telephone. There was one place there that had live music every night. Everyone would go to that one place because that was where the party was. And I loved the concept of everybody coming together.

The image of a coming-together place like the one in Negril, where there was live music and everyone was welcome, stayed with me when I returned to Miami Beach. There was now MXE (mixed use/entertainment) zoning, which allowed for a two-story building to do mixed-use businesses other than medical. Because my building was two stories, I envisioned a few cafés, retail, hotel, and offices. My nightclub-to-be, Mango's, would have the patio, and I would keep the liquor and the bar.

All the ten-year leases for the old people had expired, and I took them all out. Other than my retail people, I left the clothing stores. By this time, I was hanging around with Marc and Tony, and things were starting to happen in South Beach. Nightclubs were popping up. Cafés were opening along Ocean Drive. It was like the war is over; it was getting very cool. All of a sudden there was the Ocean Drive Association, and Tony was the president. I became the vice chairman, which I still am today. It was a whole Miami Beach groove.

There were times when I thought back to the day I was swimming in the ocean in Negril, rolling along, heading south, when suddenly Mango's Tropical Café came into my head.

Now, during a mile swim in the ocean from the Ninth to the First Street jetty and back, those words came back to me.

A lovely family had recently come down from Canada and bought a hotel on Collins in the thirties and a beautiful new garden apartment property out in Miami. "I bought two buildings," this gentleman said to me. "I'd like to have you help me convert them into care facilities, and I'd like to hire you as a consultant to do it." Just about the same time, I was shown a magnificent major property in Boca Raton right off of I-95 that could be the finest, and largest, care facility in the country.

I said to myself, I have both of these opportunities. I am at a major crossroad here. I could do this incredible project in Boca Raton, or start all over again and join in the renaissance of South Beach with a brand new business I was never in, that being a restaurant/nightclub that I would call Mango's Tropical Café. Here was this family offering me the perfect exit path from the elderly care business.

"If I do decide to do the restaurant/nightclub, I will take my entire staff and move them and my residents into your facilities," I told him. As such, none of my staff would lose their jobs, and I would see to it that all were settled in. We arrived at a price that was very substantial, because all of a sudden he'd be set up with a complete operation. It was perfect.

I had made my choice. I'd start all over again by creating the first mixed-use renovation project on South Beach that would include my opening a new restaurant/café nightclub within it called Mango's Tropical Café.

I knew that when I opened, mango daiquiris would be my signature drink, so come August I bought an entire truckload of mangoes. My plan was to close down and go into a full redevelopment in October. I set up tables on our patio, and my elderly people and I began two weeks of slicing mangoes and loving it. It was a fun activity. We sliced up thousands of pounds of mangoes on the patio and bagged them. I stored them in a rented freezer.

Some of my residents wanted to go to the Miami facility, and some wanted to stay in the hotel on Miami Beach. I went back and forth to get everybody settled. Then I closed Mango's in October and went into redevelopment.

The bank wouldn't give me a new mortgage unless I had seven leases, one of which would be Mango's. I then started high rent in Miami Beach and did the first conversion of a two-story building into mixed use in Miami Beach with the new MXE zoning law. It was a pioneer project.

I also began the—until then unheard of—concept of key money in Miami Beach. It was $50,000 for the corner to get the lease, $35,000 for the other front Ocean Drive bays as advance cash payment, and $45 a square foot triple net (which was unheard of). I also called for a straight 7 percent increase annually. I retained control of all alcoholic beverage service for Mango's Tropical Café.

Everyone said I was crazy, that no one would pay such ridiculous rental prices and terms. But miraculously, within one month, I had everything rented. I had my leases, and the bank gave me my new mortgage. We all opened together that March 30: a bathing suit and leisure-wear shop called Wild Things on the corner, a pizza and pasta restaurant, Mango's Tropical Café on the inside patio, a Mexican taco restaurant, a men's retail clothing store, and a few office rentals upstairs. We were off to the races—young, eager, and ready to ride the renaissance wave of Ocean Drive and South Beach.

Mango's would become the longest running off-Broadway show in the country. I was forty-two, forty-three, playing rock and reggae. I'd jump up and play with the band. Celebrities came in as customers, not to perform.

My father had passed away by this time, but my mother was with me. It was scary. In the early days, Gloria and Emilio Estefan and Andy Garcia came in. I believe that's where they got inspired to do the nightclub/restaurant Bongos.

For four years, we were hand to mouth. We had a grand opening, a wonderful party. But it was small. Until one day, a guy named Miguel Cruz walks in, says, "David, I love this place. I want to play here."

"Yeah? What do you play?"

"Afro-Latin jazz. I played with Santana out in LA. I will knock this place all around."

I said, "Great! Come on, let's have a good time."

He was like a psychedelic Desi Arnaz. He's playing the conga drums crawling on the floor like Jimi Hendrix. He had it going on. My girls—without my saying anything—jumped up on the bar and started dancing. The cash register started turning and burning. No more beer; now it was Black Label. I go, "Let's keep doin' it; let's keep doin' it."

Miguel played at Mango's for years. Then I brought in Erica Norimar and Brazilian Explosion. We got the samba going. All with small bands that were good club bands. A club band is different than a concert. Concert is selling tickets. Club is come in and buy a drink. And still, we were not charging to get in.

3

Along Ocean Drive

The News Café, the Versace Story, and the Return of the Models

Everything here used to be something else.

—Roberto Dessommes

MARC SOYKA: The old Jewish people were still living in the Park Central Hotel when Tony Goldman bought it, and he needed someone to go down to Florida and decide what to do with the building. I was the lucky person who was chosen to help him.

When I first came here, all I saw was sand, palm trees, whole deserted areas. I felt like I was in pioneer country or Never Never Land. Then we began renovation, and within a month, I had fallen in love with Miami. It reminded me of Israel—the small buildings, the smell of the ocean. The Deco District looked like Israel when I was growing up.

I became Tony Goldman's director of operations. We renovated building after building. But after a couple of years, with all due respect to my relationship with Tony and as much as I enjoyed my association with him, I realized I am an independent person who wants to do something on his own.

I had a passion for the hospitality business. When I was five years old, I was cutting tomatoes in the little grocery store my parents owned. But as an Israeli who grew up in outdoor cafés, the only thing I could think of was a café. I told

Tony I would like to rent the first floor on 800 Ocean Drive, one of the buildings he had purchased, and he went along with me.

Oddly enough, there were no cafés in Miami then. In New York, the idea of cafés had just begun when TGI Friday put a few tables out on the sidewalk. But in Miami, with all the sun, there were none. So I decided to open one. I called it the News Café, and with that, my independent life in Miami Beach began.

It was like a kiosk in Israel. We did a little ice cream, newspapers. For the first three, four years we didn't even cook. The only food we had were sandwiches, salads, soft- and hard-boiled eggs. But it was a café, a place where people could hang out, where they could sit down and have a cup of coffee. You want to eat, you eat; you don't want to eat, you don't. Nobody will ever chase you out.

We opened in 1988. There never was an opening celebration. I don't celebrate when I open; I celebrate only after time goes by and I know what I'm inviting people to. But the News Café soon became the Grand Central Station of Miami Beach.

The newspapers were there from the start—a wonderful selection of all the international newspapers such as you find all over Israel. Soon afterward, I opened a bookstore section; it was the first bookstore in Miami Beach and immediately successful because it attracted a combination of people, New Yorkers mostly, who came down as soon as they heard a lot is going on in the Art Deco District.

Marc Soyka. Courtesy of Marc Soyka

The News Café was an immediate destination because there wasn't much around. But then the fashion industry discovered us. They used to go to the Caribbean, but they couldn't get all the services for film, for developing, for assistance. Now, they found Miami.

From the photographer's point of view, it has the finest light. And there were so many places where one could stay. As a result, wherever you went, all over Miami Beach, day or night, you would see them: models here, models there.

We kept expanding, from twenty seats to forty, to fifty. Today we have about 350 seats and a big menu. We seat in excess of three thousand people a day, and it's not necessarily to eat. It's café life.

There's a big difference between a restaurant and a café. It's a different mentality. I had to teach my waiters and my staff that a café is a place where you sit down and have a cup of coffee. Today, the News Café has a big menu. People like to eat a lot. To Europeans, it's an American bistro. To Americans, it's a European bistro. To everyone, the News Café is oceanfront, and ocean is ocean.

When I first came down in 1985, 1986, the City of Miami was in the midst of the cocaine war between the Cubans and the Colombians. It was the era of Scarface—but in the City of Miami, not Miami Beach. Even the City of Miami Beach in the twenties and thirties was not a city of crime; it was the place where all the major criminals, people such as Al Capone, used to live.

Miami Beach has always been safe. Crack addicts are not criminals; they're not dangerous. If they need a fix, they might steal something. Although Miami Beach may have looked sleazy, like something out of *Miami Vice*, which was being filmed at the time, it was not dangerous. Actually, the only police force we saw was in the shooting of *Miami Vice*. But anywhere there's a camera and actors, it's never the wrong image.

I never came into this business with the expectation of having six or seven restaurants. I did it simply because I thought it was what I should do, which was to copy, to some degree, my life in Israel.

ROBERTO DESSOMMES: In 1990, when I first became a manager of the News Café, there was a constant parade of people walking up and down Ocean Drive. The models made South Beach famous. Calvin Klein and all the others came down here to shoot.

Gianni Versace was part of the scene. The famed fashion designer used to go around town with gorgeous models. Then he bought Casa Casuarina, the mansion across the street from the gay beach on Twelfth Street.

"I like the boys," he would say.

MARTIN JEAN: Casa Casuarina was built in the 1930s in the Mediterranean Revival style for Alden Freeman, son and heir of the original treasurer of Standard Oil Trust. He lived in the mansion from 1930 to 1935. A casuarina tree that had been brought to Miami and planted on the property had survived the 1926 hurricane, and it was thought it would bring good luck to name the mansion after it. Hence, Casa Casuarina.

JACK JOHNSON: Alden Freeman was probably gay and never married, but he had a partner, a younger man named Antonio D'amico, whom he adopted. Then he married a woman; they had a child together whom Alden considered his daughter.

The building had twenty-six units that were rented to wealthy tourists. Freeman lived on the top floor left in a unit with a balcony and with his partner's apartment right next door. Freeman lived there until he died.

MARTIN JEAN: In 1992 Versace came upon the mansion and bought it for $2.9 million. He also wanted to buy the property next door for $4 million, but the Revere Hotel was there. The preservation law protected buildings that were built up to 1949, and the Revere was built in 1950. So Versace knocked down what was the third-most photographed home in the United States and made room for a swimming pool and a beautiful courtyard that all the rooms look out on.

ROBERTO DESSOMMES: A friend of mine who was a photographer (everyone was a photographer then) was a real estate agent on the side. Once I was at a party with him, and everyone was telling him, "Congratulations, congratulations."

I asked, "Why is everyone congratulating you?"

And he said, "I just sold Versace's house."

Two years later, I was the manager for the Armani Exchange in a place that used to be an old Cuban market. This was the second Armani in the world; the first was in SoHo in New York, which had recently opened. Now I was riding my bike and passed this space where the sign AX was repeated on the storefront windows. Then I read in the newspaper that interviews for Armani were being held at the Colony Hotel just down the street.

They hired me on the spot. I was one of the opening managers. But two years later, I was back as a manager of the News Café. One day on my way to work, I saw Gianni Versace. He was walking down the street with these two male models. Soon after that, he opened the Versace store in a space that used to be a bank (everything here used to be something else) and was right next door to the Armani store.

Versace was in constant competition with Armani. They were both from Milano, Italy. Versace's longtime boyfriend, Antonio, told me they always had that rivalry.

Every day, Versace would walk down Ocean Drive to the News Café. He'd sit at one of the tables, have his breakfast, and read the paper. People knew who he was, but nobody bothered him. And then, one morning, he finished his breakfast, headed home, and was shot dead right in front of his mansion.

I was at home that day watching the news while I was having breakfast. Then I got on my bike and rode down to the boardwalk. There was a media frenzy: CNN, NBC, and the others, the helicopters, the blood on the steps of the mansion. For a week, every station in the world was on it. I was interviewed time and again and again and again. What did Versace eat? What did he drink? How was he dressed? Was he nice? Did I talk to him?

All of Miami Beach was in a high state of alert. There was a gay killer on the loose. It was someone Versace had met in San Francisco whom he'd had some kind of relationship with before coming to Miami Beach. The killer ended up being cornered by the police and killing himself in a boathouse near the Fontainebleau.

MARTIN JEAN: Andrew Cunanan had already killed four other people in a nationwide killing spree. No one knows why he did what he did. It's a dark story that people are really taken by. The story became a myth: how comfortable Versace was in Miami Beach, how he fell in love with the estate, how he bought the building. Everyone remembers the day Versace was shot dead. It was July 15, 1997, on the steps of his mansion as he returned from a morning walk on Ocean Drive.

Versace's sister sold the property to a businessman who wanted to make it a destination resort for wealthy folks. He ended up renting it to a high-end hotel that is still running and a restaurant that is no longer used. In 2013, it was auctioned off. The winning bid was by the owner of Jordache jeans, which owns the Victor and Breakwater hotels.

ROBERTO DESSOMMES: All over, everything has become corporate, but the News Café remains family owned. Marc Soyka envisioned a little café on the corner of Eighth and Ocean. And look at us twenty-five years later. People can come here, enjoy a cup of coffee or a cappuccino or a mojito, take a paper off the rack, watch the parade of people passing by for hours. And the food is really good.

Everyone who comes to Miami Beach, for the first time at least, has to stop at the News Café. It's a must. We have many repeat customers. I see them every week. Many have become my friends. And don't forget the ocean: on Sundays after work, I take it upon myself to jump into the water.

But things have changed. In the past, I saw Katie Couric just walking down the street. Same with Bryant Gumbel, Calvin Klein, Cindy Crawford. Before you could see everybody strolling along Ocean Drive, enjoying the cafés, the atmosphere, having a mojito.

Now there's a different kind of celebrity, and the attitude on the part of some of them is disappointing. I overheard Kevin Spacey telling the waiter he didn't want to be bothered. Jodie Foster walked by the other day; she wasn't very nice. The parade has changed to more regular people.

But you'll also see a drag queen parade with numbers out of shows such as *La Cage aux Folles*. The Palace on Twelfth and Ocean has drag queen shows on Sundays. The movie *The Birdcage* with Robin Williams took place in Miami Beach; it was filmed right here at The Carlyle Hotel on Fourteenth and Ocean. There are still some terrific things going on.

4

Dancing Up a Storm at Mango's

DAVID WALLACK: Tony Goldman was undoubtedly thinking of his own experience in New York when he said, "Let's do a special taxing district, and we'll get our own street manager. We're not getting the services we should be getting from the city to really make this a world-class street." So we lobbied and got the city to do a special taxing district that we all paid into. We had our own streets manager and people in Loomis Park with nice white shorts with Ocean Drive Association on their shirts and helmets, and they're telling people about this and that. This is early nineties. The street was in a high time. There were very cool cafés opening; people were starting to put in money. Not just buying the buildings, but opening businesses in them.

The Delano began the chic boutique hotels. It was very important, because on Miami Beach there were all these business hotels. Heading north, there were all these mid-sized hotels: the Delano and the Shore Club and that whole string. And then, further north, you had the Fontainebleau and the Eden Roc and the big hotels.

People came down from New York with money and style. It was a renaissance; the area became a mecca for artists of every genre flocking to South Beach and Miami Beach. Many of the hotels were bought by international owners from Germany and France.

We did the Ocean Drive Association and Ocean Drive Improvement Association. And then Mayor David Dermer came along and said, "I'm throwing all that out."

It seems we had too much power. Their attitude was, "The city will give you the services you need. We don't need you to do that anymore." But they didn't give us the services we needed. And the high time of Ocean Drive settled down. It was no longer as clean; it was no longer panache. And it became political.

It was very disheartening. There's always a war going on between the residents and business. But the thing is, when you're in business, different political administrations will come and go, but you have to keep your business going.

David Wallack and his magnificent dogs. Courtesy of Mango's

Now, Mango's was growing. There's a new record every year, and we are up there in the stratosphere, but the growth is not happening. It could be, but it isn't. They killed the new convention plan that would have been the next renaissance. They're saying, "We going to redo it differently." We're starting to meet with commissioners and tell them that architecture is key, that if they don't build a new convention hall, we'll fall right off the map. "You think you're doing good," we tell them, "but you're only going to create a disaster and then justify it by not having good business."

At Mango's, my group was predominantly Latin, and all of a sudden, they're buying booze. I said if I'm going to go broke, I might as well do it in an empty place, not with people standing around just to watch the show. I started charging three dollars at the door just to keep out the bums.

Now, we're making a lot more money. At the door, it could be anywhere from $5 to $10 to $20. On New Year's Eve, $100. Friday and Saturday it could be $20 to come in. I'd rather go out of business than give a free show, take up space, and create problems if I'm not putting any money in the cash register.

I had a line waiting to come in, so we went to $5. Then I noticed there's a line when the band goes on. When the band goes off, there's a line to get out. I've got to figure out this one.

And I thought, *choreography*. I want our girls putting on a show when the band goes off. A choreographer, and everybody else is in dance class every week: managers, busers, servers, and bartenders—all in dance class. As soon as I started with choreographies, there was a bigger line when the band went off than when the band was on. That bridged the gap and became the pattern of growth. And from that, the question became one of refinement of the music and shows, and professional dancers and deejays along with my own staff.

Everybody is contracted to work at Mango's. They can take on a gig, a private party here and there. But they don't have the time. They're working five days a week, and we're open seven days a week, so we have to have multiple people to cover seven days. We have roughly 240, 250 people working year round. We started with fifteen people.

When it was the beginning for all of us on Ocean Drive, I would sit with Marc Soyka and his partner at the News Café before Mango's opened.

"Why did we buy a liquor license? We don't sell liquor," the partner says.

"Oh, stop with the liquor license already," says Marc Soyka.

"Listen, you've got a good thing," I say.

"Just keep going, just keep going. It'll happen."

Marc wasn't cooking. He was all sandwiches and stuff. But he'd say, "My chef's not here. He was arrested last night for getting drunk. I gotta go inside and make the sandwiches."

That was Ocean Drive. And for Mango's, we didn't have a roof. Finally, I got $15,000 to put up an awning. My thought was if it doesn't rain and if we make $1,500 on Friday and $2,500 on Saturday, and $1,200, maybe, on Sunday, we'll make payroll on Monday. And that's the way it was. My mother was at the books, and if there was a little shortfall, we put it in.

Those were the early days. It wasn't like now when we'll do more than $100,000 a day. In Miami Beach, the number one restaurant is still Joe's Stone Crab. It's the classic, number three in the country when it comes to restaurants. At the Fontainebleau, Liv is the number one nightclub. But the number one restaurant/nightclub is Mango's.

Nobody can beat Las Vegas numbers. But we are third in the country outside of Vegas in nightclubs and fourteenth with Vegas.

JUNE HENDERSON: I left Belize for modeling school in New York. After a while I participated in Miami Caribbean carnivals and the hospitality business. I was thirteen years at Doral Golf Resort and Spa, now Trump Doral, twelve years at Marble Company that helped build the Doral. At all these positions I was an executive assistant to the presidents/owners. In the hospitality industry I handled various celebrities and high-profile individuals.

Having never posted a résumé before, since all my positions were strictly from referrals, I decided to seek the same positions and a few caught my eye that stated "Executive Asst./Confidential with photo." After only one month I got David Wallack's call.

We set up an interview at his beautiful waterfront home. David said it would be more comfortable for us to sit down and talk, so we went out on the terrace overlooking the bay. His home is right on the bay, and looking out at the water and seeing downtown Miami on this gorgeous sunny day in June was a special time for *this* June.

Conga at Mango's. Courtesy of Mango's

I liked David the moment I met him. He has great heart and great insights and seems passionate about all he's doing as the owner of Mango's. Just talking with him that first time, I was sure that if I worked with him, I would be kept on my toes.

I made an appointment to come in the next day. I met members of the staff and management; there was a lot of rapport. He made me an offer. I said I wanted two or three days to think it over, and I did think it over very carefully, especially when it came to the extremely busy schedule he had outlined and the work it would entail. He didn't mention how many hours a week that would add up to. Still, I said, "Yes."

The reason David wanted to get the position filled quickly was he was getting set to go to Italy for a two-week vacation and wanted to make sure he had someone in place when he was away. I became that person and have been pretty much on call 24/7 for Mango's as personal and executive assistant to David Wallack.

Courtesy of Mango's

All the managers at Mango's have been handpicked by David. All work as a team. Mango's is open 365 days a year from 11:30 a.m. to 5 the next morning. A lot of things have to be taken care of every day. The total number of employees in Mango's is about 250.

There is also security. We have our own people on hand to take care of any incidents that might take place there. We also have about 150 security cameras placed in different positions. Mango's is a very secure place.

The total seating capacity is about eight hundred including private rooms. Performers can be brought to these rooms to dance and sing. It is a gigantic enterprise.

Miguel Parra, from Venezuela, has been here a long time. He's in charge of entertainment—the look, the costumes, the music, the performers. Many of our entertainers have come from TV shows, Telemundo. A lot of dancers are from Cuba, Peru, Santo Domingo. The guys at the bar also have been here seven, eight years. They are a team.

Courtesy of Mango's

Doors open to the public at 11:45 every morning. A lot of families with kids come in, people from the beach, tourists, people from the area. It's not uncommon to see a two-year-old dancing on the floor with one or two of our dancers. Daytime at Mango's is amazingly family-oriented, but at eight o'clock the place changes into an adult environment. One must be twenty-one years old to be admitted.

Through the years all kinds of celebrities have come to Mango's: LeBron James, Dwyane Wade, Pitbull, Steven Seagal—they love it here. Versace, I was told, was a frequent visitor. But it is when David comes into Mango's that the place really lights up. Entertainers and staff members come over to greet him, give him a kiss and a hug. Some owners are untouchable. David is not; he has an open door.

More than one million visitors a year come to Mango's. We have a lot of repeat customers. Everyone who comes to Miami, whether on a business trip or a vacation, seems to make it a point to visit Mango's. We have customers from all over the world, from all walks of life, from all kinds of places: North and South America, China, Australia, England, Italy. All say the same thing: "What an amazing experience!"

DANCING UP A STORM AT MANGO'S

And it's true—there is a beat, a rhythm, a movement from the Latin music that takes over. People just gravitate to the salsa, merengue, cha-cha, rumba. When David first opened Mango's many years back, this Cuban girl jumped up on the bar and started dancing. It just lit a fire. "This should never stop," David said. It never has.

I love dancing. It's all feeling. I get up on the floor all the time, but I've never, never gotten up with the dancers on the stage. Members of the staff have been urging me to get up there, but I don't think I belong there. I belong on the floor. Sometimes I'll walk into Mango's in the morning or afternoon. A great song will be playing, and I'll get on the floor and start dancing, get the crowd going. Then I'll move on to my office. But maybe one day I will get up on the stage.

Mango's is unique to me. Every day I love it more. The salsa, the mambo, the rumba, reggae, hip-hop, salsa, the merengue, the Michael Jackson show—the music is always on. It just embraces you and fills you. There is always a beat, a rhythm, a song in the air. All those girls who come from Cuba, from Tropicana or another club, they come right off the plane and go directly to Mango's. They'll ask for a job because they know it's the place to be.

5

It's Not All about Ocean Drive

What Happened on Lincoln Road

> It was Morris who decided to bring in the tropical influences from cities around the world and present them in a modernist form.
>
> —Philip Smith

MICHAEL ALLER: Lincoln Road is the heart of Miami Beach, centered, as it is, in the center of the universe here. It is our fashion place of wonderful adventure, a mainstay of Miami Beach for all these many years. Everybody goes to Lincoln Road. When I was a child, I'd go there with my parents. We would dress up. We would go shopping. We would have dinner there.

Lincoln Road is like the Champs Élysées of Paris, it's like Fifth Avenue—only more magnificent, because it is in Miami Beach where the weather is eighty degrees on an average daily basis and the sun is always shining.

It was Morris Lapidus who did Lincoln Road. All those little pigeon stops along the way are his creations. The black-and-white stripes on the cement path, the different portico chairs, the oval that has been used for years and years and years—a wonderful stop especially at Christmastime when you have Hanukkah and Christmas trees.

PHILIP SMITH: In the thirties, forties, and into the fifties, Lincoln Road was the Fifth Avenue of the South, the chic shopping place for snowbirds. It had great stores such as Saks Fifth Avenue and Bonwit Teller, even a Cadillac dealership. And it was where you could get New York fashion.

My father had his first design studio there on the second floor of what was or is the Van Dyke building, a huge kind of loft space above a series of stores—I can remember as a kid running up and down the stairs. My father would design interiors there and had a factory that made furniture and draperies. It was so chic a destination that clients who would come to him would also come to shop on the Lincoln Road Mall at Saks and other stores.

Back in the fifties, the city wanted to take Lincoln Road to the next level. It had had its good days in the thirties and forties and was still going in the fifties. But people were moving to the suburbs while Miami Beach had basically become a retirement home for the elderly. And they were not shopping; they were walking.

Then, the architect Morris Lapidus came in, and he designed these sort of modernistic pavilions where people could sit. There would be some fountains. Most importantly, he designed the black-and-white walkway, reminiscent of Copacabana in Brazil. He wanted to give the area a modernist tropical feel. Tropical modernism started with Morris. Later on, it would be picked up by lots of other people, but it was Morris who decided to bring in the tropical influences from cities around the world and present them in a modernist form.

IRA GILLER: In 1959, Morris Lapidus proposed an open-air pedestrian mall, one of the first in America, along the six blocks of Lincoln Road. Closed to automobile traffic, it was a big hit for a time.

PHILIP SMITH: In creating the pedestrian mall on Lincoln Road, Morris drew on an international vocabulary of architecture. It was a walkable urban shopping area with gardens, fountains, and shelters, and characterized by the MiMo or mid-century modern style he pioneered.

ALAN MANDEL: When I came here from Cuba in 1961, it was the latter part of Miami Beach's mid-century glory period and still tremendously glamorous. Lincoln Road was a promenade of high style. There were eight movie theaters on Lincoln Road alone, and they were grander than any I've ever seen before or since.

I guess they were like the Paramount or the Roxy in New York. All were all air-conditioned and elegant. As a little kid, I was awestruck.

MARY NIVEN: As teenagers, we used to walk up and down Lincoln Road, eleven o'clock, twelve o'clock at night. Woolworth's was our meeting place. It was safe—a different life.

LILIA GARCIA: I'm on the board of the Lincoln Road Arts Center, the organization that changed Lincoln Road. At the very beginning, Lincoln Road was very upscale with all the top stores. But as the culture of the community changed, it became dangerous, boarded up, a place for homeless people.

Then this woman, a ceramic artist and the wife of a big grant writer, built a studio on Lincoln Road and made it her studio. She renovated storefronts for practically nothing, started writing grants, and almost singlehandedly changed the entire scene. That was the start of the South Florida Arts Center on Lincoln Road.

Artists arrived; they started working in the studios. Collectors came; they wanted to buy art. Tourists came; they wanted a place to visit. They also wanted a place to eat. So up came a restaurant. It did so well that soon another restaurant opened. Books & Books came in. But as soon as they saw a Gap, the artists started leaving. It took about ten years, but eventually all the artists moved out.

PHILIP SMITH: By the early seventies Lincoln Road was hit hard. The elegant shops had moved north to Bal Harbour, and everything was closed and shuttered. There were still some shops: a store run by a woman who sold German cosmetics and spa treatments, souvenir places that featured Miami Beach paraphernalia, snow globes with flamingos in them, picture postcards, and little shot glasses that said *Miami Beach*.

But the movie theater had closed; no restaurants were left. Buildings and storefronts were mostly shuttered with aluminum shields or plywood nailed to windows. It was like preparation for a hurricane.

JUSTIN MOSS: Virtually the totality of Lincoln Road was boarded up at that time. You walked down the street, and you felt your life was probably imperiled. Every character you saw lurking in some boarded-up doorway looked dangerous. The doorways of storefronts stank of urine; people were holed up and living in them.

There were maybe three viable businesses on the entire strip. I can remember a first-rate linen shop, of all things, that sold table linens and whatnot. But it sat in complete isolation across the street from what had been a branch of Saks Fifth Avenue. It was a no-man's-land, overrun with very troubled souls.

ROBERTO JUAREZ: Lincoln Road was really funky then, not in great shape. I remember when Robert Miller, my art dealer in New York, moved down to Miami. We would walk up Lincoln Road, and he would say, "This is like the World's Fair at the end of the world."

PHILIP SMITH: Lincoln Road, in particular, felt the decline of the area greatly with businesses moving north to Bal Harbour. It went into a period of desolation. Lincoln Road was forgotten.

JOHN TURCHIN: There was a time when I tried to open a club on Lincoln Road. I had the Lincoln Theater and the Sony Building tied up, put both sides

John Turchin. Courtesy of John Turchin

of the street under lease. For four full years I had an option, but I couldn't get a soul to invest on Lincoln Road. I had a place called Theodore. I bought the lease. You could lease anything on Lincoln Road back then for $2 a square foot, but you couldn't give it away. Now it's $300 a square foot. More.

PHILIP SMITH: I can remember when the city wanted to tear up the pedestrian mall and allow parking in front of stores. But that would have turned Lincoln Road into basically a strip mall like thousands of other strip malls around south Florida. There was a little tram service— sometimes free, sometimes twenty-five cents— that would shuttle you back and forth.

If you were looking for property, you could pick up one of the buildings for $250,000. A tall tower would have a million-dollar price tag, but they would probably take $500,000. Not much was going on.

Courtesy of Frommer Archives

MITCHELL KAPLAN: In 1989, we took a chance and opened a bookstore on Lincoln Road in the Sterling Building, a beautiful Art Deco structure. There were some rumblings, and people were beginning to invest. But it was still very early. In those days nobody thought Miami Beach was going to develop into much.

Still, there was a feeling that there would be battles to develop that whole area. When we opened the bookstore, just the fact that a legitimate business came to Lincoln Road was an event. The *Miami Herald* had a headline: "Books & Books Moving to Lincoln Road." The rent we paid has probably gone up a thousand percent since then, but at the time, it was really great news.

PHILIP SMITH: And then Lincoln Road turned around again, became the incredible destination, *the* destination today in Miami Beach for dining, people watching, shopping, even looking at the 1111 Lincoln Road garage built at a cost of $65 million, which was written up in *The New Yorker* and *The New York Times.* People go the corner of Lincoln Road and Jefferson Street to gaze at a parking garage.

Once again, it is reinventing what it was. Knocking down stores and rebuilding to accommodate bigger chain stores like the Gap, Lincoln Road has become a place where very cool people watch what is going on as they stroll down the walkways, take in the strip of high-fashion stores, dine at one of the outdoor restaurants.

Meanwhile, the rents keep going up. The little stores, the specialty stores will soon not be able to exist.

MARC SOYKA: At one point, I found the Van Dyke building on Lincoln Road. It was smack in the middle of Jefferson Road and the tallest building built by Carl Fischer, who was the founder of Miami Beach. I bought the building and opened a second restaurant, and with that, I thought everything in my life had come together.

I'm a very hands-on person. I love the restaurant business. I enjoy seating people at the News Café, cleaning the tables with a *schmatta* [rag] over my shoulder. The Van Dyke, with its beautiful restaurant and also a café, seemed to me a perfect addition. Together, they would be the two places where I'd spend my time.

But after more than twenty years, I closed the Van Dyke. I had to do it. I had never closed a place before. Real estate is about as expensive in Miami Beach as it is on Madison Avenue in New York. And I saw the writing on the wall: my lease as it would come up for renewal would go to numbers that would not make sense.

When I sold the Van Dyke, five, six years ago, it was contingent upon my keeping the restaurant that was occupying two floors including the café and the jazz room upstairs. My wishes were fulfilled by the buyer. But then, about a year ago, he sold the building. And the new people paid so much money for it that they had to raise rents to the point where it really is Madison Avenue.

The landlord decided he would try to work a deal with me. I really didn't want to give back my remaining lease, but he made it impossible to refuse, because I knew the future was not going to be as comfortable financially with the kind of rents I would have to pay.

It's all becoming corporate. It's in Monte Carlo, in Venice—the white plastic chairs that appear in every place in Europe. That's the way life is. It was the right moment, the right time, and I did it. But I still cannot go to the corner and walk by.

The News Café recently celebrated its twenty-fifth anniversary. There is a place by the Colony Theater and a big outdoor café that are mine too. It's called Segafredo, which is the name of a coffee company—the Starbucks of Europe—and we were the first ones to import it. I still keep it.

I keep everything, including my wife and my four children. I learned how to delegate and do what I do best. Today we're a big company. Even without the Van Dyke, I have five restaurants in Miami and Miami Beach and more than five hundred employees.

PHILIP SMITH: Today, in addition to the 1111 Lincoln Road parking garage, Lincoln Road features a state-of-the-art multiplex cinema, the New World Center concert hall, more than two hundred designer boutiques, local merchants, and national retail stores. It also has a wealth of fine restaurants and bars and is home to the newly restored Colony Theater, a performing arts venue, and a collection of studios and gallery spaces for artists. Street performers entertain a constant stream of tourists and locals up and down the walkways. Lincoln Road is among the most popular destinations for visitors to the South Beach area.

ROBERTO JUAREZ: You go there now, and it is chic, beautiful people, expensive stores everywhere. I have no problem with what has happened. It's wonderful that everything is kept up and taken care of and lots of people love it.

But it was nice when it was dead, quiet. For a painter, that's preferable.

6

Postwar Glamour

Ladies and gentlemen, here is Judy Garland!

—Laney Sheldon

IRA GILLER: In the postwar years, Florida was a fertile ground for building. My father was an architect; his clients were young developers who built houses in Miami Beach and out in west Miami. The hotel business was zooming. Motels—a new class of facilities that you could drive your car up to—developed.

My father designed the first motel in Sunny Isles and then the first two-story hotel in America. In the early- to mid-1950s, he designed more than 50 percent of the hotels and motels in Sunny Isles, which had become the playground for people who were more family-oriented and couldn't afford the expensive Miami Beach hotels. Most of them were low-rises, but he also did the five-story Thunderbird—that was a big building!—and the Diplomat in nearby Hollywood. I spent some time with my father while the Diplomat was under construction. It was subsequently torn down and replaced by a high-rise. But at the time, it had that postwar glamour.

CHARLIE CINNAMON: Those were the real glamour days of Miami Beach, the place to get your suntan and go back north to show it off, the time people came down to see what was called "this year's hotel." It seemed there was a hotel being built on the beach every twenty minutes. The garment district came down from New York in droves, women wearing sables and minks and diamonds. Through the fifties, sixties, seventies, all of it was wonderful.

People like me used to go back and forth to New York by car to see family or whatever. We didn't stop at hotels; we went nonstop, aside from gassing up and eating. There were very few interstates. We'd drive trying to break our own records. Later on, we flew.

PHILIP SMITH: In the summer in the 1950s, my mom, Esther Smith, who was very glamorous, would go to the hotels with my father, Lew Smith. They would drink cocktails. They would see comedians such as Shecky Greene and entertainers such as Dean Martin. They were very well dressed. My mom had a lot of handmade jewelry; she was very vivacious and very beautiful. My father would wear sharkskin suits. Because of his clients, he would often be on the front page of the Home Section of *The Miami Herald* on a Sunday. It was high society.

IRA GILLER: Art Deco had its time in the thirties. It was new, it was fresh, it was the latest thing. Come postwar, Art Deco isn't so hot any longer. Now it's the MiMo era, mid-century modern architecture. Developers move in, renovate the buildings, turn them into posh mid-century modern places that are bigger and grander.

In the thirties and forties, people went to nightclubs for entertainment. In the fifties and sixties, the nightclubs were right in the hotels. No longer did you have to drive over to Lincoln Road to go shopping, because the shops were right in your hotel. But by the seventies, Saks Fifth Avenue and the other Bal Harbour stores had taken away some of the high-fashion clientele.

My father was on the cusp of all this, because when he first started his career he worked for Henry Hohauser, an Art Deco architect who designed a lot of hotels in South Beach during the mid-fifties. That was the boom period of postwar hotels. The Fontainebleau, the Eden Roc, the Diplomat, the Deauville—they were all built during that time.

Miami beach in the 1950s. Courtesy of Frommer Archives

JEFF LEHMAN: It was the time of the big, splashy hotels. They all had entertainment. Even a forty-room hotel on Ocean Drive would have a clown performing for the kids. And if you went up north to the Fontainebleau and such, there was talent on the order of Frank Sinatra, Judy Garland, Dean Martin and Jerry Lewis. Jackie Gleason and Ed Sullivan did their shows from Miami Beach.

HELEN KAPLAN: The Fontainebleau was the first big, really gorgeous hotel that opened.

It had all the great performers, everybody. I saw Frank Sinatra there; I saw Judy Garland, who sat on the apron of the stage and sang whatever song anyone asked for. When we first got married, Joe and I took dancing lessons—mambo and cha-cha, and then we went dancing in the nightclub at the Sans Souci, a little further up from the Fontainebleau.

MICHAEL ALLER: At the Fontainebleau there were Jack and Mary Benny, Bennett Cerf, George Jessel, Judy Garland. They stayed in the cabanas when they were appearing in the hotels or for their own vacations. I was introduced to Judy Garland, whom I adore, and she invited us to her show.

I lived at the Fontainebleau with my parents from the time it opened in 1954 until 1968. We had a three-bedroom apartment on the twelfth floor overlooking the city and the ocean. Frank Sinatra was there—he took a liking to me—I was just a kid then. I used to walk him from the Fleur de Lis room to the stage door at the La Ronde, the big nightclub. He would grab the microphone and start singing in the doorway as he walked onto the stage. Sammy Davis Jr. was a constant with Dean Martin. "Birth of the Blues" was Sammy's song—it still stays with me. So does Frank's singing of "My Way."

Jackie Gleason and a young Ira Giller. Of Gleason, Giller recalled, "He loved Miami Beach, put it on the map." Courtesy of Ira Giller

POSTWAR GLAMOUR

FLOYD MAC McSWANE: I was a Fontainebleau bellman from the time it opened in 1954. I saw Betty Grable and Harry James, Frank Sinatra, Dean Martin and Sammy Davis, Judy Garland, the Beatles, Elvis, the Gabor sisters. They all entertained at La Ronde, and I took care of all of them. Sammy Davis was the nicest.

So were the gangsters. The James Bond movie *Goldfinger* with Sean Connery was filmed there. So was *Surfside 6* and *The Bellboy* with Jerry Lewis. I played the part of the bellboy. I also took care of Kennedy, Johnson, Nixon, Golda Meir—I was their personal concierge. JFK's suite was on the penthouse floor: number 1784. Marilyn Monroe's: number 1782.

I saw it all, from the days when the high rollers dealt out big bills, to the times Joan Crawford would sweep in carrying a makeup case filled with miniature bottles of vodka. The ballroom was built to be a casino that could hold nine thousand people. That never came to be, but national political conventions were held here, both Democratic and Republican.

LANEY SHELDON: When I came down to Miami Beach in 1957, I was almost twenty-one and vacationing at the Seville. I went into the dance studio there to take some lessons, and before I left, they offered me a job. I went back home and told my father I wanted to move to Florida. He said, "You can't leave before you're twenty-one."

I waited till my birthday and came down again. But now it was in-season time, and all the dancers at the Seville were working. So I got a job as a switchboard operator at the Catalina Hotel, and before long, a job as a dance instructor opened up at the Seville.

I didn't know a lot of steps; I tried to stay one step ahead of my pupils, and for the most part, I succeeded. Like all the girls in my family, I had learned ballroom dancing from my Uncle Jack. He and his brother were in show business and did the USO shows during the war. Along with my father, who also loved to dance, they would get all the girls up. They loved Latin couples dancing.

DAVE ROGERS: I used to hang around a lot with my friend Lenny Savitz, who was stage manager at the Deauville. I'd go over to the Deauville, see all the shows, go backstage and climb up the ladder into the lighting booth. That's how I saw Wayne Newton, the Smothers Brothers, Linda Ronstadt, the Supremes, Sammy Davis Jr.

LANEY SHELDON: We had champagne hours at the Seville along with dance contests. Later on we'd do shows at the different hotels like the Carillon. Every hotel had a Latin band, dance studios in the lower lobby, and male teachers. They used to give a dance class: couples, singles, whatever. I taught whatever they wanted to learn.

All the pupils tried to get fresh. But the wives were there. We all were in the same room, a lot of people from New York, New Jersey. We did mambo, cha-cha, waltz, fox-trot, rumba, tango. There were contests. We used to make up a routine for our pupils so they could get up and do a routine with the teacher and win the big trophies.

The ones I found very difficult to teach were the Latin people, because they had their own rhythm; "Mi Corazón" (My Heart). They loved to dance; they had that feel inside them. I ended up dancing with them rather than teaching them.

After I was at the Seville for a while, I was asked to go to the Fontainebleau, where friends of mine ran the dance studio. That was a step upward. It was such a big place; there was so much magic to it, so much glamour. The Fontainebleau was the first of its kind on the beach. Everyone who went there wanted to be seen.

Across the street was the three-story Surrey Hotel, where all the entertainers who worked on the beach lived. Among them was Bert Sheldon, the man who would become my husband. Ben Novak, owner of the Fontainebleau, had given Bert, who was a serious singer, a tenor who did show music and had appeared on Broadway, the job of entertainment director at the Concord Hotel in the Catskills. Now Ben offered him the job at the Fontainebleau. That was it—just a handshake. Bert was there for fifteen years.

I saw all the big acts at the La Ronde Room because my husband introduced them. He introduced Sinatra when he was performing at the Fontainebleau.

One night, I was dancing with my partner during a champagne hour in the Fontainebleau's Boom Boom Room when I feel somebody grabbing my hair. I take a look. It's Jackie Gleason. He had just done *The Jackie Gleason Show* with Art Carney and Audrey Meadows and had come to the Boom Boom Room to celebrate.

And that was how I found myself looking into Jackie Gleason's beautiful blue eyes and dancing with him. He was so light on his feet. We breezed along. That's all I remember except the song the band was playing: "Miami Beach Rumba."

Another time I was playing the maracas in front of the Latin band at the Baltimore. I finished my set, and my husband said to me, "I want you to meet somebody."

He introduced me to Edward Pierce from CBS. "We want you and the whole band to do the Orange Bowl Parade on New Year's Eve down Biscayne Boulevard," he said. That was New Year's Eve 1968. The temperature was a beautiful seventy-five degrees. They picked us up in a limousine.

The Supremes, Danny Thomas, performers in all the acts of the day were in the floats, moving to the music of "La Bamba." Every Cuban in town lined the streets; even babies in diapers were dancing. We made the front page of *The Miami Herald*.

Whenever Sinatra came to the hotel, it was electric. Ann-Margret, Sammy Davis, Jackie Gale, who introduced Sinatra every night—they were all there. Sinatra would be filming during the day, *Tony Rome*, for example, and doing the shows at the hotel at night. He was married to Ava Gardner then.

I remember the time I was standing in the lobby by the maître d's desk. The show is ready to go on, and this vision comes into the La Ronde room: tall, dark, statuesque, gorgeous; in a green velvet outfit that was probably painted on her, with black velvet cuffs and collar. People part the aisles as Ava Gardner goes down to the stage, sits down, and watches Sinatra. For me, it was like a tennis match, looking at one and then the other.

I used to watch Frank Sinatra every night. I never really spoke to him—you could tell he didn't want to be bothered—but we used to go to the Gigi Room, and when Sinatra was there, he and his people would stay on until five o'clock in the morning.

He certainly didn't mind, however, when Elvis Presley came to the Fontainebleau in 1960. He had just gotten out of the service, and Sinatra threw a big party for him in the La Ronde Room. Still in uniform, Presley sang the Sinatra standard "Witchcraft," while Sinatra sang "Love Me Tender."

Once my husband got a call backstage: "We have a problem. Debbie Reynolds is sick and can't go on. Do you think there's a chance we can get Judy Garland to go on at the Eden Roc and do a couple of songs?"

"Of course."

They send the limousine over. It makes a huge turn into the Fontainebleau. Judy had gotten her hair done by her stylist and whatever else she needed. She gets into the limo. Meanwhile at the Eden Roc, the people are waiting for Debbie Reynolds. They're going nuts already because they're waiting and waiting. They've eaten up their minimum, and there's nobody on stage.

Suddenly the band starts playing "Over the Rainbow." There's the announcement: "Due to the sudden illness of Debbie Reynolds, we have a surprise for you. Ladies and gentlemen, here is Judy Garland!"

Wow! The place went wild! She did a number of songs. She's a hit at the Eden Roc.

But there's a backstory to all of this. The owners of the Fontainebleau and the Eden Roc hate each other. In fact, Ben had put up a big wall—they called it the Spite Wall—to block the sun from the Eden Roc's pool. After the show, we go back to the Fontainebleau. My husband is getting ready to work when he gets the word: "Novak wants to see you." He goes into Novak's office and explains that as a performer he always tries to help another performer.

"I'm sorry if I did something out of line, but this is what I thought I had to do," he says.

"Don't ever do it again," Novak tells him.

A couple of days later, Debbie Reynolds is fully recovered. We go over to see her. No sooner do we walk next door and go into the nightclub, then the maître d' of the Eden Roc lays down on the floor so we could walk over him. They couldn't do enough for my husband.

We start walking down to the stage when suddenly my husband turns to me. "We're not going any further," he says. "Novak's sitting there at a table for twelve."

But move on we did and take our seats. In the middle of the show, Debbie stops. "As you know I was under the weather this weekend, and Judy Garland graciously did the show for me. I would like to introduce you to the hotel owner who allowed her to entertain here."

Ben Novak gets up, waves to the crowd, eats it all up. He's the hero.

JIM LAWRENCE: After their performances, all the famous entertainers used to go to Denny's. At the same time, it was the place where any guy could take a date. You got three little sandwiches, pastrami, corned beef, all the pickles and coleslaw you could eat. One night we were there when the place was packed, and they gave us one of the big round tables in the back. Someone tapped me on the shoulder. I turned around. "Kid," he said, "do you know that man sitting over there?"

I looked and said, "Yeah! That's Uncle Miltie!"

Milton Berle smiled and said, "See? I'm not dead."

LANEY SHELDON: Christmas time, the gardens of the Fontainebleau were made to look like the gardens of Versailles. The property was turned into a circus with tents, clowns, elephants, and monkeys. That was outside.

Inside, the ballroom was turned into a carnival with all kinds of little booths. There was so much going on. Cocktail parties, continuous music—nonstop, every day.

LISA COLE: When Steve Muss bought the Fontainebleau, one of the first things he did was to remove the drapes from all the lobby windows. He wanted to see the ocean, the beach, the pool.

He did the pool over before he had the rooms renovated. Then he added Cookie World—a children's fantasy water playground with a waterslide, raft ride, and Cookie—a gigantic water-spraying octopus. It was for the kids, but everyone loved it.

FLOYD MAC McSWANE: Back then, the marble floors were polished every night. You couldn't walk into our lobby after five in the evening if you didn't have a jacket and tie. Back then, the bellmen used to have a dress code; I'd keep jackets and ties in my locker. Back then everyone used a bellman. Now they roll their own luggage.

LANEY SHELDON: When it was party time at the Fontainebleau, I'd teach, go out, do shows, come back, hang around the lounge, run home, take a shower, go back to teach. It was a great life; I wouldn't change it for the world. Everything I learned was in Miami. I grew up in Miami.

JOSEPH KRUTEL: This was the Riviera; this was where it was. The day of the Fontainebleau, Frank Sinatra and Dean Martin, the Rat Pack. These guys were the biggest of the biggest. I saw them as a child, although I wasn't old enough to grasp what was going on.

Look at the original photographs in the Fontainebleau that Morris Lapidus built for Ben Novak, the columns and the marble, the craftsmanship, the ice-skating rink. Who puts an ice-skating rink in South Beach, in a hotel? There was such respect, such style. Even the valet parkers were dressed up.

There was a very famous photographer, Terry O'Neill, who took photos of a movie being made in 1968, the year I was born. It was a black-and-white shot of Frank Sinatra's double walking to sit with security on the second level of the cabanas in front of what was our cabana. Cabanas were a huge thing. They were set to the side in a curved double layer like a boardwalk, and it was made of wood. My mother used to warn me not to walk on it barefoot. But I did, and often I would get a splinter. They'd call out for a doctor; there were so many doctors around. The doctor would put on his glasses, take out a tweezers, and remove the splinter.

The people who rented the cabanas were largely local. You could rent for the day, or you could do it by the month. The menus were fabulous. Hotel food was great. The service was impeccable. The food would be wheeled out on a tray with a fresh flower in a vase, with silverware, china, a cloth napkin.

There were all the other hotels. The Eden Roc, for example, which Morris did as well. It attracted a lot of great stars of the day such as Elizabeth Taylor, Humphrey Bogart, Lauren Bacall, Frank Sinatra, Katharine Hepburn, Ernest Hemingway, Sammy Davis Jr.

But the Fontainebleau was the Fontainebleau. It had the Poodle Lounge. Jerry Lewis would be there and Lenny Bruce and Alan King, who was a compulsive gambler, and Larry King.

My father was great friends with all of them. I met them all.

IRA GILLER: The Miami Beach community had that attitude of, "We're Miami Beach. If you want to see us, you're going to have to come here." Starting in the fifties, the jet plane made it very easy to get here from the northeast. But, at the same time, it opened up traffic to other places: the Caribbean, Vegas, Mexico, Europe.

The result, by the early seventies, was stagnation. There were many family-owned hotels, apartment houses, small retail businesses. But the families were tired; they didn't want to do a revision. The strip had lost its charm.

JEFF LEHMAN: In the sixties it was the Rat Pack at the Fontainebleau. Then it was the Mariel boatlift. We had no infrastructure for all these people, and the entire city collapsed. Drugs, prostitution, crime on every level—that was the Miami Beach of the seventies. Then the leaders rose to the stop. The most obvious group was the Cubans.

LISA COLE: By the late seventies, entertainers who once played at La Ronde found they could make more money, attract bigger audiences in Vegas. Those were sluggish years. Miami Beach kind of fell to its knees. The Fontainebleau wasn't getting the tourists; they weren't fixing up the place. The La Ronde always had some kind of show. However, in the summer it would close down.

LANEY SHELDON: Things had changed. We heard about these four guys from England and went over to the Deauville to see them. "They sound nice," was all I said. I really didn't know that kind of music. The twist came in, the rock bands. I wasn't a fan. I stayed away from them.

Somehow, it ended. The baby boomers grew up; the older people had gone to different areas. It was gradual; and then all of a sudden, it stopped. I got out of the dance business and went into conventions, "meet and greet" at hotels, hospitality, tours.

When the hotels started to go down, I was out of it. The stories and memories of the Fontainebleau are still in my mind. But I had reached a point where I didn't want to keep dancing.

7

Morris Lapidus

Architect of Joy

He had a light within him.

—Michael Aller

IRA GILLER: I'm not big on hyperbole, but Morris Lapidus certainly made his mark on American architecture. He was half a generation older than my father. They were colleagues but competitors as well. We'd see him Thursdays for lunch at the Kiwanis Club; my mother-in-law and his wife played bridge together.

MICHAEL ALLER: As a member of the Kiwanis Club of Miami Beach, I was often present when somebody didn't show up for a meeting. Those times Morris Lapidus would always be asked to speak. He would tell tremendous stories.

IRA GILLER: Although he started out as a theater-set and store-window designer in New York City, when he came down to Miami he began designing the hotels that became his most famous work. He did hotels in New York as well—the Americana, the Summit—but his base was Miami Beach.

PHILIP SMITH: Morris sort of defined Miami. He not only defined, he invented Miami glamour in the fifties, sixties. Glamour is not really an American concept. It is totally European and something that until the past decade or two was alien to the American culture, because we were largely very puritanical. But when it came to Morris, the glamour was there from the start. You walked into his hotels, and you were in a glamorous environment. You felt glamorous. You felt privileged. You felt you were royalty. This was a vocabulary that he invented. It didn't matter whether you were a busboy or president of a foreign country.

I don't know enough about how much Hollywood influenced him, but his buildings are pure Hollywood. You walked into one of the palaces he designed and you were on a movie set. He wanted to elevate people in such a way that they would feel they were in front of a backdrop that lent them glamour.

You can go to the Pierre, the Plaza, other high-end hotels in New York, and they have their European regal glamour. But the Fontainebleau, the Eden Roc, all those places Morris designed in Miami Beach had a new kind of glamour, a certain kind of pizzazz.

Ben Novak, the son of Charles Novak who owned the Catskills' Laurels in the Pines, selected Morris to be the architect of the Fontainebleau. It was the first hotel Lapidus did in Miami Beach. And my general impression was that it was wonderland, grand. Everywhere you looked there was an unusual detail: the sort of fluting around the elevator, the incredible staircases, the open gardens in the middle of the hotel, the rococo surfaces, the many unorthodox shapes he referred to as "woggles." The Fontainebleau was a locale that existed nowhere except in the world of Morris's imagination.

LISA COLE: That Morris Lapidus was all about innovation can be seen in most of the 1,200 buildings and 250 hotels worldwide that he designed. In the 1950s when everything was boxy, his look was revolutionary, all about circular lines.

Morris was into making entrances and catching attention. He had a terrarium with live alligators installed in the Fontainebleau lobby. He designed this enormous swirling stairway that went from the lobby up to the mezzanine. Today the hotel's offices are located there, but half a century ago, there was nothing on the mezzanine except the top of the stairway.

On their way to dinner and an evening at La Ronde, the women would get off the elevator on the mezzanine while the men would continue on down to the lobby. Then they would proceed to the foot of the stairs and watch as the ladies, in their couture gowns and glittering jewels, descended.

When Steve Muss bought the Fontainebleau, he had all the carpeting taken up. Underneath were white, square-shaped marble floors that had a little black triangle in each corner. The triangle of one tile would meet the adjacent one forming the image of a bowtie, a signature motif of both Morris Lapidus and Ben Novak.

IRA GILLER: The Fontainebleau was overstated. It made use of twenty-seven colors of paint. If you look at the hotel's exterior, the sweeping curve, you think it's a fantastic idea, but the interior elements are equally over the top.

When the Fontainebleau first opened, Lapidus called it "the world's most pretentious hotel." He said it was "flamboyant" and later on declared: "I wanted people to walk in and drop dead. I wanted them to say, 'My God, this is luxury.'"

PHILIP SMITH: I interviewed Morris Lapidus for *GQ* in the very early eighties when his career was sort of forgotten by most people. When I met with him in his small office in Miami Beach, he was forthcoming about himself and his career. He was wearing a bow tie—back then architects favored bow ties—and he wasn't particularly distinguished looking. But he carried himself with dignity.

I don't think he was getting many commissions at the time. There didn't seem to be a lot of work coming in for him. Miami was dead. Nobody was building down here. His glory days had been the sixties. People asked, "Who's this guy?" No one saw his genius.

Morris had done some commercial glass and steel buildings in the seventies, but I don't believe his true spirit came through in those works. In a way, they were a little bit anonymous.

It is very hard when you have accomplished acts of genius and then are deserted by the public, deserted by the critics, deserted by the marketplace. Your lifestyle becomes more modest; it becomes very, very hard to maintain your dignity. But he did. At the same time, I am not saying he was impoverished by any means; he was estimated to have billed $50 million in his career. But Morris Lapidus had much more to give, and he was not given the opportunity. He had to deal with the ups and downs of a creative career, which is never easy.

I do not think the article I wrote about Morris for *GQ* received a lot of attention, because by that time he had largely been written off; his time seemed to have passed. He had written a monograph—*Morris Lapidus: An Architecture of Joy* with Deborah Desilets—but it didn't get a lot of play.

Here in America, we tend to go through people very quickly. We use them. We exploit their talent, buy it and sell it, and then forget about it. The market curtailed his creative activity, which was really a shame. The critics and other architects made fun of him.

IRA GILLER: Frank Lloyd Wright, whose buildings had detail but in an understated sort of way, was scathing in his judgment of Lapidus's work.

PHILIP SMITH: Morris had a very rough time career-wise. What he was able to do at the height of his career was amazing and welcome, but the architects who didn't know how to design buildings were largely brutal to him because his work was not the prevailing orthodoxy at the time. It was inventive, creative, unlike anything else that existed then. But they did not understand how to process it, and not knowing, they destroyed it with words.

You have to look at what he did in context. Although he wasn't limited to hotels, Morris is most remembered for them. He had the idea that people wanted to see and be seen, and therefore the lobby is a social element of a hotel. He very much took to that concept. He had a good sense of design and a good sense of what he was about. He was also a good storyteller who told his stories not only in words, but in buildings.

MICHAEL ALLER: Morris was the son of Russian immigrants who grew up in a ghetto and liked to talk about going to Coney Island and seeing the gleaming light and shine of Luna Park. Morris Lapidus had a light within him.

PHILIP SMITH: He was a talented man, a man of great vision, a man who was ahead of his time. When he designed the Fontainebleau, the traditional architectural community rejected it vehemently as being too outrageous, too indulgent, not serious architecture. But today—fifty years later, sixty years later—they look at it and think it is great work.

I am thrilled that he got rediscovered in the late 1990s and 2000s, that people started having symposiums on his work. There is still a lot for any architect to learn from that work. Just think of the sort of bubbles on the exterior of the Fontainebleau, for example, how they evoke Art Deco, Modernism. To formalize that in architecture is a huge accomplishment. It still works; it will always work.

He wanted people to walk in and feel majestic. And I think he accomplished that. What they have done today to his hotels is sort of tragic. They have lost his spirit. They have been decorated, for want of a better word, and not successfully.

Morris understood aspiration. He captured that more than any other architect I can imagine. If you go into the Taj Mahal, you'll find it is pretty aspirational. But Morris's architecture will sweep you off your feet. You'll forget who you are. You'll become someone else. That is a very rare accomplishment.

Morris did not cater to the cliché Miami colors of pink and turquoise. He used very sophisticated coloration. There were woods and golds and black-and-white and some turquoise in the background. It was a very decisive palette. The garish Miami colors were not prevalent. His work was incredibly sophisticated.

What remains of his work should be designated as historical heritage sites or something like that, because there are so few left. They are so unique. God help us if someone wants to tear them down and put up big twin towers, seventy stories high.

It was innovative and visionary and uniquely his own signature. So many architects throughout his period and into today imitate each other. They don't have a distinctive brand the way Morris did.

Miami just didn't know what it had. It did not know how to respect and honor this guy and the gifts he gave them. I don't think there is anybody who came to Miami in the fifties, sixties, seventies and went through his hotels and did not go back to Wichita or Philadelphia or Akron or Houston without realizing how unusual an experience he or she had been through. Morris provided the structure for them to enjoy themselves and the environment. What more could you want from an architect?

Courtesy of the Ritz-Carlton Hotel

DIEGO LOWENSTEIN: Toward the end of his life, Morris had an apartment in one of his buildings on Belle Isle, a federally funded structure designed for moderate and low-income people. Morris got himself the equivalent of a penthouse there. It wasn't a tall building, but he had a very nice corner and water view, and he fixed it all up.

PHILIP SMITH: As it turned out, my mother had moved into that building in the eighties or nineties. Morris had a duplex apartment in that building as well. We would run into him all the time.

DIANE WOOLFE CAMBER: A reporter from New York City once asked me whether I thought the Fontainebleau would be considered a historic building one day. I said, of course it would. It's considered an iconic building.

When I learned Morris Lapidus was closing down his office, I asked him—in my role as director of the Bass Museum—if I could have his archives for the museum. "Why would you want them?" he said. He had been slammed by New York architecture critics, such as Ada Louise Huxtable, who wrote terrible things about him. It had made him very depressed.

But I thought his work was terrific. The buildings he designed were the purest Bauhaus-inspired fifties architecture; they were considered the epitome of good taste. He was into spectacle and drama, into making stairways to nowhere.

Toward the end of his life, people started writing about him and taking notice. He lived to be ninety-five, ninety-six. He was getting dressed up, going out, and appearing at buildings he had designed that were going to be restored. And I did get the archives for the Bass.

Morris had said, "The one thing I'm eternally grateful for is that I lived to see my work appreciated and recognized."

IRA GILLER: Morris often expressed to me how nice it was that my father and I worked together and how well we worked together.

He was dramatic and daring. He had that freedom in his thoughts, which I think came from his early theater background. He didn't have the inhibitions, withstood the criticisms, outlived all his critics. And before he died, he had gained the respect of the architectural community that he lacked throughout most of his career and most of his life.

PHILIP SMITH: In New York, Morris Lapidus had focused on shops and buildings that were very sophisticated; those experiences remained with him. Then he came to Miami and saw a city with a quality that he captured and formalized—the spirit of Miami, a glamorous, continental place.

No one has ever come close to doing what Morris did. His buildings are and will always be unique. I don't think there were many copycats of his work, because people just couldn't copy him. He had such a complex vocabulary that he could take pieces from Versailles and Art Deco movie theaters and blend all of that creatively into one.

What came out was unique to him, all of it transformed under his direction. And it worked in a way that no one else could have arranged. No one came close.

8

Early Days

> There would be GIs on the trains playing harmonicas and guitars, singing the songs of the times like "I'll Be Seeing You."
>
> —Jim Lawrence

IRA GILLER: My family's been in Florida since 1905, in Miami Beach since the 1930s when the Art Deco hotels blossomed. Some were restricted, some were not, but the clientele they appealed to was a moneyed class, people who came by train from Chicago, New York, Boston, Philadelphia. I can still remember watching the trains come in, the trunks and porters. People would stay at the hotels for the winter and then go back to their homes for the summer. All the hotels would shut down then; you'd drive along Collins Avenue and A1A, and everything would be closed.

DIANE WOOLFE CAMBER: I was born in Miami Beach, but between the ages of three and eight, I lived in the city of Miami proper. I remember going down to the waterfront in Coral Gables where Pan American Airlines was based when they began the first overseas flights from the United States. There were those seaplanes that landed on the pontoons. The first airmail was from there. Now the old Pan Am terminal is Coral Gables City Hall, a historic Art Deco building with a gigantic globe in the center of the lobby.

A postcard from Miami Beach's early days

My father was a self-trained artist who came to Miami in the early twenties. He was supposed to help George Merrick promote the development of Coral Gables, but Merrick died, and my father got stranded because the money didn't come through. Still, he liked it here, because he could hunt and fish and also because he could paint outdoors. He was quoted in a newspaper of the time saying, "Miami is an artist's paradise."

He met my mother in 1924. Her family had come here from Akron, Ohio, where my grandfather became a very successful contractor. During the first wave of construction in Miami Beach, he built seventy-five of the Art Deco buildings in the historic district. One of them is the Hotel Victor, which is named for my uncle Maxwell Victor Miller, an attorney and the first Jewish judge in Miami Beach.

After my parents met, my father realized he could never make a living supporting a family as an artist, so he began doing different things. The day after Prohibition ended, he opened a restaurant called the Village Tavern on Espanola Way off Washington Avenue. The décor was like an English tavern. Very famous people went there. And an eighteen-year-old Desi Arnaz performed as a guitarist and singer.

In the thirties, kids hanging out, Miami Beach. Courtesy of Robert Zuckerman

In the thirties, my father started a construction business. There were houses that he built and some apartment buildings, but mainly he got into real estate. He was an outgoing person and good with people.

I remember taking the bus with my parents and going from Miami Beach to Miami, where we saw productions at the Gusman Theater, which was a gorgeous place, like a Venetian palace. There was always an organ performance and a stage show. And I can still remember seeing Charlie Chaplin's *Gold Rush* at what was the Grove Playhouse (now it's the Grove Theater) and *The Wizard of Oz* at the Parkway Theater on Coral Way.

BERNIE ROSEN: I got to Miami in 1947. I was from the Bronx, and I had just gotten discharged from the army and decided there was nothing for me to do in New York City. My parents were immigrants from Poland. My father just eked out a living, and it was tough. I wanted something better.

I went through the University of Miami under the GI Bill. At first I was majoring in business. I wasn't that smart, but someone said to me, "If I were you, I'd get the heck out of that major and try the radio and television department. I think you'll find that a much more interesting situation." I followed the tip.

The University of Miami was a very small school. When I first arrived, I lived in leftover barracks close to the airport. Shortly afterward, I moved into a house

A happy FDR shows off his great smile and a Miami Beach suntan at the back of the presidential train. Courtesy of Library of Congress

with four other guys. We were five guys in one apartment, two bedrooms. We just shared. To get to the college every day, I went out on LeJeune Road and hitched. I had no money. I didn't have anything.

In September 1949 I became an intern at the television station, WTVJ, Channel 4. It was a brand-new station, had only gone on the air a few months back—March 21, 1949. Funny the things you remember. It was a CBS affiliate located in the former Capitol Theater in downtown Miami and the only TV station in the state of Florida for nine years, the sixteenth in the United States.

I was a gofer; I used to sweep the studio. I was also a studio cameraman and a part-time director, which led to everyone knowing about my interest in sports and my becoming a sports producer. I used to take the bus to shoot the stories, because I did not have enough salary to own a car.

I started working at the television station on a part-time basis making $50 a month. The next year I made $150 a month. It was very primitive television. In the early years, we did not have much in the way of network affiliation. We had 125 live television shows in a little studio. Each show was different. We had to run around and reconfigure the studio to accommodate each show. It was hard work but a lot of fun.

We were pioneers in the industry, the very early fifties. The television sets: small, black and white. Not many people owned televisions. They used to watch TV in store windows from out in the street.

DAVE ROGERS: I came to Miami in 1941 when I was seven years old. My mother had gotten divorced, and she came to live with an aunt of mine. I grew up in Miami Beach, graduated from Miami Beach High School.

Miami Beach was very pristine in those days. It was like new, ten blocks wide, and about eighty blocks north to south. I knew everyone, because I was always in Flamingo Park. My friends and I would play basketball with guys who came down from New York. Girls from Hunter College would come down from New York as well. We'd take our pick. I had hair then and a good build. We'd take the girls up to Sunny Isles Beach and tell them: "They've got submarines out there, and they have races."

"How can you tell?"

"Well, there's a red light, and white light."

"You have this beautiful cleft in your chin," they'd tell me.

"Why don't you kiss it?"

"Oh," they'd say, "you're so cute."

BASHA SCHLAZER: I spent most every Miami Beach summer of my growing-up years at Flamingo Park, which opened in 1950 in the heart of South Beach at Jefferson Avenue and Eleventh Street. It was a beautiful place, spread out over more than thirty-six acres with wonderful recreation programs, well-groomed tennis courts, a big amphitheater for summer revues, arts and crafts, dance and tennis classes. We'd play Ping-Pong. We'd sit on the ground and play jacks. I used to walk all the way there in the morning, spend the whole day, and walk home. No worries.

The Miami Beach Flamingoes, a minor league baseball team, played at the park. I'd go to the games with my parents. My father especially loved sports. One night we were sitting and watching the game when this man wearing a big trench coat and a little hat walked by. He was sort of hunched over, and he was waving to everyone.

"That's Babe Ruth," my father said.

DAVID WALLACK: At Flamingo Park, I enrolled for baseball and tennis summer camp. We'd get there by bicycle or roller skates. Roller-skating was very big. There was a time when my father went bankrupt, and we moved to my grandmother's palatial estate in New York. But then we moved back to Miami Beach, where I had a wonderful growing-up time with my sisters and cousins in South Beach, roller-skating, hula-hooping, and building castles in the sand.

The Beach was the Beach, but Miami was Miami: totally different worlds. The Beach was its own world with the original sand—which was like butter, different from the dredged sand. I had friends who lived on Hibiscus Island. I would go over the causeway on my bike, and all of us would ride out to Miami, where there was a little bowling alley.

Now it's part of the Performing Arts Center. Then, for thirty-five cents a game, we'd bowl two games, have a hamburger, a Coke, french fries, and go through the sporting goods section in Sears, which was nearby. Then we'd get on our bikes and ride back.

BASHA SCHLAZER: Although I was born in Philadelphia in 1937, I remember nothing of that. All I know is suddenly it was 1940, and I was in Miami. I was an only child and lived with my parents in downtown Miami close to where my grandmother had a boardinghouse. Miami was becoming a big city by then, but it still had a small-town feeling. We'd drive around in my father's big black Packard with running boards. It was the kind of car you'd see in old-time movies.

Miami Beach was a baby then, only a few blocks from the beach. It went north along Collins Avenue only as far as Forty-first Street. There was no Fontainebleau, no Eden Roc. We lived at Eighth Street and Pennsylvania Avenue, right behind the Blackstone Hotel, which became an army air force base during the war. Every morning soldiers would line up and fall in for muster on Pennsylvania Avenue, and every night at five o'clock they would fall in again for reveille. All the little kids would form a line behind them, standing up straight like the soldiers. When they saluted, we'd salute. And then we'd fall out. It was a lot of fun.

Air raid marshals were on the scene wearing those little white helmets. Army trucks were driving down the streets. The war was very close to us. You knew the water was out there. You heard submarines were out there.

REY BAUMEL: I recall one summer day when I was on the beach with a high school buddy.

There weren't that many people around. Then, all of a sudden, platoons of solders were coming down to the beach. They did calisthenics on the sand, and when they finished, the drill sergeant rushed them into the ocean to cool off. A few seemed terrified of going into the water. They protested, but they went.

CLAIRE WARREN: During the war, the army air corps took over my father's hotel, the Anchor on Sixteenth and Washington. The hospital Mt. Sinai became the Nautilus Hotel and was used for rest and recreation for soldiers when they returned. The streets were filled with soldiers marching up and down. There was a USO on North Bay Road, where we'd go to jitterbug with the soldiers.

DIANE WOOLFE CAMBER: Miami had always been a place famous for its proximity to water and a place to learn how to fly planes. Now airmen were being trained. There was officers' training to go overseas for American as well as British servicemen. Hotels were taken over by the military. People who lived there had to move out, although they must have been compensated. World War II changed everything.

JIM LAWRENCE: During the war, we would come down to Miami Beach by the Florida Limited, a Pullman with stops at different cities. There would be GIs on the trains playing harmonicas and guitars, singing the songs of the times, such as "I'll Be Seeing You" and "Don't Sit under the Apple Tree."

Of course, they got first seating, but when my mother and I came on, they'd always get up and give us their seats.

ANN BROAD BUSSELL: My brother and I, together with another brother and sister pair, ran the lemonade stand on the Bayshore Golf Course for the soldiers who were practicing on the calisthenics field.

There was always a scrap drive. We would recycle to get the metal to make ammunition, pile the metal into a little red wagon and take it to Foo Man Shoo, a Chinese restaurant on the south side of Forty-first Street that was owned by Jewish people named Goldman. That was the collection point. They gave a prize to the one who brought in the most metal. My brother usually won.

Hundreds of thousands of troops trained on Miami Beach during World War II. The United States government took over approximately 70 percent of the three hundred hotels, dozens of which were owned by Jews.

HELEN KAPLAN: When the war started, the Blackstone Hotel became an army camp, and all of Flamingo Park and the golf courses became training grounds. I'd ride my bicycle through the park wearing blue shorts, and as I passed the soldiers, they would sing out: "The girl in the blue shorts/parlez vous." I'd wave and laugh; it was such a fun time.

On the edge of First Street there was a huge USO. I was pretty big for my age, so my sister would babysit me and take me there. Boy, was I a jitterbugger!

JIM LAWRENCE: My parents bought me two uniforms: an army one and a navy one. The hat, uniform—the whole darn thing. Along with the other young children, I marched on Biscayne Boulevard with the soldiers.

There was no television; my family listened to the radio constantly. We kept hearing about war in the Pacific and Europe. When my parents would take me to the movie theater, there'd be newsreels showing the war and messages to buy war bonds.

ANN BROAD BUSSELL: During the war, we realized that among the soldiers training, there were Jewish young men. We got to know some of them. There were few hotels that were allowed to operate as hotels during the war. Most of them served as barracks for the army air force that trained on the beach; the navy trained in the City of Miami. All the young men were in the army air force or the navy air force. There was no separate air force.

My father, Shepard Broad, organized the effort to purchase and refit three ships—*Hatikva*, *Geula*, and the *Jewish State*—on the Miami River. Then he made the ships available for the journey from Miami to Europe to rescue seventy thousand stranded Jews.

When the war was over, many decided to begin their grown-up life in Miami Beach. That was when Jewish people in any great number started to come to Miami Beach on a permanent basis.

With the GI bill, many of them went to school at the University of Miami, and everything permanently changed. The introduction of air-conditioning made a big difference.

GEORGE NEARY: "Sand in your shoes" is a popular phrase meaning that one will return to a place with fond memories. But it was replaced by "sand in your boots" for the December 7th reunions held on Ocean Drive for veterans who had trained in the oceanfront hotels during World War II and then returned and got married here. They were big events with bunks, Jeeps, and tents. But as the veterans aged, fewer came. It ended about 2005.

CLAIRE WARREN: When the war ended, it was bedlam! Fireworks, parades, soldiers in Jeeps coming down Washington Avenue. Many of the GIs had fallen in love with the Miami weather. They went back to Ohio, Illinois, all over the United States, got their families and brought them down. The government helped by building houses for many of them—project houses: three bedrooms, one bath, a big lawn.

MARGARET GRIFFIS O'BRIEN: I remember watching the army people march up and down the street. At South Beach Elementary School, the teachers used to close the windows because of the dirty songs the soldiers would sing such as "Drinking Beer from a Girl's Brassiere."

MICHAEL ALLER: The USO Club on Dade Boulevard had long, rectangular tables and a stage where performers such as George Jessel and the Andrews Sisters would entertain. They charged nothing. They just got on the stage and cheered the people. If Jessel was appearing at a hotel, he would invite a table of servicemen and servicewomen; all of them did it. There were these long, rectangular tables and a stage. George Jessel would go over and entertain whoever was in town.

ALAN MANDEL: After the war, guys who had been stationed here came back. They had great memories of Miami Beach and wanted to bring their families for vacation. Those great hotels in the Art Deco area, many of them small, all of them family friendly, were filled with them. Many went on to buy property here.

JIM LAWRENCE: When I was six or seven years old and the war was over, I used to play with other kids in the gardens of the old Royal Palms Hotel next to the Brickell Bridge. Flagler had built the hotel in the teens and twenties. It had since burned down, but the remnants were there. Across the street was where all the military trucks and Jeeps were parked. There were the deserted barracks that the army had left behind, and the famous poster of Betty Grable hanging on the wall, looking beautiful in a bathing suit with her hair in an upsweep. That was left behind as well. I'd go there with friends, and we'd play cowboys and Indians. It was empty area then. Today it is Brickell, all built up.

From 1940 to 1957, my parents, my brother, and I would come down to Miami from our home in Philadelphia for the winter months. I'd go to school here, but the schools up north were much more advanced, making it difficult to go back and forth. And you didn't know what you were studying.

On my way to and from school, I would have to cross the train tracks where the Florida Limited ran. If the train was there, I couldn't cross. One day I was late and got on the train thinking to walk through the cars to the other side. But the train started to back up a little, and I had to jump off. I never did that again.

I remember when the banana boats would come in at the Port of Miami. We would agitate the longshoremen until they'd give us a hand of bananas. I'd bring mine home, and my mother would say, "Get out of here with those bananas."

Back in the fifties, I went to a high school in the southwest section. There were tomato fields that I walked through to get to school. I also carried a saltshaker with me so I could have tomatoes for breakfast.

I went to Catholic school where the girls played on one side and boys on the other. The girls would torment me, so I would chase them. The nuns would catch me and smack me on my arm and other places. This lasted until fifth grade when my parents pulled me out. They sent me to public schools from then on.

I played in areas where there were only vacant lots. Now they are the sites of huge buildings. School trips were to fire or police stations or Wholesome Bakeries—a favorite because you'd get doughnuts or pastries. There were no art galleries, no museums. Artists would show on the streets or in movie theater lobbies such as the Miracle Theater in Coral Gables, circulating their works between South and North Miami, Coral Gables, Miami, and Miami Beach. Two weeks here, two weeks there.

My dad would give me a quarter to go to the movies on Saturdays and Sundays. It was fifteen cents to get in, a nickel for popcorn, a nickel for candy. There were Westerns, scary movies: always a double feature.

Sometimes the Dorseys or Guy Lombardo would come down, but generally in season. A lot of employees would go up to the Catskills for the summer. It was very quiet after the winter season. Air conditioning had first arrived in 1925, and that was in a theater. It really took many years before it fully took hold. But we had transoms all around the apartment that allowed the breezes to come in.

MARGARET GRIFFIS O'BRIEN: My father was a Floridian who ran a bunch of movie theaters: Cinema, Plaza, Art, Flamingo, Sheraton, Beach, Lincoln, Roosevelt. All of them were old style. Barbara Capitman would come into one of those old Art Deco theaters that were built in 1936. They were closed, but my father took care of them.

"You know, you need to preserve all these Art Deco places," she would say in her high-pitched voice.

I was ten and obnoxious, and would say, "Yeah, yeah, yeah," and think, *Lady why don't you just buy these places and do whatever you want with them.* Which is what I think she did.

The theater on Washington Avenue and Twelfth Street—today it's called the Mansion—had vaudeville shows. They were great. I was the youngest shiksa to see them. Sometimes I didn't know what was going on because they spoke mostly in Yiddish. My father had to learn Hebrew to paint the signs.

BASHA SCHLAZER: The movie *They Were Expendable* was shot on Miami Beach. This was after the war when the soldiers had gone. The performers in the movie stayed at the Blackstone Hotel. One night the bus stopped right at the corner of Eighth Street and Washington Avenue, and actors of that time came out—John Wayne, Ward Bond. My mouth dropped. But the actors were very friendly. That was the way things were in Miami Beach.

We moved to Coconut Grove when I was in seventh grade. It was after the war. My father opened a grocery store on Grand Avenue. There were four stores in a row all owned by whites.

It was the original Miami. There were lots of older people there who had been in the Grove when Miami was just starting. As children we would say we lived in Coconut Grove. But we always were corrected. They would remind us, "You live in the original Miami."

At that time Coconut Grove had "White Grove" and "Black Grove." The whites lived on one side and the blacks on another. We were still segregated. Our grocery store was in "Black Grove." My father had only black customers.

I loved Coral Gables High School. I was in the band, the orchestra. I was a majorette.

It was wonderful there. I cried when I graduated in 1954. I did not want to leave.

RED HELLER: I was a change-of-life baby, the child of Russian Jews who had immigrated to America at the turn of the twentieth century and spoke only Russian and Yiddish, leaving me, at the age of five, with little understanding of the English language. My father was a butcher with two meat markets. But both failed during the Depression, and he left my mother and me in the Bronx while he went to Miami Beach hoping to make a living there. He sent for us after a year.

At the start, we lived on Euclid and Third Avenues. Then we moved several times. There was a Jewish population living in Miami Beach at the time, mostly elderly Eastern Europeans. Cultural prejudices were evident, as seen by "Restricted Clientele" signs posted in conspicuous places in many apartment buildings and hotels located west of Jefferson Avenue, north of First Street and along Ocean Drive. Very few Jews lived north of Lincoln Road.

My first day of kindergarten, my father brought me to school, led me to the classroom, and said good-bye. Then he abruptly left for work. I can distinctly remember the ringing of the classroom bell and how I sat in quiet despair gazing at the teacher as she spoke. I could not comprehend what she was saying.

Confused and frightened, I raised my hand to indicate I needed to go to the restroom. The teacher acknowledged my request. I rose from my seat, opened the classroom door, and ran down the front stairs and in the direction of the kosher butcher shop on Washington Avenue between Fourteenth and Fifteenth, where my father was working.

Tearfully, I told my father that I hated school and the teacher; that I wanted to stay with him. I begged him not to send me back.

My father, a kind and gentle man, removed his soiled apron. He laid down his carving knife and meat cleaver on the butcher chopping block, grabbed my hand, and back to school we went. I will never forget how he spoke to the teacher in his clipped broken English and thick accent. He argued that the teacher should be patient with me because of the language barrier. He told the teacher that I was a good boy. Then, confident that he had made his point, he left and returned to the shop. That was my first day of school in Miami Beach.

When I was six, my mother and father put me on a train. My brother, who was sixteen years older than me, was to meet me in New York City. I still could hardly speak English. My mother put two dollars in my pocket, safety-pinned it, and gave the conductor fifty cents to watch me.

I remember when it was time for breakfast, I would make my way into the dining car and pretend I didn't know what I was doing until someone would say, "Come here, sonny. Are you hungry?"

"Yes," I'd say.

Oh, I tell you, I was a little *ganef* [rascal] then.

IRA GILLER: There was a magic to Miami Beach High School. People who grew up here still come back to relive the times. People who graduated in the thirties, forties, fifties, sixties still talk about their high school days, recall their great memories. Mickey Rourke, Andy Garcia, Robert Rubin, Barbara Walters—all of them grew up on the beach.

My wife, Honey, and I were high school sweethearts. In 1967 we were set to go to our senior prom, which was to be held in one of the smaller banquet rooms at the Fontainebleau Hotel. That night, my parents, who were active in the

Democratic Party, were set to go to a big fund-raiser for Hubert Humphrey that was also at the Fontainebleau, but in the grand ballroom. Frank Sinatra would be performing there.

My parents said, "Frank Sinatra is going to be entertaining tonight. Come on over; we'll take you to see his show."

So Honey and I walked down the aisle with my mother, and all of a sudden we're at the table where Sinatra was. A bodyguard was standing behind him. You had to wait. My mother nearly fainted. But Sinatra couldn't be nicer. He gave us autographs, and then we stayed and saw the show.

When people talk about that prom, we say: "We saw Sinatra; we saw the vice president." But that's what Miami was like in the sixties. Sinatra used to come to town regularly. So did Sammy Davis. Once I was with my father-in-law, an attorney who brought his clients to this club called the Footlighters, where Sammy Davis was entertaining. His was the filthiest act, but funny . . . we couldn't stop laughing. And there I was with my father-in-law.

When I was in high school, we'd cruise up and down Collins Avenue. Sinatra would be in town; the whole Rat Pack would be here. We'd see the names on the marquees. My wife saw the Beatles when they were here. I have a picture of me with Jackie Gleason when I was in high school. He loved Miami Beach, put it on the map.

9

Still the Segregated South

My life turned on that single encounter.

—Clarence Dickson

SETH BRAMSON: Prior to it being called Overtown, the town that the black people lived in was called Coloredtown. Prior to that, it was called Darkytown. The black people lived there because they had to. Florida was a cracker, hillbilly, redneck, racist, anti-Semitic state. That has changed for the most part since 1964.

Unless they lived with the family they worked for on Miami Beach, black people were not allowed to live there. They had to leave at sundown and go back to town. So if a black person saw another black person with a car or getting into a bus, jitney, or trolley car, it was:

"Where are you going?"

"I'm going over to town."

That became Overtown.

One of Mr. Flagler's favorite people was a carpenter, a black man named Dana Dorsey. With Jim Crow and during the years of segregation, if a black person could save enough money and if there were no deed restrictions, he or she could buy property. Mr. Dorsey bought lots of property in what today is downtown Miami, including the property that Burdine's, now Macy's, sits on.

When it became time for Miami to incorporate, July 28, 1896, of the people voting for incorporation, more than a hundred of them were black. They were allowed to vote to incorporate Miami as a city even though Miami was segregated, and black people had to live in Coloredtown.

But they went all over to work. They took the trolleys and later the bus, which had signs up front: "Coloreds sit from the rear." In the stores there were four restrooms: white men, colored men; white women, colored women. There were two water fountains: white and colored.

When Federated Department Stores bought Burdine's, Al Daniels was sent down from Abraham & Straus in New York to become the vice president and general manager of Burdine's. He saw these obnoxious signs and got very upset. Coming from New York City, he had never seen anything like this before.

The workers told him, "Oh, this is the law; we gotta have it."

It ate at him for about five and a half years. Finally, in late 1960, he issued an order that as of the first business day in 1961, all signs separating the races in the Miami and Miami Beach Federated Department stores would be removed. He also ordered that all Negro customers would be seated in the coffee shop as guests at the Hibiscus Tea Room on the fourth floor. And he mandated that black customers would be allowed to try on clothes, use the dressing rooms, and return unsatisfactory items to the store.

It was groundbreaking. But there were no protests. Everything went on as if nothing had happened. That was not the case with other stores in the area. Mr. Daniels was the only one to have the guts to say, "These signs are coming [down] to try to make things equal." No other stores did what he did at that time. The poor treatment of blacks went on as if nothing had happened.

There were a huge number of transplants in Miami at that time. We had moved here in 1946. I shopped in all the stores as a kid. It was a different world. But this was Miami. Not Miami Beach.

In Miami Beach there were no black kids. There were no black kids in Miami Beach High School until forced integration in 1970, and then it was a disaster. It took years to work its way out until the black kids coming over from Miami were not horribly resentful of all these white Miami Beach kids. It was a bad time. But it's not a problem anymore, and Miami Beach is once again the great high school it had been.

I have the largest collection of memorabilia of signs declaring "restricted gentile clientele" and "references for reservations" as well "suitably restricted" guest lists in Miami Beach. Bal Harbour, which was once deed restricted, is now all Jewish. You can't let people forget, or it will happen again.

FERDIE PACHECO: I was born during the Depression, December 8, 1927, in Tampa, Florida. My father had a little apothecary store with nails that he kept on the back of the wall where he'd put prescriptions. Customers had to pay for their prescription if they wanted to get waited on again. Most people came back and got a second prescription.

There was this fellow named Santo who came from Sardinia. He was a great organizer and founded a big industry for himself in Tampa. The man was ruthless. He did not bother to argue with people. I mean, if you fucked with him, he'd kill you.

As time passed, my father had a huge collection of prescriptions in the name of Santo. "Don't worry about that nail, I am going to pay you for every prescription," he would say to my father. "I am just getting started. When I get established, you can have anything you want in this city. But you stay honest. Don't join me in what I am doing."

That man was Mafia. They did a lot of bad things. They also did a lot of good things, like Robin Hood. They found out who needed help, went to people's homes and gave them a turkey, helped with the rent.

My father was qualified as a doctor, but he couldn't be bothered to get a license. In those days, you went to the druggist, who treated you with drugs. If the treatment did not work, my father would make the customer go to the doctor. He did operations; from the time I was twelve, I would be watching and helping him with autopsies. He carried a gun. He got shot at a few times. People didn't always agree with him. He was so honest, straight. He became a conciliator. That was how I grew up.

My father's rigid sense of honor came along with me when I got to Miami in 1954. It was a segregated town. This old doctor who sold me his clinic at Southwest Eighth Street was making five hundred bucks a month, which was a lot of money back then. His office was indescribably dirty: old medicines and old instruments. He had an EKG machine that was one of the first ones ever made.

I set up my Miami practice in the ghetto. I practiced medicine out of my little bag, treating patients with symptomatic medicine. You didn't come up with any exotic treatments; you just took care of what the important thing was.

I did not become a doctor to make a lot of money. I did it to help people. If you came in, you wouldn't have to wait. If you didn't have the money, you wouldn't have to pay. I had lots of poor people coming in. The ghetto was nothing but poor people.

LUISITA PACHECO: Ferdie treated patients for five dollars a visit. He didn't charge people over sixty-five or children under two. He treated all the boxers and their families for nothing, including Muhammad Ali.

FERDIE PACHECO: I couldn't stand treating people with nothing wrong with them and wasting my time. The hypochondriacs, those who wanted a narcotics prescription, I kicked them out. "Get the fuck out of here. There's nothing wrong with you," I would tell them. I cleansed my office of all drugs. Drugs were absolutely the worst thing that happened in the ghetto.

GEORGIA AYERS: Miami was a segregated town with the black community concentrated in Overtown, a neighborhood northwest of downtown Miami. I remember Overtown as being my world. Whenever I anticipated enjoying life, I'd look to Overtown. It was to blacks what Miami Beach was to nonblacks. That's where we went to see black entertainers such as Nat King Cole, Cab Calloway, Harry Belafonte, Ethel Waters. They'd perform in Miami Beach hotels, then come to Overtown to spend the night. Black entertainers could entertain on the Beach, but they couldn't sleep on the Beach.

FERDIE PACHECO: The big black bands such as Duke Ellington and Count Basie would come into the Fontainebleau and the other big hotels on the Beach. But they could not play past twelve o'clock. So they would get in taxicabs and ride on over into Overtown, where they would play the rest of the night. In the ghetto, every night was entertainment night.

BASHA SCHLAZER: If a black person was in Miami Beach after nine o'clock at night, they had to be working at a hotel or in somebody's house as a maid or something.

REY BAUMEL: If they had a card showing they were working somewhere, it was okay. If they had no card—and that included anybody, and it did not matter who they were—they would be taken to police headquarters.

LANEY SHELDON: Even Sammy Davis, when he came to the Fontainebleau, was told he had to carry a pass.

But Sinatra stepped in. "If Sammy is not allowed at the Beach, I am off the Beach," he said.

HELEN KAPLAN: My mother was really bothered by segregation. She had this cleaning woman, Donna, who would sit down and have tea with us, and her friends would comment, "The *shvartsa*?" And my mother would look at them with such disdain. "She's a person," my mother would say. It was very different in New York. We would march with our Italian friends when they had religious processions. But I never did see a lot of blacks.

Later on, we'd see black entertainers such as Lena Horne, Billie Holiday in Overtown. People would say, "You may be jeopardizing your law career being seen here." But we never cared. We'd go with a whole group of people. Then they opened up the Clover Club in Miami Beach, and Lena Horne entertained there. There would be a lot of blacks there, especially the tap dancers. I loved tap dancing, and they were great tap-dancers. As long as they had a job and identification, they could be there. I never thought about it. *That's the way the world is*, I thought.

Courtesy of Clarence Dickson

CLARENCE DICKSON: The first one who refused to leave the Miami Beach hotel where she was entertaining was Dorothy Dandridge. She broke that barrier.

REY BAUMEL: Harry Belafonte followed. So did Lena Horne, who stipulated in her contract that not only would blacks be admitted to her shows, but that they would not be seated in the rear.

FERDIE PACHECO: When you went in to hear the Ellington band play in Overtown, it was for free, and moreover it was not the nice white jazz they played at the Fontainebleau. It was the music they played for themselves. That was real jazz!

I met every one of those guys, every last one of them. I got to meet Duke Ellington. Count Basie was a good friend of mine. Any entertainer who was black and came to Miami saw me as a doctor and a friend, whether it was Lena Horne, Ella Fitzgerald, Cab Calloway. There was an innate trust for me.

DAVE ROGERS: Brownsville was a town "on the other side of the tracks" where great jazz was played during the days of segregation. People such as Duke Ellington, Cab Calloway, Cassius Clay/Muhammad Ali, Malcolm X, Sam Cooke, Nat King Cole, Berry Gordy, even Martin Luther King would gather there to see some of the top black musicians in America in late-night performances.

The Hampton House Motel in Brownsville was a gathering place for black and white jazz aficionados. Maître d' Charles Martin, dressed in a gold lamé tuxedo jacket, would seat patrons. Black as well as white entertainers such as Milton Berle would be there.

GEORGIA AYERS: Living in New York for two years early in my life taught me that all people are created equal, that we are different colors of roses in God's garden. That left me with the feeling that I'm ahead of the average person who never left Miami.

I did housework; I worked for individuals. Some were nice. For others, you had to enter their back door. I worked in the kitchens of hotels in Miami. When we wanted water, we had to go to the back of the restaurant. But I was never treated like a nigger: never. Having worked in New York, I knew the difference.

The Harlem Theater in Overtown, the Lyric Theater, the Morgan Theater—they were all segregated. I went to some of the shows, but I had to be home before dark. My grandmother raised me, and she was born in Tallahassee. She didn't believe in you hanging in the street.

There were two buses where I came from: the 21 for white folks, the 21A for colored folks. My father was in the Veterans Hospital in Miami Beach, and I was going to see him.

STILL THE SEGREGATED SOUTH

When I got on the bus, the driver put his hand over the place where you drop your money. I asked, "Why are you doing that?"

He said, "You're supposed to wait for the colored bus. This is the white folks' bus."

I said, "How did it get to be the white folks' bus? I don't see anything that would discriminate one from the other."

The fare was only a dime. But I took my dime and threw it on the floor. I said to the driver, "When my father went to war to fight for us, he didn't go for white folks or black folks. He went for all God's children."

When he came home in 1945, my father did domestic work because he was not educated. He was a very quiet humble man, the opposite of me.

I was thirteen years old when I received the name Spitfire. Professor Holmes, who was the principal of the elementary school, gave me that name. That was what they called me and still call me: Spitfire. I was always outspoken. My grandma would tell me, "Girl, those white folks are gonna kill you with your big mouth."

I said, "Grandma, I got one life to live before I die." It angered her that I spoke out, that I was not afraid.

In my elementary school, there were all black teachers. We would go on field trips, but as black folks, we had to go in the back door of everything. I remember one time we were on a field trip. A bus was taking us to the White Milk Dairy. Mr. Dupre owned the White Milk Dairy, and that was where his cow pasture was.

After a while, the bus stopped. "Everybody off the bus," the bus driver said, and the kids got off.

"All right, get off now," the bus driver said to me, because I hesitated on the steps.

"What for?"

"They're goin' to show you how to milk cows."

"I'm not goin' to school to learn how to milk no cows," I said, and I got back on the bus.

Because I got back on the bus, the other kids got back on the bus, and we were all taken back to the school.

The teacher wanted to know why we returned so early. The kids said, "Georgia told us she's not going to school to milk no cows, and we won't go to school to milk no cows too." I felt that way only because I had gone to New York and been in integrated schools.

When we got back to school, Miss Holmes called me up to the front of the class, grabbed me by the collar, pointed her finger in my face, and said, "Georgie, you too outspoken. When you speak, you spit fire!" And that's how I got the name Spitfire.

DIANE WOOLFE CAMBER: There were "colored only" bathrooms in the department stores when I was a kid. I grew up with discrimination. I didn't socialize with African Americans until I went to college at Barnard.

JIM LAWRENCE: The slogan then was, "If you're black, stay back. If you're white, you're right." Segregation was in full force. The Richard Department Store had separate water fountains and bathrooms.

GEORGIA AYERS: If you go to any store downtown, you go in the back door. The whites had separate try-on rooms. You want a pair of shoes? They put you in the shoe room. You had to try the shoes on in the shoe room. You want a hat? You have to put this thing on your head first.

I've always been police conscious. If the policeman has to protect you, he has to protect me, too. During the 1968 riot, which started in the project, the highway patrol came and sat in the center of Twelfth Avenue and Sixty-seventh Street, shooting tear gas. The county manager and assistant county manager were tear-gassed in.

I was on the Dade County Community Relations Board by then. I said, "You're doing wrong shooting tear gas. How are people going to live and breathe?" People started to run. I was with Archie, my husband, but he didn't stay with me. "That's because you went the wrong way," Archie used to say.

We had black police officers there, but they couldn't arrest white folk. Back then, you stop a white person, you have to call a white police officer to take him in.

I saw Martin Luther King Jr. go into my church, St. John's Church on Eighth Street in Miami. It was in the early days. People were afraid to come down because of the Ku Klux Klan. Dr. King wanted us to be humble, to keep the peace. I agreed with his teaching, but I'm the kind of person who isn't taking any shit. I don't care what or who you are.

I worked for an all-black insurance company. If anything happened in the black community involving whites, they would always call me. And every day I'd keep people out of jail. I've been doing this since 1963.

I've always been open-minded. My grandmother lived to be one hundred years, nine months, and thirteen days. She never taught us hatred.

MARY NIVEN: I used to go to school on the public buses and saw the black people sitting in the back of the bus. It was so strange to me, because in Cuba there was no difference between black and white. There was prejudice against the Cubans, too. You were not well liked if you spoke Spanish.

CLARENCE DICKSON: I was still in the air force in 1957 when I was transferred from Texas to Miami. A year later, I was discharged, but I stayed on in Miami. I liked it right away—it was very segregated but a healthy, bustling place. I was a lowly airman who didn't have any money. My first place of residence was in a room over a bar, and I knew I had to get out of there. So I moved into an apartment building in Liberty City together with my wife for about $13 a week, and I got a job in Miami's Children's Hospital in South Miami.

I was up and around at 4:30 one morning waiting for the bus that would take me to the hospital when a police car drove by. I had had no experience with police officers at the time: none at all. This one drove by, and I said to myself, *"You know what? That guy's coming back."* Sure enough he did, pulling up in front of the bus stop. I could see he was black.

"Hi," he said. "What are you doing here this time of night?"

I said, "Actually it's morning, but I'm waiting for the bus so I can get to work."

"Really? You're going to work?"

"Yeah."

"You got any identification?"

I showed him my ID.

"Where's your car?"

"Well, my car didn't like getting up so early in the morning. It was busted."

"I tell you what. If it was my car, I'd shoot it."

"Well, I don't have a gun," I said, "but I do have a baseball bat."

He asked me questions, interrogated me in a conversational manner. I knew what he was doing. In a respectful way, he was getting information that he needed from me. I really liked that.

"You would probably make a fine police officer," he said to me.

Clarence Dickson as a newly minted police officer.
Courtesy of Clarence Dickson

I laughed, because that was the furthest thing from my mind. But he went on: "You should go down and take the test. You'll make a good cop."

I thought about it as I went to work. Sitting around in the janitor's lounge that morning, I told the guys about this cop and what he told me. "I'm going to take the police test," I said. They laughed, "Yeah, right." But I went to City Hall and applied for the exam.

A few weeks later, I took the test, and a while after that I received the letter that said, "Mr. Dickson, you are qualified to become a police officer." With the formalities out of the way, the next thing I knew I was told to come in and begin the course at the Police Academy.

Now this was what I didn't know: Until I interviewed for the Police Academy, no blacks were allowed to render that service. The black people who were working there had not gone to the academy; they had received on-the-job training. At that time, the Miami Police Department had one of the best police academies in the country. But even though they'd been fighting to get into the academy where they would get sixteen weeks of training and education, blacks were never allowed there.

It was strange to be amid all those whites. The other cadets didn't know that I was the first black man there. Neither did I. The first inclination I had that something was wrong was about two weeks into the academy when a white police officer came around with papers that he handed out to everyone in the class except me. I raised my hand, but the instructor put his finger to his mouth signaling that I should keep quiet. I caught the signal right away and put my hand down.

What this guy was doing was inviting the cadets to join the Patrolmen's Benevolent Association. I couldn't join because I was black. That was why I didn't get a paper. I didn't know this. But afterward, when I asked one of the guys what was going on, he told me. "I got the paper," he said, "but when I saw you didn't get one, I threw mine in the trash."

This man became a good friend of mine. I was ready to drop out at the time. He saved me.

I had grown up in Palatka, a little town in Florida, fifty-two miles east of Jacksonville, where the Ku Klux Klan was marching all the time. As kids, seven to ten years old, we'd go down and watch them; we played with their kids, swam in the same river. Twice a year, the Klan would march through the town with their hoods on. We'd laugh at them.

The whole black community of Palatka had nothing to do with the whites. I never heard stuff about race in my house. I had the chance to grow up and not feel inferior because I was black. I think the general mood of that small town was like that. Racism was there, but there was less room for conflict and violence. The black kids and white kids would sneak down to the St. John River, the river that flows north, and swim in the dark, swampy waters. We'd play stickball, blacks and whites together in the fields. The parents didn't know we were doing that. We never talked about it. But I remember it, and I think it had an effect on my joining the air force when I was twenty-one and my getting into the Police Academy.

One day, about the sixth week into the academy, we were told, "You guys are real police officers now. On weekends you go out and get experiences. Then you come back and tell us what your experiences were like."

My classmates went outside and got on the bus that was waiting there. But I was told, "Clarence, you wait right here." Then they put me in a police car. I saw the bus with all the cadets going one way, and I'm going the other way. "What's going on?" I said.

They took me to the black precinct. I didn't know there was a black precinct in Miami, let alone that it was the first black police precinct in America. I was in regular cadet khaki; I carried no guns. The next day I went back and reported for work. There was a roll call of the officers. All of them were black.

After the roll call, the sergeant said, "Okay, men, there is a new recruit in the academy, and he is the first one of us. I know you guys have been waiting for this, fighting for this till we find the man, and here he is." That's how I found out I was the one who integrated the academy.

This big black police officer was there. He said, "Hey, rookie, how are you doin'?"

I said, "Okay."

Clarence Dickson in his uniform as chief of police. Courtesy of Clarence Dickson

He said, "Don't let us down. We fought hard to get you here. Don't let us down."

I had quit school before I joined the air force. I wasn't ready for the academic world; I had trouble with the math. In the academy, you could flunk only two tests. If you fail the third one, you're out. But I failed only two and graduated number three in the class.

It was from that point on that the department accepted blacks as equals. Before blacks were patrolmen, whites were policemen. The pay was the same, but the authority was not the same. Blacks couldn't arrest whites.

I did go through some trying time in the academy. I was told the reason blacks were not going through the academy was because they could not cut it. The instructors at the academy tried to make it difficult for me so that I could not graduate. That's why it was so tough. Of the forty students who began my class, only thirteen graduated. On graduation day, when we all got our uniforms, I was the only black man there.

I graduated from the academy in 1960, joined the police department, and got my badge that same year. They took a class picture of all the graduates. I had it over the years. Then somehow I lost it. But unbeknownst to me, they took another class picture, and this one hangs in the academy. That is the official class picture, and it's without me.

I only learned about this years later when I became chief of police, and the *Miami Herald* did a story on me. Looking through all the materials, they came across that picture. "This is the chief's class," they said, "but where's the chief?" I guess, at the time, they didn't want to show me.

I began as a patrolman in the black precinct and went out on patrol with a training officer. I was still on probation. Our beat was right near Overtown. Blacks didn't police the white area. We couldn't cross certain boundaries into the white part of town. If we stopped someone, we had to call a white police officer; we couldn't arrest anyone.

Overtown was a mixture of a slum area and a vital business community. It was very crowded. There were forty-four thousand people living there when I started out compared to six thousand today, which is why people moved out and into Liberty City. They extended the boundary so blacks could have more room to live. There were gangs, numbers, prostitution, robberies, but no murders. And there were clubs where the famous black entertainers slept after they performed in Miami Beach.

GEORGIA AYERS: What happened to those who lived in Overtown was the second coming of the establishment and replacing blacks to allow room for whites. My neighborhood was the first displacement of black people some forty years ago. Fortunately, they had places for them to go; they were given some sort of subsidies in order to find other housing. They placed those persons who didn't have a place to stay in what we call emergency housing centers. It wasn't a surprise to me, because I had lived through it from the divided—colored—subdivision from where I came. The system itself perpetuates displacing blacks.

It's like what happened when they drove the I-95 through Overtown. They wanted to make commuting for the "haves" who live in the south and the north end more convenient for them to come downtown. So they decided to build I-95 or the expressway. And in order to get downtown they had to come through Overtown—which meant, "The niggers had to go."

So they came out and talked to all of the property owners and told them that by eminent domain, this property is needed to build this expressway. "Growth is coming on," they said, "growth is coming on. And sometimes some people lose, and invariably it's blacks who lose."

A few whites were displaced too, but Overtown was destroyed because of urban renewal and the expressway. There was all this anger and frustration in Overtown, and it brimmed over into the worst race riot in America when four white policemen were acquitted in the killing of a black businessman. It lasted five days and caused seventeen deaths.

All of my life, I have been fighting for survival against racism, oppression, economically and every other way. I am fighting for a better way of life for my children. I understand now, for a fact, that my children don't have to drink in the black fountains as I did. When they go downtown, they don't have to go in the back and sit in the back to try on a pair of shoes. They don't have to buy a hat and take it home because they cannot try it on. We have integration as far as the white man says it's there. My thing is to take what you have, make something of it, and never be satisfied.

CLARENCE DICKSON: In 1962, another black cop, Robert Ingram, and I were asked to leave the black precinct and go downtown. We would be traffic cops, joining the traffic unit, which was all white. That was the first attempt to integrate the department. Newspaper clippings speak of how the two black cops were sent downtown to work in the all-white community. The first day people sat on the curb and watched as I directed traffic, blowing whistles. They wanted to know what was going on.

I didn't like working downtown. I didn't like directing traffic. I really wanted to be a cop on the street. But this was an integration thing. When I started working downtown, some white guys quit the department in protest. That was because they didn't want to work with a black cop. But I gotta hand it to the white guys. Most of them were very supportive of me and my friend. They told me, "Clarence, that guy was gonna quit anyway."

After being a traffic cop for four years, I asked to be put back on patrol, to do some real police work. I had had enough incidents working on traffic downtown. One I'll never forget was the time I was standing in the street on the corner next to a paper stand when a big white guy up on the curb pulled an automatic on me. I saw the holster hanging down from his coat.

"You got a permit for that there gun?" I asked. He looked at me and said, "Get lost. I'm FBI."

I knew right away that wasn't true. FBI don't talk to cops like that. But I said, "Okay."

Just then the light changed, and the noise comes on that means all traffic must stop so people can cross. He took off across the street. By the time I crossed, I saw him again standing with the gun in his hand waiting on me. I kept running toward him while trying to find some cover. *"I'm dead,"* I thought, and I drew my gun.

Just then, two little old ladies walked right between us. And I saw he was looking around. Apparently, he was trying to find me.

I had my gun in my hand, but I didn't come out firing because there were too many people around.

Instead I began to yell, "Drop the gun. Drop it."

At that moment, I saw Office Henley come up behind him and tackle him. Then I moved in, and we took that army forty-five away from him. He had forgotten to release the safety in his gun. That saved my life.

When he was arraigned, we found a machine gun on him. We learned he was a newspaper reporter from Texas, had been here for only a month, and he was on the ten-most-wanted list.

I had a lot of years climbing up. By the time I made lieutenant, there was already a rule that said the department had to have a black executive officer. Major Smith, the first black executive officer with a rank above captain, was getting ready to retire, and I was made major.

When that happened, I thought that as a high-level police officer, I would be able to make a difference. But the chief at that time sent me to the black police officers' graveyard: community relations. That's where all the black officers were sent. But I was needed in patrol, because things were getting out of hand.

Cocaine was in the atmosphere. Drug pushing was out in the open air, in your face. You'd get out on the roadway, drive into Overtown, and you'd see these guys standing there on the streets with nothing in their hands. You stop; they ask what you want. It was like a flea market sale. There was crack cocaine, the most addictive—you can get addicted from a single use.

But this happened around the same time that we were coming off the Rodney King riot, the Martin Luther King assassination. We were shell-shocked from all the riots. And so it became the policy of the police department to back off the minor crimes in the black community. Police officers were encouraged by their supervisors, by the brass, to put on the blinders, to show how community-minded they were, that they were not aggressive, abusive, disrespectful.

So whenever they were called to the black community, the police would go in, do their job, and immediately get out without causing any disturbance. By this time, all the cops, white and black, were working together. They didn't care about the segregation business; they were too affected by this policy of nonconfrontation. There was overindulgence from the mayor down to the police officer.

This backing off brought the drug people and criminals into the streets. Without the good cops doing progressive police work, they felt safe standing out there selling their drugs. The policy of looking away helped the cocaine business. A police officer would see someone smoking marijuana and just go by. I saw this happening over and over, and I didn't like it.

I kept asking to be moved to patrol. Then the major in patrol did something wrong, and that opened the door for me. The police officers were brought away from community relations to focus on crime, and it turned from the worst into the best of times. We stopped the backing off. We took off the horse blinders. We went back to the streets.

It's altogether different now. The department is back on its feet. People will call you when they need you to accomplish something. We go there, we take the side of the victim. We stay until the situation is resolved.

I moved up to deputy chief, assistant chief, and finally chief, which is where I stayed from January 1985 to August 1988.

When I retired in 1988, a black police chief followed me. People had said they liked what I did; they said they want another guy like me. When he left, another black police chief took over. I feel like I left a legacy.

One of the main things I was able to accomplish was to speak out for the victim. I remember one night when I was working on the desk, I got a call from a citizen who said, "I need a real police officer right now. Not one of those good guys who wants to make everybody happy. Send me a real police officer." I felt for that person. She wanted help. I went there myself to help her out.

Every once in a while, I think back to the morning I was waiting for the bus to get to work, and this black officer struck up a conversation with me and told me I'd make a good cop. Years later, when I was a cop, we met again. He seemed above me, an established guy whom I couldn't measure up to. Then I learned that, like me, he was born and grew up in Palatka, Florida.

It remains one of those amazing coincidences in my life, how we shared the same hometown, how he happened to drive by as I waited for a bus, how my life turned on that single encounter.

10

A Little beyond the Law

It was not legal, but it was acceptable.

—Claire Warren

DIANE WOOLFE CAMBER: Every hotel had bookies in the cabanas. On Forty-third Street there was a little cigar store where they took bets. There were casinos in the nightclubs.

LISA COLE: Before Vegas, the Fontainebleau and the Eden Roc were the happening places. They had gambling under the table, coming in from the back door. That was big; very big.

ANN BROAD BUSSELL: Miami always had a history of things outside the law going on. It has always been a center for smuggling. During the Civil War, Key West was a Union outpost and the site of smuggled arms.

CLAIRE WARREN: My dad built these little stores from Sixteenth and Washington Avenue almost up to Española Way. I can remember when I was twelve years old, my dad would go around and collect all the bets and run them up to the horse room that was on Fifteenth and Washington. An office supply was downstairs, and upstairs was the horse room where you placed your bets. I was a runner when I was twelve years old. It was not legal, but it was acceptable.

There was a whole world that existed a little beyond the law back then, and it was totally safe. We left the door unlocked day and night. We didn't know from drugs and things like that except that Gene Krupa, who played the drums in the hotel bands, used to smoke marijuana.

We had the S and G Syndicate down here. They controlled the prostitution and the gambling, and it was all very clean and open. There were no streetwalkers, but there were call girls. If you walked into the Fontainebleau and saw a girl sitting there with her purse on the table, you knew she was for hire.

The big gambling was out in Hallandale. But on Miami Beach, there was jai alai and the greyhound track across from Joe's Stone Crab. My dad taught me how to drive on the dog track.

I knew Meyer Lansky. I called him Uncle Meyer. He was immaculate, very bright, a likable man. He and his buddies used to eat at the Heart Institute, which had a wonderful cafeteria. He did a lot of business in Cuba, before Castro, when George Raft was the maître d' at the Naçional Hotel in Havana.

If you needed money for a cause, you had powerful people to go to. During the war, Meyer Lansky and the others lent support. "You need a battleship? Here's the money," Meyer would say.

Joe Kennedy was a major receiver of gray money—money you get from tax evasion. For every bottle of scotch that came into this country, Joe Kennedy got a cut. Even the Jews couldn't do that.

ANN BROAD BUSSELL: The movie *The Godfather* made many aware of Meyer Lansky. It was said his real name was Majer Suchowlijaski, and that he was born about July 4, 1902, in Grodno, Belarus. But we knew him as a regular at Beth Jacob, the Miami Beach shul that became the site of the Jewish Museum of Florida in 1986.

Everybody knew Meyer Lansky. You'd see him walking his dog, Buster. It was common knowledge that he was running these illegal bookmaking operations in the cabanas of the hotels, the Sans Souci, the Saxony. What he did in everything else, I'm in no position to comment on.

My father had a connection with Meyer Lansky and worked with him to help secure and outfit boats with Panamanian registry for Aliyah Bet, which took displaced persons from the south of France and Italy and Bulgaria to run the

British blockade in Palestine in 1947. He also secured guns for the state of Israel when they were really needed. However, when he wanted Israel to take him in as a Jew, they sent him back. He did a good deed by getting weapons to help the Jews.

JOHN TURCHIN: My father and the men of his generation used to eat at the Embers; among them was Morris Landsberg, who owned the Eden Roc and the Deauville and brought all the entertainment into Florida. They were tied up with Meyer Lansky and those guys.

HAROLD ROSEN: There was gambling in different spots around Miami. Everybody was so happy; everybody had a dollar from the gambling. The waiters, the waitresses, the taxi drivers—they'd open the doors for you. Then Senator Kefauver was invited here by one of our commissioners. He investigated, closed everything down.

I had gotten involved in the gambling because of a guy by the name of Jack Gross. He lived in the apartment next to me when I first came down. His brother was Harry Gross, a big racketeer. He used to send Jack $250 spending money every week. I was living on $60 a month.

My mother was a compulsive gambler. She ran the junkyard. When she came down, she used to go to the racetrack in the afternoon, dog track at night, and after the dog track, she would play cards at the hotels.

Meyer Lansky was a good friend of mine. He was very knowledgeable, Jewish conscious, knew his way around. We'd talk about world issues.

We used to eat in Wolfie's. Meyer and I would sit at a table in the back, a special table. Nobody sat there but us. We had a favorite waitress, a black lady who used to take care of us every morning. The waitresses used to pay to be in the front lines, because they did so well with the tips.

They took a thousand pictures of me with Meyer. They also did an article in *Reader's Digest* about me: "From Mob to Super Mob." Like I was the politician. I didn't even know what was going on.

I used to do a lot of litigation. "Oh, you're a good friend of Meyer Lansky," the judge would say.

"Don't ever forget it," I'd answer.

Robert Zuckerman self-portrait. Courtesy of Robert Zuckerman

ROBERT ZUCKERMAN: In 1999, I was doing photography for *The Crew*, a film about aging mobsters, with Burt Reynolds and Richard Dreyfuss. We were filming at the Rascal House on Sunny Isles Beach on a hot summer day when Lou, the makeup artist and a veteran in the industry, walked out to the front of the restaurant. With him, shuffling along, was a guy in his mid- to late-nineties. "Hey, Robert," Lou said, "take a picture of me with Jimmy Blue Eyes." I couldn't believe it. Back in the days when Miami was the Wild West, Jimmy Blue Eyes was top lieutenant of the Meyer Lansky organized crime group.

11

Ali and the Fifth Street Gym

Cassius Clay was born in Louisville. But Muhammad Ali was born in Miami.

—Ferdie Pacheco

DAVE ROGERS: The Fifth Street Gym on Fifth Street and Washington Avenue was iconic. People came there from all walks of life. There was no air-conditioning. It was musty. It smelled of sweat—boxers' sweat. There was a back room with a bed and mattress, a place where the boxers would shower, towel off.

BERNIE ROSEN: There was no elevator. You had to walk up two flights of steps to the first floor. Sitting right there at a table would be Chris Dundee, who ran the gym. He used to charge twenty-five cents to let people in to see the fighters train. If he knew you, you paid nothing.

LUISITA PACHECO: I remember one guy didn't want to pay the quarter because, he said, he was the press.

"Press my pants," he was told.

BERNIE ROSEN: In 1960, after Ali—the young Cassius Clay then—won the Olympic light heavyweight championship gold medal, he was managed by the people who made Seagram's Whiskey in Louisville, Kentucky. Those people had him come to Miami to be trained and managed by Angelo Dundee, who got him a little apartment in Overtown.

FERDIE PACHECO: That was when I met Cassius Clay. He came to my office in the ghetto in Miami at North West Second Avenue and Tenth Street. I thought he was the most exceptional looking individual I had ever seen in a boxer. He was beautiful, he was shapely, all his muscles were in the right places. And he was extremely fast—fast with his mouth; talked all the time. He was not an intelligent man in the conventional sense. He was totally instinctive—just did the right thing—and he was very funny. He could charm anyone, even my usually uncharmable old Baptist Church nurse, Miss Mabel Norwood, who summed him up: "That boy is either going to be the champion of the world, or he's crazy."

Ali was a solitary figure then, with nobody to keep him company; an eighteen-year-old, new to the big city of Miami, trying to find out what it was like. He had no guy friends. He had no girlfriends. All he had was the Fifth Street Gym and Angelo Dundee and Chris Dundee. That's who he had. But inside of two months, he had taken over. He was a magnetic figure. The whole town was following him around. If you hung around him, you became attached to him and were under his spell.

LUISITA PACHECO: Ali was such an unassuming person. He didn't care about getting dressed up; he would always wear black. He was so kind to everyone. He would collect antique cars, ride around in the cars, and talk with Ferdie.

I was a dancer and dance teacher, and from my expert point of view, he was very light on his feet.

DAVE ROGERS: Sarria, a Latin guy, would massage Ali in the back room, work his muscles with the cream and all that. Once when Ali was getting his massage and workout, I tried to get into the room, and this big black Muslim guy—he was wearing one of those hats that look like yarmulkes—was standing at the door, blocking my way. "Man, you can't come in here," he said.

But Ali overruled him. "Hey, that's my man Jesus," he said. That came from the time I was wearing a little beard like Mephistopheles, and the cut man, Angelo

Muhammad Ali, Ferdie Pacheco, and their daughters. Courtesy of Ferdie Pacheco

Dundee, introduced me to Ali, saying, "This is my friend, Jesus Christ." After that, and for all the years that I knew him, Ali called me Jesus.

I saw things between Angelo and Ali that most people didn't see, didn't know. There was such a close tie. Ali seemed to have a great love for Angelo, and Angelo for him. He would put his arm next to Angelo, who was Italian and had dark skin, and he'd say, "Angelo, you a nigger; you more of a nigger than I am." But lovingly.

BERNIE ROSEN: Angelo and his brother, Chris, founded the Fifth Street Gym in the early fifties. Angelo was one of the top trainers in the twentieth century. Chris was a promoter of the fights in the Miami Beach auditorium, the place where Jackie Gleason would eventually put on his shows. I would go over every single Monday and do a preview of the fights, and Chris would put on shows every Tuesday night. We used to shoot one of the fights and run it back to the station to have it processed and put on the air. That was a huge thing back then.

DAVE ROGERS: We used to go to Wolfie's after the Tuesday night fights: Angelo, Chris, Ferdie Pacheco—the fight doctor who had a medical practice in Liberty City and would regale us with all kinds of stories—and Jimmy Ellis, the fighter. They were all part of Ali's entourage.

"Angelo, give me a couple of dollies," Ali would say. Dollies, not dollars. Angelo would support fighters who needed money. He kept one pocket for singles and one pocket for larger bills.

Every day, I'd pick up Angelo, and we'd go to the gym. A lot of people came to the gym, guys from all walks of life. They would come off the street, up the steps, and there on the right would be this little guy sitting at a desk, always with a cigar. That was Sully Emmet, a true Damon Runyon character.

I was in the insurance business and insured a place on Twenty-third Street called Ollie's. It had great steaks and hamburgers with special seasoning.

Ollie had a girlfriend, Terry. They would argue; the language was terrible. Whenever he and Terry had a fight, he'd go out in the back and smoke his cigar. He was always smoking a cigar. Sometimes the ashes would fall on the hamburgers. "Ah," he'd say, "that's what makes it good."

I took Ali to Ollie's. There was a bus outside filled with a class of kids. Ali went over to the bus and made like he was boxing, hitting the window of the bus. Then we went in. I said to him, "You'll get only one *Ollie burger*. That's all you'll get." (In those days they would name a burger after someone.)

Ali said, "I want another one."

"You can't get another one."

Then Ollie came over. "Ali, for you, there's another one."

Angelo brought Moe Fleisher along. He was a guy who sold boxing shows from New York and was publisher of *The Ring* magazine.

We'd go out for lunch, and Moe would invariably say, "I have to go meet the girl." The girl lived in the Tropics Hotel on Collins Avenue and Fifteenth Street—I wrote the insurance for the building. He was eighty-six at the time; she was eighty-four.

Once I was with Moe in the Convention Center. We go to the bathroom. He's standing next to me in front of the latrine. Before anything starts, he looks down and he says, "Son of a bitch, you died before I did." That was Moe Fleisher.

Another time at the Convention Center, Ali's standing next to me. "Muhammad," I tell him, "one of the fighters at the gym is gay."

He says, "Who is it?"

"I can't tell you; he'll beat the crap out of me."

"Tell me. No one's gonna touch you."

"I can't tell you."

"Come on, you gotta tell me."

I say, "Bend over, I'll whisper it to you."

He bends over. I kiss him on the cheek. He slides down the wall, hysterical.

I called Ali the Pied Piper of Hamelin. He would talk to everyone, give autographs to everyone. He was a really good guy.

LUISITA PACHECO: When Ali was at the Fifth Street Gym, chairs were lined up all around the ring. People would scream and yell as he shadowboxed around. Other fighters were training there, but it was never packed the way it was when he was there.

JOSEPH KRUTEL: I'd see Ali there, watch him spar, sit on his lap. The Fifth Street Gym had to be the greatest one location on Miami Beach when it came to sports. I used to go there with my father and a group of guys. We saw Sonny Liston fight there. My father would be in the huddle in the ring; he shot it on 16 mm. My father was best friends with Angelo Dundee. I saw the training that was done with Angelo. I saw Ferdie Pacheco, the most famous fight doctor ever known in sports, and his wife, Luisita, at the gym. They were my mom's dear friends.

FERDIE PACHECO: The Fight Doctor name for me was New York stuff. That was hardly all that I was. I was a scholar who gave lectures at Harvard and all over.

I liked every boxer I ever took care of. I was a hero to people, because I was taking care of their heroes. There is something ennobling about taking care of people who are on their last legs: eighteen, nineteen years old, and they don't know what to do with themselves.

The Cuban boxers were my favorites. They came to Miami completely lost. They were political exiles and had been oppressed horribly. I took them into my house and let them sleep in the garage. I had a Cuban maid. She was a great cook, and she cooked the food they liked, lots of it. They all made money and all became champions.

I met Angelo Dundee around the time I came to Miami to live. "I like boxing and jazz," I told him. "Any boxer who gets cut: I will sew him up for nothing. I will take care of his medical needs. For the rest of your life, you will never have to write out a check for me. On the other hand, I want a ticket to every fight you promote—for me and my wife, and maybe more if I want to bring friends."

He got a good deal. So did I. He saved himself at least a hundred, two hundred thousand dollars. For my part, because of Ali, worlds of interest opened up to me that I had never known. I met the Queen of England, Winston Churchill, Malcolm X, the Beatles, Elvis. Through the 1960s and 1970s, everyone who was anyone was at our door. They all wanted to be with Ali.

I met Budd Schulberg. He liked being at the Fifth Street Gym. He loved boxing. He was a great writer, a perceptive writer. He wrote *On the Waterfront*, *The Harder They Fall*, among other top writings. I had written a very good novel of my growing up. It delineated the society of Tampa and Ybor City better than anybody else has ever written it. I asked him if he would read what I had written.

We agreed that he would come over to my house at ten the next morning. He asked me to have a good bottle of vodka for him. I had a case ready. He went into

Pacheco and Ali on the streets of Miami, 1970s.
Courtesy of Ferdie Pacheco

the backyard with the manuscript, sat under the shade tree, and began to read. He stayed with me for two days and read it straight through. He edited it for me and did not make many changes. He said he liked it a lot and if it didn't get published, it would be a shame. However, he couldn't get it published for me. I couldn't get it published either.

But Schulberg was extremely helpful to me, and I was extremely helpful to him. And that was because of Ali. Because I knew Ali, people wanted to know me, to help me.

RED HELLER: I was in charge of the Police Athletic League, and one time I got Ali to come down and pose with some of my fighters. We wanted to put him in the ring with this young kid. Ali put on his gloves. They both got in the ring. The kid was shaking like a leaf. But Ali, who was just beginning to have Parkinson's then, just patted him on the head. It was a special moment for everyone.

Of course, he would clown for photographers. He would recite poetry. He would brag that he was the greatest. He even would predict the round he'd knock out his opponent. But in the ring, in a pure boxing match, he was all business.

Maybe the most dramatic moment in my time with Ali was February 25, 1964, at the Convention Hall in Miami. It was Cassius Clay versus Sonny Liston—the heavyweight championship of the world on the line. It was a pure boxing match. Nobody, they said, could beat Sonny Liston. Nobody. He was considered totally indestructible—huge, muscular, murderous: a murderous man.

In the opening seconds at the weigh-in, Clay called Liston "a big ugly bear." The champ was stunned. His eyes burned with anger at this young pup of a challenger. Clay was a twenty-two-year-old, still like a high school kid, as innocent as could be. He had learned from the people in the gym that the people in the penitentiary were scared of only one kind of person: a crazy person. Sonny Liston was the only kind of person who could kill you inside the gym, inside the ring, inside the penitentiary.

There was no one around outside of Angelo Dundee and me who thought Clay would win. There were forty-six writers who covered the fight; forty-three predicted Liston would be the winner. He was a seven-to-one favorite. But once you saw the way the young man trained, you knew he was going to beat Liston.

No one was faster or stronger. Never was there a heavyweight champion built by God like Muhammad Ali. Not many remember that his record was 19–0. That is what earned him his shot against the heavyweight champion, Sonny Liston.

BERNIE ROSEN: I will tell you a story. I was at the Liston-Ali fight. We had a camera set up in Sonny Liston's post-interview room. Everyone had a camera in there. There was no thought that Cassius Clay could win. He was the underdog of underdogs. But just in case, I had a second camera set up in Clay's interview room.

FERDIE PACHECO: Liston was a two-step fighter. He shuffled two steps forward and then jabbed. But once the fight started and Liston did the two-step, Ali timed it and saw that he was able to handle it. Liston was used to hitting people once and knocking them down. He was hitting Clay, but Clay wasn't budging, and Liston wasn't hurting him. "I felt good 'cause I knew I could survive," Ali said.

BERNIE ROSEN: Liston had a substance on his glove. Back then they were not that active in checking everything.

FERDIE PACHECO: In the fourth round, Liston rubbed some substance into Ali's eyes. The round ended. Ali came back to the corner. "My eyes burn," he said. "They put something in my eye. I can't see. Cut off my gloves, Angelo, cut off the gloves. I want to prove to the world there's dirty work afoot. I want to end the fight now."

Angelo calmed him down. I got the sponge and poured water into his eyes, trying to cleanse whatever was there. Angelo put his pinkie in his eye and then put his pinkie into my eye. It burned like hell.

It turned out that Clay's eyes were rubbed with a substance from Liston's gloves. Angelo expertly threw more water in Clay's eyes and yelled, "Run, run, run," until his eyes cleared.

As Clay went out for the next round, Dundee told him "Just run, run. Keep away as much as you can."

Clay did run and shuffle. He landed shots as the rounds moved along, and his eyes cleared. Liston went on the defensive. He did not answer the bell for the start of the seventh round, leaving Cassius Clay a TKO and the world championship. "I shook up the world," Ali said afterward. "I shook up the world."

LISA COLE: My father, who was a fabulous public relations guy, was a friend of the Dundee brothers. "Hey, Julian," they said to him, "we need you to do something for us." And that was how my father became Clay's publicist for the fight. He also arranged for that famous photo of the Beatles when they came to Miami Beach to meet Cassius Clay where the Beatles are lying down on a boxing mat, and Cassius is standing over them with his fists in the air like "I am the greatest!"

Now, Cassius wanted to announce his becoming a Muslim, but my father and both Dundee brothers told him, "Listen, let's focus on the fight. After the fight you can do whatever you want. Let's not distract from what we have to take care of."

FERDIE PACHECO: The next morning the champ confirmed reports that he was now a member of the Nation of Islam and that the name Cassius Clay was one he would never answer to again. Eight days later on a radio show, Nation of Islam leader Elijah Muhammad gave the new champ his new name: Muhammad Ali.

The transformation from Cassius Clay to Muhammad Ali was overworked. The writers, the guys looking for shit, they did that. It was a very amazing thing. He was a young man in a world that was very confusing to him. He had come from Louisville. There was nothing in Louisville. He came to Miami. It was Paris and the ghetto: jazz and the civil rights movement on every corner.

He fell in with the Muslims. They were a gangster bunch. Some were ex-cons who had killed people. They were violent. Ali was not violent. But he liked their philosophy of black is best, of not wanting to be with the whites. The ideas they presented to him appealed to him. They would take care of his wants. He could go wherever he wanted. That was very important to him. It worked for him.

Ali was naive about becoming a political pawn. His handlers and bosses in the Nation of Islam wanted to fire Angelo Dundee and me and bring in their own people. Ali refused. We remained. A bunch of hangers-on came aboard. Howard Cosell came on the scene and enhanced himself. He was a tall man, stooped over from carrying the weight of his importance on his shoulders.

What was it like to be Ali's physician? At times it was like being Queen Victoria's gynecologist. The title didn't mean much, but the view was spectacular. I remained with Ali as corner man and physician, but as the years went by, I was concerned about his physical condition. In 1977, he took a terrible beating in a championship fight with Ernie Shavers.

BERNIE ROSEN: He was a great, great defensive fighter. But you can take just so many shots to the head.

FERDIE PACHECO: I told him, "You have to quit, retire from all this." He would not, so I left his camp.

LUISITA PACHECO: I was proud of Ferdie when he left Ali, because he knew Ali was being damaged. Ferdie was a physician first and a cornerman second. He could not stay and watch this happen. Always concerned about Ali's health and his injuries. His hangers-on, and there were so many of them, did not want to lose their meal ticket.

For me, it had been a tremendous run with Ali. People wanted my autograph, too. I was *Showtime*'s on-camera boxing analyst for fourteen years. I even won an Emmy.

DAVE ROGERS: From the time it opened in 1950 to the time it closed in 1992, Chris and Angelo Dundee made the Fifth Street Gym a place for the boxing champions they trained. They included Sugar Ray Leonard, Willie Pastrano, Carmen Basilio. I met Joe Namath at the Gym, Melba Moore, Barry White, Burt Lancaster, Jackie Gleason, Frank Sinatra, the Beatles, Joe Louis, John F. X. Condon (the voice of Madison Square Garden).

But by the time the Fifth Street Gym closed, the boxing thing had run its course. The place had gotten rotten.

12

Looking through a Lens of Culture

Back then, it was a kind of culture in exile.

—Philip Smith

DIANE WOOLFE CAMBER: There was opera in Coral Gables when I was growing up. It was the oldest cultural institution, but there wasn't much else. We had touring performers; things came to town. But it was a movable feast.

COCONUT GROVE

PHILIP SMITH: My mom used to go to the Coconut Grove Theater to see a play or have lunch; she met Tennessee Williams and Edward Albee there. It was a kind of culture in exile. People were hungry for culture, but they were a small group. Most of the people living in Coconut Grove at the time were rednecks.

The rest of the country was a separate country from Miami Beach. When some comedian my mother wanted to see would be appearing in one of the hotels, my mother would come in to see him. There was little "fine dining."

CHARLIE CINNAMON: I graduated from NYU in the 1950s, and I knew I didn't want to spend my life in the subways of New York. I wanted a little sunlight in my life. My sister told me, "You have to go out and find your life." Friends of mine who lived in Miami suggested I come down and give it a whirl.

So I came down to Miami, where I went to the library and met a librarian named Helga Easton. I told her I hardly knew anybody but very much wanted to get started as a press agent. She invited me to come with her to the home of Helen Alpert, publicist for the Empress Hotel in Miami Beach. Tennessee Williams would be among the guests that evening, I was told.

Alpert was a big fan of Tennessee Williams. On the top of her fireplace was a whole collection of glass animal figures that she called her "glass menagerie." Tennessee Williams failed to show that night, but Helen Alpert, a wonderful and very colorful woman, got me my first job as her assistant at the Empress Hotel. Working with her, I began to learn my craft.

It was tough. I used to write releases and send them out. They would come back with comments like, "This is terrible writing," and that kind of thing. I was brand-new. I had no money. I lived in one room with no cooking facilities and ate out all the time, cheaply. But then my first big break came when Helen Alpert left her job at the Empress. I took over and was able to make some money and move down to the Beach.

You have no idea how competitive it was then. Just to get a client mentioned was a major accomplishment, even though there were two daily newspapers. But I grew into my business, became part of the scene. In that time you had two lives. You worked during the day. You went home. You changed your clothes and went out again to try and do more business. That was how I developed more and more contacts.

I started to represent other hotels and nightclubs. My first client was Patsy Abbott, who ran a little club. She was what was called an off-color Yiddish comedienne. I worked for Patsy for twenty-five dollars a week. That was the beginning of my career. Then I started to stretch.

While I was representing the Empress Hotel, the Coconut Grove Playhouse reopened on January 3, 1956, with the American premiere of Samuel Beckett's *Waiting for Godot.*

At that time, I was friendly with a woman known as Sleepy Time Gal who had a late-night radio show where she talked about her imaginary love affair with singer Tony Martin. Now, she asked me to escort her on the opening night of the play. It was a black-tie social event that lasted some time before the first act finally began. By then, everybody was half tanked. At intermission, everybody was leaving. They didn't like the play, didn't understand it.

"Let's go," Sleepy said to me.

But I protested. "No, please let me see the end of this show."

I had to beg her to stay. I'd never been to a play like this before. It was a great and groundbreaking work, a whole new language of the theater performed by a pair of exceptional actors: Bert Lahr and Tom Ewell.

Waiting for Godot may have been a flop in Miami, but it became the beginning of an exciting new movement: the Theater of the Absurd.

I used to put out a weekly gossip sheet at the Empress Hotel. Now I wrote a rave review of *Waiting for Godot* and sent it off as a thank-you note to my friends at the Playhouse. They showed it to Playhouse owner George Engel, who had it run in both of Miami's dailies. At that point, producer Zev Buffman hired me as his publicist, and I became the Miami theater person. I got a lot of publicity for the show and also did good for myself.

In October 1963, I was promoting the musical *Irma la Douce* in Coconut Grove. It starred a French actress named Genevieve who used to appear on a late-night talk show called *The Jack Paar Show*.

It was tough to get people to come across the causeway in those days in order to get to the Grove Playhouse. I was looking for some kind of gimmick. Then I thought because the show was a musical about a Parisian policeman who falls in love with a prostitute, why not turn the streets of Coconut Grove into a Left Bank neighborhood? I called it The Street Art Show. We created this miniature version of the Left Bank of Paris on the streets around the playhouse, complete with a sidewalk café, an art exhibit, even a poodle contest. And it worked! Blocks around the playhouse were jammed with artists showing off their stuff. We got a ton of publicity.

At that time, the Grove was the home of artists, really daring artists, and they began coming out like wild. It was so successful that we formed a nonprofit organization: the Coconut Grove Association, later renamed the Coconut Grove Arts and Historical Association, and what began as a kind of Parisian clothesline art show has turned into a mile-long display of hundreds of artists' works from around the globe.

Today the Coconut Grove Arts Festival is considered one of the premier arts festivals in the country. It shows the works of more than three hundred artists to some 750,000 visitors and brings in at least $40 million in tourist business. Through the years, many celebrities on the order of Milton Berle, Eva Gabor, Charlton Heston, Alan Alda, Gloria Swanson have taken part, and the festival keeps growing.

LILIA GARCIA: The festival is a three-day event over Presidents' Weekend with artists in thirteen different categories and music, dance and culinary—top chefs—under tents. People come to buy art. It is the education for Basel, the way people can come and talk to artists and get to know art, and it's not threatening. We spend more than $80,000 in promoting.

CHARLIE CINNAMON: But the playhouse, although it's still standing, has been closed since 2006. No performances. It has become a political football. The Grove was a big part of the hippie generation; art was what defined it. Miami Beach had bubkes; they didn't know about art then.

LILIA GARCIA: When the playhouse closed, it killed that part of Coconut Grove. It was a $4 million loss. But we have an international theater festival here where we bring in people from other countries, and Coconut Grove is a green place with great gardens, with wild things growing, with lots of plants.

THE FLORIDA GRAND OPERA

JUSTIN MOSS: As a child in San Francisco, I learned to read music and studied violin, which was a requirement. Now I was on the stage, rehearsing along with the other singers, holding my green Schermer piano vocal score, following annotations, when suddenly I had an epiphany. "This is what I've been waiting for my whole life!" I said to myself. It was a life-changing experience. I began spending all my money on opera tickets, attended all the opera seasons.

In college, I studied English literature and managed the art music library at the University of California in Santa Barbara. The summer of 1969, I graduated from college and was looking around for work. A friend and I were hired to do properties for the Music Academy of the West opera production of *Tales of Hoffmann*. It had a famous stage director and famous conductor. From there, I moved on to other positions in the field.

I was general director of the Boston Lyric Company—a troubled landscape at the time—when I got a call from the artistic director of the Opera Guild of Fort Lauderdale telling me the general director of the Greater Miami Opera had died. I thought this could be a promising opportunity.

The Opera Guild of Greater Miami (later known as Greater Miami Opera Association) was founded in 1941 by Arturo di Filippi, an accomplished tenor and voice teacher at the University of Miami. In 1945, the Opera Guild Inc. of Fort Lauderdale was founded with the mission of presenting performances of Opera Guild of Greater Miami productions in Fort Lauderdale. The relationship continued until 1994, when the two companies merged to form Florida Grand Opera.

I had been to Miami for an Opera America conference some years before. I stayed at the Fontainebleau then, and being in Miami for the first time, I took a long walk down Collins Avenue and found Ocean Drive. At that time, all of the Art Deco

Luciano Pavarotti and Joan Sutherland perform in Miami in 1965.
Courtesy of the Greater Miami Opera Association

hotels were basically retirement/nursing home. Set upon the boulevard and porches of the hotels were oceans of recliners where elderly people were lounging.

When my wife and I moved to Miami in 1994, it was the year after Hurricane Andrew. A series of hurricanes that came and went had worn down everyone. We lost 100,000 trees in Miami Dade County. We were living in an apartment on the twenty-fifth floor of a building on Biscayne Bay. We knew the hurricane was coming and had taken precautions. My wife had gone to bed before me. Now I stood looking out the window when the power grid went down. We were in the black—no electricity.

I went to bed. After a while, I got up and went into the dining room, where my wife was seated at the table with her head down, furiously playing solitaire. I started walking over to the window when she cried, "Don't look out!"

I looked up instead and saw the chandelier swinging back and forth. I realized it was the building that was swaying, so much so that the chandelier was swinging along with it. I could feel it. Waves were being driven up the building.

But we survived that hurricane and others that followed. And the Florida Grand Opera, the oldest in the state, where many of the world's leading opera singers have appeared and continue to appear, has also survived, its performances being staged at the Adrienne Arsht Center in Miami and also Fort Lauderdale's Center for the Performing Arts.

ALICE ARSLANIAN FIFELSKI: All of Miami was watching and waiting as the Adrienne Arsht Arts Center, Florida's largest performing arts center, opened in 2006 on the site of the former Sears department store. And the consensus, early on, was it was worth the waiting for. The concert hall can seat 2,200. It has a stage that extends into the audience for additional seats and space in the rear for a chorus of two hundred.

People tell me it reminds them of the Vienna Philharmonic Hall. Its sight lines are perfect, the acoustics phenomenal. What's more, the orchestra level can be transformed into a grand ballroom for dining and dancing events that can accommodate 850 people.

Every year, the New World Symphony performs here twice during the season. The Cleveland Orchestra comes down for a residency. Miami City Ballet does ballet for young people; first access passes fly out the door. We have free gospel on Sundays, and Broadway shows. There's always something. And two thousand students are here through the year for different performances. That's what the Arsht Center is here for—to get students to be interested in the arts, to see live performances.

SUSAN T. DANIS: As the general director and CEO of the Florida Grand Opera, I have the ultimate say in everything; I receive the entire team. My entrée to Miami was on October 12, 2012, and I was immediately aware that I was in one of the most dynamic cities in America. There was such energy, such a sense of growing possibilities, and a view of the Atlantic.

JUSTIN MOSS: When I first began working with Florida Grand Opera, there was a population of elderly donors who had been active in the founding of the company, and I became close to many of them. Hearing their stories, I developed an understanding of what Miami was like in the 1920s, '30, '40s. They are all gone now, but I was terribly fortunate and honored to have known them.

For years I had heard about the uniqueness of the FGO. Whenever I was working in Florida, I would come over to see productions. It is one of the oldest opera companies in America and has a history of performances by some of the biggest opera stars. I had come here from a level-two company. This was level one.

From 1941 through 1972, founder and General Manager Arturo di Filippi regularly brought leading artists from the Metropolitan Opera to south Florida. The young Italian tenor Luciano Pavarotti made his American debut in the 1965 production of *Lucia di Lammermoor* starring Joan Sutherland in the Dade County Auditorium in downtown Miami.

Dr. di Filippi retired in 1973 and was succeeded by Robert Herman, who had been assistant general manager at the Metropolitan Opera under Sir Rudolf Bing. It was during his administration that Greater Miami Opera became one of the country's leading opera companies.

As much as south Florida is known for its tourism, it's also much loved for the amount and quality of its cultural offerings—and that includes the fine arts. Although it's true that the people who come as tourists stay in hotels, go to the beach, the nightclubs, and that sort of stuff, whereas only a small percentage of visitors attend and support performances of arts organizations, there's another "transient" population here—a vast community of Central and South American and Caribbean people who maintain homes here and connect with the cultural institutions.

When I first came here, almost twenty years ago, there was a piece of shared wisdom: the opera audience was elderly and white and elite and dying off. But over the years, that has been proven false. Stand in the lobby of the Arsht Center, of the Ziff Ballet Opera House—especially for a weekend performance—and you'll see as the audience enters that it looks exactly like this community. The ethnicity breaks down; it's fascinating to see the inclusiveness, the number of young people who are coming to the opera.

We distribute dress rehearsal passes to about a thousand students for each final dress rehearsal. You may not be making opera fans of them, but in every assembly there will be some students who connect with the art form, who have had the epiphany I had long ago, who say to themselves, *"Ah! This is what I've been missing all my life!"* Sitting in the opera house, hearing a live performance, there's nothing like it in the world!

One of the things I love is our "Unexpected Opera in Unexpected Places" series, which takes place in totally different venues, both interior and exterior. There's one planned for a space in the Design District. Another one will be in an American Airlines terminal, where you'll be sitting next to someone and all of a sudden he or she will break into an operatic aria. An opera house is a huge structure; it can be a scary thing. I will do anything to break down the darn opera stereotypes, to bring people in. That is the main thing.

Our maestro, Ramón Tebar, out of Valencia, Spain, is the first Spanish conductor to be appointed music director of an American opera company. He's young, enthusiastic, accomplished. He excels in his command of the opera and orchestral stages.

RAMÓN TEBAR: I am from Valencia. I was a pianist and started to play for big names in opera in Barcelona. From there I started conducting in distant places such as Amsterdam, Istanbul, Paris. Then I won a big competition and met a conductor from Rome, who offered me the opportunity to be his assistant in America. After I did two or three seasons at the Palm Beach Opera, he invited me to be music director of the Miami Grand Opera.

That was on June 1, 2011, and for me, it was love at first sight. Since then, I have been the one with the baton, conducting all the productions, supervising the music, the chorus, the singers, the orchestra. The general director and I make the decisions about the season. At the same time, I am still the artistic and music director for the Palm Beach Symphony, where I conduct the symphony orchestras.

My biggest challenge is to translate or to be as faithful to the composer and the score as I can be. I prefer to have the score before me, but a score is just a guide, a bunch of dots. I have the lines of each person in the orchestra and all the singers, and my role is to get them to play together as one. There is much more work in conducting an opera than a symphony.

When I was with the Italian conductor, he invited me to join him in Palm Beach as the second conductor. There I became known as the conductor with "the nice arm." You can teach a conductor how to perform, but to achieve what the piece is capable of is something you have to be born with. Unlike a painting, a piece of sculpture, or a novel, music is vibrations in the air. It has no concrete physical existence. It exists only as you feel it.

Miami was the first American city I came to. It was my first time in the "New World"—in Spain, we still have an attachment to the New World. Growing up in Valencia, there were two countries I wanted to go to as a musician. One was Germany, the other America. When I got the offer in America, I didn't think twice. And Miami turned out to be very special for me, because it is here that I met my wife. She is Venezuelan and came to Boston to study voice. Later on, she decided to switch to psychology. But she was singing in the chorus when I met her.

I'm the first Hispanic music director in America. And it is of a great opera company. There was never a Spanish music director in America before me. I am the first one.

I feel the Spanish connection here in Miami; I believe destiny brought me here. Miami is an American city, but it is also very much like a city in South America. In fact, when people say Miami is the capital city of South America, I can understand what they mean.

When I proposed to do the opera *Nabucco*, I did it for two reasons: first, because it is by Verdi. I love Verdi. For me, he is the best of all opera composers. Second, because Miami is the second largest city of Holocaust survivors, and *Nabucco* is about the diaspora. But there is also the fact that the story is so connected to the

Cubans. The same thing that happened in *Nabucco*'s time is repeated here. Both are about exile, about losing your home. There is this verse in Italian that says, "Oh my beloved country, so beautiful and lost." This is the tragedy of all people who left Spain when the Catholic monarchs ordered the expulsion.

When you see Michelangelo's or da Vinci's masterpiece, you are seeing the same piece every time you look at it. You may see something you haven't noticed before, but it's still the same piece of art. Music changes every day.

If today is sunny, I may conduct differently than if it's a gloomy day. Your interpretation of the music changes with the circumstances. Every day it's a different opera.

JUSTIN MOSS: We want to have some really well known artists during every season. We want to have one production every year that is either technologically or from a scenic perspective mind-blowing. There will always be a warhorse in every season. It's the way into opera for a lot of people. We want to make sure we keep that.

THE MIAMI BOOK FAIR INTERNATIONAL

MITCHELL KAPLAN: It was when I became a bookseller in 1982 that I began to meet artists and writers. It's a complicated story, the story of a city, of different decades.

I was an English major in college who loved books and writing. Then I went temporarily insane and for two years was a student in law school. But it was not for me. What I really wanted to do was be involved in literary culture one way or another.

NYU used to have a publishing institute that I attended at that time. Then I discovered I would be offered salaries on the order of $6,500 a year. So I came back to Miami and made a choice to dive into a world that I was always attracted to: books and literature. All I wanted to do was bring authors together with their readers. When someone asked me what I planned to have in the store, I said "Books and books."

And it was wow! Perfect! We opened Books & Books Coral Gables in 1982, a small, literary bookstore of five hundred feet with a specialty in the arts. In 1989, we opened in Miami Beach, and in 2000, we moved back to Coral Gables but double the size and with a café, something we always wanted to have. We've been in business now for more than thirty-two years.

About six years ago, we opened a store in Bal Harbour, and then we began embarking on these strategic partnerships where we don't own the places, but we give the owners our name and let them be part of our marketing plans. Beyond that, we have something downtown called The Newsstand in the southeast financial center. It's a little place with books, newspapers, beautiful pastries.

For me the beauty of being a bookseller is being part of the renaissance of Miami. We opened in 1982, and in 1984 we started the Miami Book Fair, which is huge. I was the cofounder with Eduardo Padrón, president of Miami Dade College, which I think was probably like what Brooklyn College was like originally.

Mitchell Kaplan. Courtesy of Frommer Archives

The Miami City Ballet started around that time; so did the Miami Film Festival. Art Deco became a cause. The world had shifted, and one began to see the colors of Miami. The gay community came down. Style over substance began to mean something in Miami Beach. At the same time, the drug culture and the cocaine cowboys came into being. You no longer had the serious sixties and seventies. You had the "me decade" and the excesses of the eighties. Now we're seeing that played out even more.

When we started the Book Fair in 1984, not much was happening in Miami. It wasn't even sun and fun. You had the cocaine cowboys, the effects of the Mariel boatlift, poverty, racial strife. It was a very complicated town. The downtown was kind of crumbling. South Beach wasn't as what we think of it today. *Time* magazine had an article with the headline "Miami: Paradise Lost?"

For a long time, Miami had been a pretty bleak place. There wasn't a lot happening; it was not a place where very serious stuff went on. On the other hand, there were a lot of independent bookstores, and they were probably responsible for more than 50 percent of all books sold. Having recently opened the bookshop, I knew what people were reading, and it wasn't as sophisticated as elsewhere in the country. Miami wasn't thought of as a literary town.

But it was clear from the start that Miami was sophisticated enough to support a literary community.

When we began, book fairs were scarce around the country. Only two major ones existed. One of them sold books, and the other held readings. We wanted to do both, to be a kind of cultural center with readings and events. That turned out to be so appropriate when our very first reading was by Isaac Singer, the Nobel Prize–winning writer.

So many people showed up for his reading that we could not accommodate them all. One of my early thrills as a young bookseller was bringing him up to my residence along with all of the books he couldn't manage to sign at our tiny store. I spent a good two to three hours with him, time I will never forget.

In 1989, we took a chance and opened a store on Lincoln Road. In those days, nobody thought Miami Beach was going to develop into much, but in a very short time, we became a hub. We had events. There we had readings by Susan Sontag, Annie Leibovitz, Anne Rice. We also had a lot of celebrity visitors such as

Madonna. Miami was beginning to develop, and so were we. The feeling was that we were building something for the future.

I was a young guy when we started, twenty-four, twenty-five years old. The idea of doing the fair was kind of organic. There were about fourteen of us who met initially and decided to start the fair. It had not been an easy sell in the early years, but we pressed on, and we have seen it evolve to be an extremely important feature of the entire city. Today we are the biggest book fair around.

When we thought of what we would have to do in order to make it a region-wide book fair that would celebrate the diversity that was and continues to be Miami, we decided to bring authors and publishers together to show what books were being published. When James Baldwin was the speaker at our book fair, he flew in from Paris. But somehow his plane landed in Fort Lauderdale, and he had to take a cab to get to Miami. About ten minutes or so into the program, he came walking in and absolutely dazzled the audience.

I presented the great poet Yevgeny Yevtushenko. He was a showman with a persona that was larger than life. His reading was very big, highly dramatic. You could tell that he came from another generation of poets who were also performers.

Over the years, we have had maybe eight thousand writers at the fair: Joseph Heller, Saul Bellow, Mario Vargas Llosa—you name them. Audiences came for the most serious of writers, and that helped to change the perception of Miami as a superficial place.

One day when I was in the Coral Gables store, I got a phone call from Oprah Winfrey. She had an apartment in Miami Beach and wondered if I could meet her at the bookshop on Lincoln Road. This was when she had started her own book club. We met. I showed her all kinds of different books. She was very nice and very interested in books.

There have been numerous articles written about Miami from writers who were here for the first time. At one time we had all the living Nobel Prize–winning poets appear at a fair event, each one introduced by a younger poet. Outside, people were scalping tickets. It was magical, a very special event.

We had about two thousand people show up for Anne Rice when she was in her heyday. Hunter S. Thompson was here in 1988, inebriated and not very coherent. He opened an event with a question of his own for a full audience: "Does anyone

Miami Book Fair street view. Courtesy of Frommer Archives

have any Wild Turkey?" Two men in the audience dashed out, returning in time to thrust a bottle at him. Wrapping up his event, Mr. Thompson dove into a big, bold Cadillac convertible. My last glimpse of him was of legs thrust skyward from the backseat.

Norman Mailer was a very nice guy. He gave a very full talk, took every question, and was not a prima donna. When he appeared at the fair, it was toward the latter part of his life when he was very engaged in politics.

Early, early on, Garrison Keillor came to the fair. He was at the height of his power with his radio program, and at the end, he led the entire audience in the singing of "Amazing Grace." Miami had just emerged from a very difficult period at that point, and to see the auditorium filled with people who were singing in a united voice was quite magical.

Lauren Bacall was a very interesting guest. She couldn't wait to get to Joe's Stone Crab. They actually kept the place open a little late to accommodate her.

One of my more difficult experiences was interviewing Gore Vidal onstage when he was not in the best of humors. I would ask him a question in the hopes of a thoughtful response, but his answer was consistently, "No." I got through it, and so did the audience.

The way I view talks and readings and lectures is that when you are dealing with someone of great importance, it almost doesn't matter how good the event is, because what the audience is getting is the experience of being in the presence of a significant figure.

The Miami Book Fair International was the name we had from the start. We were always into the fact that Miami was an international city. The thing I am most proud of is that the book fair is a very big tent under which there is something for everyone. It is not an elitist fair. It is not a superficial fair. It is not just literary. And it is not for one segment of the community. There are things for kids and their parents and grandparents. We have a big Caribbean program, a Haitian program, Spanish-language programs. We have things that go on in French.

The fair mirrors Miami. It is a microcosm of the Miami way. Exactly. My job is to put the programs together. I am out there organizing. I have been at so many of the events, but if I had to pick out a personal favorite it would be Isaac Singer. I was a great fan of his. I am so taken by his stories. And he was one of the first of that literary class that I got to know.

I always go back to those people who are no longer with us but who meant so much to that literary class at one point, people such as Roger Straus (of Farrar, Straus & Giroux), Isaac Singer, Joseph Heller, Saul Bellow, Norman Mailer . . . I could go on and on and on.

When I opened our first store, I never imagined what it would come to be. I don't think I thought that far ahead. But I have since learned something about myself: there is a producer gene in me that allows me to get a lot of satisfaction when I produce events that are meaningful for an audience and meaningful for a writer as well.

Although independent bookstores have been under attack for the past ten years or so from the Internet, from chains, from Amazon, I think people are starting to come back to them and to understand their importance. I don't think we will ever lose these kinds of stores, because they maintain the literary tradition that is so important in storytelling. And after all, storytelling makes up our cultural life. That is what we are really about—sustaining culture through traditions, through stories.

Miami Dade College President Eduardo Padrón with Mitchell Kaplan and guest at the Miami Book Fair. Courtesy of Frommer Archives

Over the course of some thirty-three years, we have presented thousands of writers, most of the great writers of the last half of the twentieth century. The 2014 fair had five hundred authors and roughly 200,000 attendees. It has been a wonderful run. Even if it ended tomorrow, it would be a wonderful run. As a former English major and teacher, I pinch myself when I think about the kind of writers I've been able to meet.

To me, it's all about literary culture. I'm not a merchant at heart. As long as we can expose people to the great writers of the last part of the twentieth century and the early part of this century, we've done our job.

ART OF ALL VARIETIES

SUE BRUSTMAN: In New York, I lived at the Chelsea Hotel, which was the center of an arts scene. Now I see it here in Miami Beach. The Wolfsonian-FIU is the only museum of its kind in the world, one that highlights propaganda art, the art that took place in the early- to mid-twentieth century years: cooking things, very unusual things that pushed forward a country's political statements, also WPA posters, marionettes, Art Deco items.

And there's Wynwood. About ten years ago, Tony and his group began accumulating properties in a scruffy warehouse area where the architecture wasn't good, but the footprint had wonderful graffiti art. They expanded upon it. They built the graffiti street museum with Jeffrey Deitch, who had a very important gallery in New York and championed graffiti people. Today this area has become our new emerging arts district. You'll see more graffiti art there than you've ever seen in your life.

At first Wynwood was attracting artists but remained deserted and forbidding at night. Then Tony Goldman and his son Joey began buying up properties. They opened a full-service restaurant, an upscale pizzeria called Joey's, and unveiled a permanent art installation called Wynwood Walls, three sprawling courtyards decorated by some of the country's top graffiti artists.

MARLO COURTNEY: That is Tony's masterpiece. It's our graffiti park, open for the world to see.

We are very, very busy with what is now called the Wynwood Arts District. It's Twentieth Street on the south and up to Thirty-sixth Street on the north and bordered by the Design District. It has 120 art galleries and some very famous family art collections, and two restaurants that are very busy. It gets press all over the world, because it's the hippest, edgiest neighborhood we do. The buildings are not historic, but they are all one- and two-story buildings, so it has a kind of SoHo sensibility.

It's a very important area. It all began in 2004, but over the past two or three years, it's really been exploding. We've developed an attraction for tenants. We've created office spaces and retail spaces. People want to work there.

In the fifties and sixties, the Wynwood section used to be the garment center of Miami. It was all manufacturing and warehousing. Then when the garment center went into the crapper, because the industry moved to the Orient, they moved into shoes. All the shoes would come in from China by boat. The boat would come into the port, and they'd bring the shoes to Wynwood, which is close by. Then it would get repacked and go right back out to the Caribbean or wherever.

But now the area is gentrified to a certain extent and very artsy, hip, chic. We have a lot of creative tenants. Aside from Joey's Italian Café, there is Wynwood Kitchen and Bar—a bit of an offshoot of the SoHo Kitchen and Bar—which is a very large restaurant with an indoor-outdoor feel. We also have a property in what is considered Town Center, which is Wynwood Walls, an outdoor art museum. The work of some of the finest artists who were ahead of their time in graffiti art or street art—I prefer street art, because it is another medium—is shown there.

People of all ages go there, all day, all night. Our walls are on private property. When you walk there, it feels like you're in a park. But we own the three-acre site. It was Tony's idea.

We are lucky enough to have Art Basel, a collection of the top 250 galleries in the world that come here. Miami is largely known as the doorway to Latin America, and the Art Basel people, from Basel, Switzerland, were looking to get entry not only to the American market but the Latin market as well. They were looking to bring the European art buyers and the new art buyers and the California art buyers to one destination, and Miami seemed a natural selection. When they came in, all these incredible collectors and gallerists, the eclectic groups of art fairs were all around them.

A lot of Florida artists are being sought after by collectors from Art Basel. Galleries are blooming all around here; corporations are into supporting the arts and art programs. It's humongous.

The season here used to begin around Christmas. Now Art Basel, which is usually the end of November, beginning of December, takes the season and moves it up two weeks, bringing a tremendous amount of revenue. Other art fairs come in. The whole complexion of the art season changes.

Miami is a gorgeous resort area with snowbird apartments, great places to design, beautiful architecture, a cultural center. I feel like I have seen it all.

BASS MUSEUM

JIM LAWRENCE: I worked for five years at the Coral Gables Museum as head of security and then five years as curator and registrar. I took care of the collection and did shows of traveling exhibitions.

The Biltmore Hotel was right next door and so elegant, so beautiful. It was built in 1926 by George Merrick, who was known as the man who founded Coral Gables. During the Second World War, it was used as a military hospital, and after the war it became a veterans' hospital. And it was the first location of the University of Miami. But perhaps the Biltmore is most famous for stories about it being haunted by ghosts and their wandering around the higher floors.

When the Coral Gables Museum closed down, I moved on to the Bass Museum in Miami Beach and began working as building manager. I was there twenty-two years full-time and another four years part-time.

The Bass was Miami Beach's first public library and is its oldest municipal museum. Its shell was made of coral rock that was brought from Key West in 1929. It was named for John and Johanna Bass, Austrian Jews who lived in New York City and wintered in Miami Beach. Mr. Bass planned to give their collection to the Metropolitan Museum of Art in New York City, but Mrs. Bass prevailed upon her husband to give the entire collection—more than five hundred pieces, mainly European old master paintings, textiles, and religious sculptures—to the City of Miami Beach. The building was redone to fit their collection.

Mr. Bass was in the museum every day. Although it was his collection, he said it was a gift for the people of Miami Beach to enjoy at no charge.

DIANE WOOLFE CAMBER: From the beginning, as museum director, I was determined to professionalize the institution, to get the museum accredited. I was very interested in enhancing the collection to include design and architectural aspects. The exhibit "Precious Legacy," a collection of European Judaica from a museum in Prague that had been taken by the Nazis, was an early example of how the Bass could serve as an important cultural destination. At the same time, it highlighted the need for an expanded facility.

SILVIA KARMAN CUBINA: The City of Miami Beach did a national search for a museum director when Diane Camber announced her retirement. I applied, and after many interviews and a long process, got the job.

Although I was born in Miami, I grew up in San Juan, Puerto Rico. But I knew about the Bass, was friendly with Diane and eager to begin on October 1, 2008, even though the recession had officially started. It lasted through two tough recession years. But after that it really has been quite sparkly and brilliant.

At the start, I had no idea what to plan for with huge external forces complicating our plans for the museum. The first month we converted five offices into one exhibition gallery, expanding the space where art could be displayed.

Time has flown by quickly. I'm into my seventh year now. Recently we celebrated our fiftieth anniversary. Museum members and current and past board members were among the guests at the gala who witnessed the presentation of a million-dollar endowment. This would be for a second expansion that would increase programmable space by roughly 50 percent.

The Bass is a boutique museum and one of a kind. Because it's smaller than other museums, we try to see to it that visitors and members have a kind of personal experience not often present in larger museums. We have a rare historical collection of Egyptian art, Renaissance art, Greek vases. Our landscape collection is ever changing. Half a century is behind us, but our contemporary programming brings us into tomorrow.

At our fiftieth anniversary gala November 4, 2014, some of the biggest names in Miami's art scene were present. All of the 285 guests had added touches of gold to their formal attire to mark the celebration. As a backdrop to the cocktail hour, a musician played a gold-leafed Steinway piano that once belonged to the Bass family's original collection.

Miami Beach is continually growing as a city of art and culture. Our institutions are maturing, not only in terms of building, but also in becoming more textured, stronger, more involved in community. We want to make sure we have a finger on the pulse of what is going on globally, and that the Bass is part of the international dialogue on the art stage.

DESIGNER SUNGLASSES

ERIC DOMEGE: Christian Roth and I consider ourselves citizens of the world. We have been traveling since young adulthood. My first time in Miami was in 1978 just after I finished high school. Miami was kind of at a standstill back then. It was not European; it was not in good condition. Ocean Drive and Collins Avenue had problems. But to me, Miami was a beautiful beach and a blue ocean, and that added up to a wonderful place.

Christian and I knew each other through friends in Europe when we met up in New York in the early 1980s. In those years, Miami was somewhere we went for business purposes and to escape the harshness of the New York weather. But we both liked to collect sunglasses and eyewear, which made our partnership a perfect match.

We had a friend, a very young prominent designer back then, who told us, "Guys, if you find me a great pair of sunglasses, I can put them on my runway." Those were the days when fashion shows were not as elaborate as today. Still, we found these great vintage glasses and painted them. The photograph of a model wearing them and walking down the runway made the cover of *Women's Wear Daily*.

It led to our becoming leaders in designer sunglasses. We saw them as fashion accessories, and that brought us close to the people surrounding Andy Warhol at

Sunglasses are de rigueur in Miami. Courtesy of Frommer Archives

that time. They supported what we were interested in doing, and that led to our founding the firm, Christian Roth, in 1983.

When we began our business in designer sunglasses, there was very little on the market. The eyewear industry was lacking. Big designers would give away licensing without caring much about the design of the glasses. We had a vision of creating something different.

CHRISTIAN ROTH: The turning point for us was at the start of the new millennium in 2002. It was then that we met with creative people and began to see what Miami had to offer in addition to beautiful beaches and a great climate. We realized with the technology available, you can be a designer anywhere, everywhere. And Miami is where sunglasses are needed year-round. Pictures of people wearing them go back many, many years.

We realized there was no better place to design sunglasses than in Miami. Although we travel to see customers and our factories in Italy and Japan, Miami is our base; it's where creativity takes place. There are so many different types of people in Miami now, so many very daring individuals not afraid to wear colorful, specially shaped designer glasses. And people wear sunglasses more in Miami than in New York or LA.

ERIC DOMEGE: Christian and I still do all the designs ourselves. When we first started, sunglasses were not really considered a fashion item, an accessory. When we began our business in designer sunglasses, there were very little on the market. We were among the leaders in designer sunglasses becoming fashion accessories.

Today Christian and I are very proud to say that our designer collection comes out of Miami, because it is here that we find the excitement, the inspiration. It is a city that has reinvented itself so many times—not only as a playground, but as a great area for business. You have a melting pot of Europeans, Americans, South Americans—an international city with a gay population, a mix of backgrounds, of diversity.

We do not design for one kind of person. We design for multi-types of faces. We see them all in Miami—so many different types, different skin tones, different shapes.

CHRISTIAN ROTH: Jackie Kennedy Onassis really brought the large-looking glasses to the mainstream. She was very beautiful with her high cheekbones and beautiful features. I would have loved for her to wear our eyewear. Her sister, Lee Radziwill, did!

ERIC DOMEGE: So did Elizabeth Debicki, who wore our vintage round tortoise shell sunglasses in the movie *The Great Gatsby*. Our designer sunglasses have been favored by celebrities such as Rihanna, Sharon Stone, Lenny Kravitz, Nicole Kidman, Kate Moss.

For us, it has all happened in Miami.

13

A Beautiful Friendship

Jeff Lehman and The Betsy Hotel

I like to manage a hotel. It's my thing.

—Jeff Lehman

JEFF LEHMAN: My senior year of high school, while my friends were deciding whether to go to Stanford or UCLA, I opted for Maui, Hawaii, where I became a pool attendant at the Royal Lahaina Resort in Kaanapali Beach. I found my job enjoyable because interacting with such different people, from places I had never even heard of, was so eye opening and cool. It came naturally to me to find out more.

The pool experience defined hospitality: "You never worked so hard, but little is as rewarding as this job done well." My thought was, *if I'm going to work my whole life, what could be better than in a place where people vacation?*

I moved along in the travel and tourism industry, seeing the world from the decks of cruise ships and behind the front desks of hotels. Experience has been my teacher. There isn't a job in the business I haven't had, from doorman to front desk to housekeeping. There isn't a guest or employee experience I can't relate to somehow.

In the 1990s, after time in Hawaii, Japan, and Tahiti, I was back in the United States working as corporate troubleshooter for Bass Hotels, going from place to place trying to problem-solve.

The glittering façade of The Betsy Hotel in South Beach. Courtesy of The Betsy Hotel

In 1992, I was sent to Cocoa Beach, Florida, and it was there that I heard about Miami Beach and in particular the development of South Beach. But being from Los Angeles originally, I felt that nothing that was happening in Florida could be really hip.

I had invited my two brothers to come to Cocoa Beach to watch a night launch of the space shuttle. Afterward, we decided we'd go down to Miami and pick up a cruise. But when I got to South Beach, I took one look at the place and said, "I'm going to live here."

What I saw is that I could live here long-term, and I hadn't lived anywhere long-term before. The Art Deco renaissance was happening. I was so impressed with the hotels—the architecture, the nightlife. Everywhere you looked were beautiful people. It was so alive.

When I had left LA, it was right after the riots. The city was going downhill at that time; it was depressing and dangerous. South Beach, on the other hand, was so open and free. I got a U-Haul and moved down to South Beach.

I had been working since I was fourteen years old. At that point my goal was not to work for eighteen months. I lay on the beach, went to clubs, got to know Miami Beach's history and consider its future.

To keep my unemployment going, I had to seek jobs regularly, which is why I applied for the front office manager's position at The Palms Hotel—then it was called the Miami Beach Ocean Resort. Even though the position was a step down career-wise, I figured I would do my forty hours a week for a while.

I got to know the Krause family, owners of the hotel, who were early pioneers of Miami Beach. They were terrific. Their work ethic matched their guest ethic, and it was quite refreshing. From the day I started, they made me feel the place is mine, the guests are mine. It was never like I'm working for somebody. It's more like I'm working with family. This attitude was expressed by the entire staff.

Built in the 1960s as the Sea Isle Hotel, The Palms had been renamed the Miami Beach Ocean Resort when the Krause family bought it in the early 1990s. It was a very nice three-star tourist hotel, which was just what Miami Beach needed at the time. Eventually, they also purchased the 150-room National Hotel on Seventeenth Street, a long-neglected Art Deco masterpiece that was built in 1939. They bought it for overflow business, never planning on the extensive restoration that they eventually undertook. However, historic preservation was really gathering speed and power at that time.

I had always been impressed with the great Art Deco buildings in LA. Now I found myself moving in a new and unexpected direction. Before I got into it, I did not know much about Art Deco. I learned as I went along.

Art Deco was always part of this area. The revival actually started in the late eighties. The Delano came up in 1995; it was probably the first. All these buildings are designated historic, and you can't touch anything. A fair amount was lost; much of it was in a state of decay.

In restoring an Art Deco hotel, I was becoming an art historian of sorts, helping to preserve a valuable piece of our American cultural heritage. We worked with the Design Preservation League, the Historic Preservation of the city, anybody who could give us insight into the way it once was. We found the original blueprints by architect Roy France, who designed many Miami hotels of the 1940s, and discovered that originally there was a mezzanine that overlooked the lobby. We had one put back in.

We were told that the hotel would be an authentic Art Deco restoration. The Historic Preservation Board, led by William Carey, told us, "Don't even think of anything but Art Deco restoration." The new owners had no options but to do it, and do it magnificently. It was, at the time, the best Art Deco hotel restoration in the city, the model for restoration, what every other hotel was held up to in terms of authenticity. It was also my first hotel as general manager. I became so aligned with that hotel that to this day I get phone calls about it, many years after I left.

The name for the hotel came from the Hotel Naçional in Cuba. My first job was to get services and operation up to our desired level, which was tough because a hotel built sixty years ago doesn't have the bells and whistles of a new hotel. The next focus was on architecture and design. The National had lost its architectural identity. The pool was a small square shaded by the buildings for most of the day. Cabana rooms facing the pool had open corridors almost like the ones in a public housing project. There were gaudy chandeliers and a white 1955 T-bird in the lobby that made no sense whatsoever.

The National was on Collins Avenue, a few short blocks from Lincoln Road. It was flanked by the highly designed Delano to the north and the minimalist Sagamore to the south. Large hotels such as the Ritz-Carlton (formerly the DiLido) and the Loews were still many years away. There was only one national chain represented in Miami Beach back in 1997 when The National opened. All of the hotels were independent at that time.

Revival actually started in the late 1980s. All the buildings were designated historic, and you couldn't change much. Most of the buildings in those days were in a state of decay. But when the Delano came up in 1995, it changed the landscape dramatically.

We scoured the world for Art Deco features and furnishings. We purchased 120 period light fixtures for the lobby area alone. A wall of floor-to-ceiling oak bookshelves in the ballroom was found in Chicago. It was used for wine storage.

Miami Beach was a destination that had to grow up, and in the early nineties, everything was waking up. It had nearly died. Yet, it was like a sleeping beauty in a way. The coming changes attracted me. I found it thrilling to take a city and see it being transformed.

At that time, there was a sentiment of Americana in the area. It was the fifties, the golden decade; the architects were building one glorious Art Deco building after another. Three hotels were in this northern part of Ocean Drive. The Betsy is the single one remaining.

In 2007, a wealthy French developer named Claude Dray bought The National Hotel. He and his wife, Simone, were avid Art Deco collectors, but they had no plan for how to run the hotel. Dray's plan was me, and theirs was not my style at all.

So without having a plan, I left thinking I was the most hirable guy in Miami Beach. But the recession was on; nobody was hiring. I ended up taking a consulting job with a little hotel called the Claridge and was there for more than two years. I also helped my partner run our flower business for hotels and restaurants, which is still going today.

During that time, I learned that a man named Jonathan Plutzik had purchased The Betsy Hotel on Ocean Drive. I started reading articles about the hotel and thought it might be a good place for me to work. So I sent in my résumé.

Jonathan never saw that résumé. A management company was handling personnel hiring for him at the time, and they never let him connect with me. I later realized they knew The Betsy didn't need a management company; it needed a good general manager, and if they and I got together, they would be out. Finally, they realized things were not going so well. They told him, "Your solution is this guy," and introduced me to Jonathan. After several interviews with him and his sister, Deborah, I signed on as The Betsy's general manager and began my career in June 2010.

I had actually walked into The Betsy once before, in 1994, and I thought it was just another neglected hotel. There were still a lot of them back then, and as a hotel guy, I enjoyed seeing old broken-down hotels and looking through the grime and neglect to what they once had been.

When I returned to The Betsy as general manager, I was very impressed by a few things: beautiful design, culinary excellence, a passion for culture and philanthropy. For the first time in years, I felt challenged again.

Jonathan encouraged me to bring in the best hotel people I could find, and, of course, I immediately thought of Ed Ponder, our award-winning director of guest services. I knew Ed when he was our concierge at The National and The Palms. He was the kind of guy I wanted to have around.

ED PONDER: When I got the shout-out from Jeff to join him at The Betsy, it was like being recruited to play for the Miami Heat when LeBron had his game going well at the American Airlines Arena. I could tell from the start that The Betsy was a class operation. It was great to be linked again with Jeff.

JEFF LEHMAN: I like to manage a hotel. It's my thing. Because everything in the hotel was already built, it was a question of "How can we improve this?" A good example was the BBar Lounge, which was being used as a little nightclub venue. It's a great room, beautifully designed, but losing money. In a city like New York or LA, you could pull off a small lounge like that, but in Miami Beach, which is the king of the nightclubs, it didn't work. So we changed the business model there, made it a place for private events, parties, bar mitzvahs, birthdays. And it works.

The Betsy—for Betsy Ross—was designed by L. Murray Dixon, one of the more prolific architects of his day. It was built in 1940, a time when an aura of Americana was part of the scene. The ceilings are definitely Art Deco, but

The Betsy Ross Hotel in 1941. Courtesy of The Betsy Hotel

The Betsy is not an Art Deco hotel. It is the last surviving example of what was called "Florida Georgian" architecture on Ocean Drive. At that time, there was a sentiment of Americana in the area.

We have sixty-one rooms, a restaurant, and close to two hundred employees, with the biggest piece being the restaurant. This illustrates our commitment to the guest experience. When you find a three-to-one employee-to-guest ratio, it's typically because the hotel has a giant catering situation. Our catering business is boutique at the moment. There is nothing small about our commitment to service.

On a business level, we have a very unique model at The Betsy. Our mission and philosophy revolve around what we call our PACE program, which stands for philanthropy, arts, culture, and education. PACE is Jon's passion.

JONATHAN PLUTZIK: After buying The Betsy, we closed the hotel for renovations. When we reopened, it was a totally new product with a defining cultural commitment.

In 1962, the University of Rochester, with the support of the then CEO of Xerox, Joseph Wilson, established the Plutzik Reading Series in honor and memory of our father and his work. Hyam Plutzik had been a professor of poetry and rhetoric at the University of Rochester, a finalist for the Pulitzer Prize in poetry, and a man deeply devoted to the public reading of poetry. In his name, the Plutzik Reading Series welcomed many Pulitzer Prize winners, National Book Award recipients, and Nobel laureates to share their work with the Rochester community. Our father's work and the impact of this series had a profound impact on my sisters, brother, and me as we were growing up.

Now, as The Betsy was going through renovation, I began to think about creating a series at the hotel, and I shared my thoughts with my sister, Deborah Briggs. She agreed the hotel could be a serious place for writing and presentation, and we began work on developing the concept. By the time the hotel opened, the poetry series was part of The Betsy experience.

What we do is invite poets to be our guests at the hotel. Most come alone, stay for approximately five days. We have them sign a contract with a single obligation: a public event, which could be teaching a master class in a high school, or conducting a salon, or being part of a reading. We want them to touch the community.

We added a writer's room for them—it was the last room in The Betsy to be finished. We had the walls lined with cork—it is silencing, and also it provides a space where work can be put up during the creation process. The poets bring their own technology—often a laptop, although some will bring an old typewriter. We may be a long way from the Algonquin, but we keep in mind what Matisse said: "Creativity takes courage."

The Writer's Room is a reflection of what we learned at home. We grew up in a house that embraced creativity. My father passed away when I was quite young, but my mother, who is still alive, was and continues to be a great support. She embraced the creative arts and raised us in a place that values people who value art as a whole. That is something that I must have absorbed, because I carry it to this day. Cultural elements are essential to me, and I credit my mother and my extended family for setting the example.

To date, the poetry series, established in my father's memory at the University of Rochester, has welcomed some three hundred poets, all prizewinners—Pulitzer Prize winners among them. That continues. There may be writers in residence in Portland, maybe a few in New York, but south of that, we are the only ones doing this kind of thing, providing a setting for a serious engagement with the literary arts, poetic and dramatic presentations, writing and discussions. That is the essence of PACE.

JEFF LEHMAN: The cultural aspect is infused into The Betsy's mission. It is what drives us. I tell new employees that if you don't get that, you'll be frustrated here. It's not frivolously done; it's done with authenticity, and it spreads throughout the entire hotel. There's nothing staged here. It all comes from an inner place, something this place teaches you.

Not long ago, the first African American head of nursing at Mt. Sinai Hospital celebrated her ninetieth birthday at The Betsy. That birthday day turned out to also be the date of Martin Luther King's birthday, and to celebrate it, Deborah arranged a perfect little Betsy-like gathering.

One of the guests talked about the journey of African Americans in Miami Beach. Another was an opera singer, and she started singing "We Shall Overcome." A group of modern-day jazz singers, who were also hotel guests, joined in. Soon the whole lobby was singing. It was one of the most stunning, inspirational moments of my life.

DEBORAH BRIGGS: We use twenty-first-century technology; I have a marketing list of 100,000 names. But when we do our salons, sitting around a long table in the private dining room, we generally have maybe a dozen people. Our rooms and suites have open shelves and walk-in closets. You can turn on the shower without getting wet. Every part of the design fits in. Design is so important—every little thing, even pencils. There are books in each room—a mini library. In many places, the decorator buys the books. Not here—we buy the books and the art. It is a collaborative effort. The Betsy model is not about six degrees of separation; it's two degrees of separation.

JEFF LEHMAN: Miami Beach has been really good to me. I worked with families first at The Palms, then at The National, now at The Betsy. There were a lot of similarities in the three properties. I had a dream or vision, and then I went about actualizing that dream. Turning a dream into a successful business is what I do best.

From the start, I had a great staff to work with, an incredible staff, all of them aiming to provide a great guest experience. Customer-relations management is a basic philosophy for me. I want guests to feel this is the only place they can go to. If there's something wrong, I want to hear about it. You can't think you got it right because in this business, it changes. We're not in this for a season. We are in it for years, for the long run.

To be sustainable, a hotel has to make money. I love to make money, and that's what I bring to the equation. As I get toward the latter part of my hotel career, I see a lot of friends around my age, doctors and lawyers who are still paying off their student loans. I don't have that problem even though I never stopped learning. Only I didn't have to go through the formal education process.

JONATHAN PLUTZIK: When we bought the hotel, the floors were covered with marble that was considerably damaged. So we took it out, replicated what we thought the original floors would look like with terrazzo tiles. The young man who came to do the work was the grandson of the man who originally laid the floor. There were so many things like that.

DEBORAH BRIGGS: The area is so protected. You can't change anything on the penalty of death. When it's happening to you, of course, you can't stand it. But we wouldn't want it any other way.

JEFF LEHMAN: Back when I started at The Palms Hotel years ago, there was one branded hotel on the Beach, and that was the Fontainebleau, which was a Hilton. They're all here now. The brands coming in along with the global marketing that came with them were major factors in the growth and development of Miami Beach.

The Betsy is not a national brand, but it's a brand. What we are, what we do, is unique. People try to emulate it, but nobody does it the way we do. The Delano is old news. Ian Schrager sold it. Now it's a company hotel. The Four Seasons, the Ritz-Carlton—great hotels, but they don't identify a city. The Betsy has a certain image. It is high quality, what one envisions and expects a top hotel in South Beach to be like.

Naturally, The National will always be my special love. But The Palms is special to me as well—it's where I got my first chance in Miami Beach, and there's always a place in the heart for the first one. There's also a place in the heart for the one you especially care for. And that is The Betsy—the now, the best of them all.

14

The Jewish Presence

There is a *haimish* feel to the place.

—Ira Giller

THE JEWISH MUSEUM OF FLORIDA

Courtesy of Frommer Archives

JO ANN ARNOWITZ: In 1913, Joe Weiss and Jenny Weiss opened up a small lunch counter at the tip of Miami Beach that served fish sandwiches and fries. They had come down to Miami on the recommendation of the doctor who treated Joe for his asthma condition in New York. Joe learned how to make stone crabs. A few years later, the couple opened what was to become the world-famous restaurant: Joe's Stone Crab.

IRA GILLER: Miami Beach was a sleepy southern town back then. Hotels had signs advertising "No Jews, no Negroes, no dogs." The islands had restrictions against Jews buying land.

ALAN MANDEL: Before the war, there was an ordinance that Jews could not own property north of Fifth Street. That's why Joe's Stone Crab is so far

An early postcard of Joe's Stone Crab Restaurant.
Courtesy of Frommer Archives

The Jewish Museum of Florida. Courtesy of Frommer Archives

downtown. But after the war, things changed. Jews were among the returning veterans, and you couldn't deny a soldier his rights.

JO ANN ARNOWITZ: In 1927, Beth Jacob, the first synagogue on Miami Beach, opened at 311 Washington Avenue between Third and Fourth Streets. About nine years later, when it turned out that Beth Jacob was too small to service the congregation, a second building opened next door at 301 Washington Avenue. It was designed by the well-known architect and congregant Henry Hohauser, who designed more than three hundred buildings in the Art Deco style. The idea for the *bimah* [raised platform in a synagogue] was Rabbi Moses Mescheloff's; he used a bar of Ivory soap as his model. He also designed eighty beautiful stained-glass windows.

When the 301 building opened, the original *shul* [synagogue] became the social hall, and the two buildings served as Congregation Beth Jacob, which would ultimately become the Jewish Museum of Florida.

IRA GILLER: The building at 311 Washington Avenue became the place where minyans were held, while the newer main building at 301 was where the High Holidays were celebrated.

The structures were badly damaged during Hurricane Andrew. I can remember walking on a wood floor that had been eaten by termites; high heels would go right through it. Raccoons were up in the attic. Pigeons had gotten inside. A synagogue that was supposed to be a vibrant part of the Jewish community was in terrible shape.

JO ANN ARNOWITZ: In the early nineties, Marcia Jo Zerivitz, the museum's founding executive director, put together a traveling exhibit of Jewish life throughout Florida—"Mosaic: Jewish Life in Florida 1763 to the Present."

The exhibit defies the common thought that Jews first came to Florida after World War II. We can document that Jews lived in Florida as conversos until 1763 when Spain lost control of Florida. It was then, when Florida came under British rule, that they first were allowed to live freely as Jews.

Now, touring Florida and then Washington, D.C., and Philadelphia, it became clear that a place was needed to keep all the material. "You can't just give it all back and go away," Zerivitz argued. What was needed was a museum to house the six hundred objects that had already been collected and would continue to be collected to preserve this history.

IRA GILLER: Marcia was living in Orlando at that time and was involved with the Jewish community. That led to her making contacts with people from other parts of Florida, which, in turn, led to the traveling exhibit. Now, she turned her attention to her idea for a museum.

A cousin of mine who lived in Orlando knew Marcia. "Go see my cousin Norman in Miami," he told her. "Maybe he can help you out."

Norman was my father. I can remember him telling me, "Marcia Jo Zerivitz is coming to talk to you about an idea for a Jewish museum. She's looking for a donation. Throw her a few bucks and send her on her way."

But she intrigued him. He was retired by then and looking for a project. "I'll get involved with it," he said.

Marcia was another version of Barbara Capitman. Her vision was not as grand as Barbara's, but she had tenacity. Ultimately, she raised millions of dollars to support the creation of the museum.

Once Marcia started dealing with my father, I became involved as an architect. At that point, we had grand plans of restoring the synagogue, but we couldn't afford to do it all at once, and there weren't any contractors who were willing to take it on a start-stop basis. So I said I would take on the job.

In 1994, the museum made a deal to lease the building at 301 Washington Avenue for fifty years with another fifty-year option. My father had become president of the museum, and I helped negotiate the acquisition of the property at 311 Washington Avenue. It was an Orthodox shul—it didn't start out as one, but it became one. Then the shul ceased to exist. Meanwhile, the congregation kept getting smaller and smaller, and we had one museum made up of two buildings.

JO ANN ARNOWITZ: There were plans to sell the properties, both of which are on the Registry of Historic Places. At that time, you could tear down a building, but if you left it, you had to restore it to its original state. The board decided to renovate the space.

IRA GILLER: When I became president, we were able to acquire the museum from the synagogue. I renovated the smaller building and became the architect and contractor who converted the main building from a synagogue that was in poor condition into what it is today. Floors were replaced. But the chandeliers, windows, and the bimah remained. The *mehitzah* [separate seating sections for men and women] was upstairs. It was built theater-style and therefore visible to everyone.

JO ANN ARNOWITZ: The synagogue officially opened as a museum in 1995. In 2008, the two buildings were connected via a long arched hallway named Bessie's Bistro. This was for Bess Myerson, whose parents lived on Euclid Avenue. The first and to date only Jewish Miss America, she was asked by the pageant's organizers to change her name but refused. She did love the museum, though, and wanted to do something for it.

IRA GILLER: Being both an architect and general contractor is unusual. But throughout my career, I've always wanted to be a builder, so doing the design and building for the synagogue has been a fulfilling experience. I named my company Design Building Construction. It went back to the old master builder. I not only design a property, but then I build it, and in doing so, it becomes a labor of love.

There is a *haimish* [homey] feel to the place. After seventeen years, I can still go to a meeting, sit and watch the colors move across the walls and floor, the peach-colored light stream through the stained-glass windows. My grandfather's brother Ben Giller, who was active in the congregation, donated one of the windows when it was still the original synagogue. My family rededicated it.

The past few years we've had High Holiday services there. There's been an effort by Temple Beth Shalom to bring in young people who are unaffiliated for an open service during those days. The museum has been an important part of my professional life. It gives me great joy to know that I've done this, have served as president, and am still on the board.

JO ANN ARNOWITZ: Rabbi Moses Mescheloff left his pulpit in Miami Beach for Chicago in 1956, the year before I would be born in the same city. All through the early years of my life, he was my rabbi. He gave me my name, officiated at my

Museum interior. Courtesy Frommer Archives

bat mitzvah and later on at my wedding. We lived a block apart. I was in his home so often. He did the same project of stained-glass windows in the Chicago synagogue that he had done in Miami Beach. And he lived to be ninety-eight years old.

Years later, when life brought me to Miami Beach and to what had become the Florida Museum of Jewish History, it was a kind of coming home. I think of it now—how Rabbi Mescheloff was my rabbi for so many years, and then unknowingly I move to the place where this brilliant, artistic man lived and worshipped and created such beautiful things. And all I can think is, it's *beshert* [destiny].

CONTENDING WITH ANTI-SEMITISM

DIANE WOOLFE CAMBER: Sometime in the 1930s, Bernarr McFadden, a naturopath known for his regime of healthy eating, built the extravagant McFadden Deauville Hotel on upper Collins Avenue. A big sign out front said: "No Jews, No Dogs Allowed."

When my father heard about it, he went up there and said to McFadden, "If you don't take that sign down, I will take it down." He was a brawny man, a boxer, and he had all these friends who—like him—knew how to handle guns. The sign was taken down.

My father had to contend with anti-Semitism often. People he hung out with didn't think he was Jewish because he was such an outdoorsman, and my parents were not particularly observant Jews. But they were Zionists and very active in the Hebrew Immigrant Aid Society.

"Always a view, never a Jew," read a hotel ad from the 1930s. The Coronado Hotel advertised: "Air-conditioned rooms available. Oceanfront luxury at low cost. Gentile clientele." Other hotels made it clear that they only serviced a restricted clientele.

There were parts of Miami Beach where you couldn't buy a house if you were Jewish. When I was growing up, the Ku Klux Klan came to an empty lot near a development where Jews had moved in and burned a cross.

ALAN MANDEL: Today there are Jewish members of the country club La Gorce, but in the earlier days they were not permitted to enter. Churches everywhere bore signs that said "No Jews Allowed." So did the apartment buildings along the west side of Collins Avenue.

DIANE WOOLFE CAMBER: At North Beach Elementary on Forty-first Street, we Jewish children were in the minority. The principal was anti-Semitic. My cousins changed their last name from Lutsky to Leslie because of the discrimination they experienced there. Still, I was selected to play Mary in the Christmas pageant because I had long blond hair. The teachers thought Mary looked like that.

ANN BROAD BUSSELL: When I was in the sixth grade at North Beach Elementary, the art teacher and the fourth grade teacher were in charge of the Christmas pageant, and they picked me to be the Virgin Mary. The anti-Semitic principal didn't want me to be the Virgin Mary and told the two teachers to get someone else in my place. But they argued that the Virgin Mary was Jewish anyway, and they won out over the principal. So there I was: holding the baby and everything else. I liked it. Why wouldn't I like it?

In every other way, though, it was all Christmas, no Hanukkah. There was much prejudice against Jewish people in Miami. Hotels and golf courses were restricted. We knew to behave ourselves, and that was it.

My parents had moved to 3700 Prairie Avenue in Miami Beach so we could walk to school. There weren't many Jews in that area then; it was not until after World War II that the Jewish population started to grow. My girlfriends were non-Jewish and had their birthday parties at the restricted club. I would get invited and I'd always go. But my mother always said to me, "If they say anything about Jewish people, don't say anything; don't get in trouble."

I was a good student and never had any problem in school. Besides, by 1952 when I graduated from high school, the Jewish kids outnumbered the Christians in the graduating class. Many of them were southern Jews. They were different from northern Jews. It depends on where you were raised.

BASHA SCHLAZER: It was a Jewish world I grew up in. There was an orthodox shul south of us and a small theater on First Street where they showed only Jewish films. I would go there with my grandfather, who lived with us. The movies were all in Yiddish. My grandfather would laugh and laugh. I didn't understand too much, but I loved being there with him, and he loved to take me.

After the war, I would see older Jewish people with numbers on their arms. My grandpa told me what the numbers meant. We saw Pathé's "March of Time" newsreels. Once I saw pictures of lampshades made of human skin.

PHILIP SMITH: There was a lot of anti-Semitism around. Arthur Godfrey ran a radio show from an apartment in Bal Harbour and was vocally anti-Semitic. Many of the clubs were restricted; synagogues were few and far between. But with a name like Smith, no one knew that I was Jewish.

ALAN MANDEL: The Beach was overwhelmingly Jewish. We Cuban kids went to school and became Cuban Jewish American. We had even more reason to integrate, because there was such a welcoming Jewish community.

When I was a kid living on Fourteenth Street in the heart of South Beach, I'd walk home from elementary school and pass maybe ten Jewish bakeries, half a dozen or more delis. South Beach had become the enclave of the Jewish working class.

But there was still plenty of anti-Semitism. My dad took me to see the sign outside of the Kenilworth Hotel in Bal Harbour: “No dogs and no Jews.” They didn’t mention blacks.

ADJUSTING TO A NEW AMERICAN LIFE

MARCOS KERBEL: The Cuban synagogue in Miami was founded on September 22, 1961. Its original name was the Cuban-Hebrew Social Circle of Miami.

In 1964, I came to Miami from Atlanta, where I had been studying, and reconnected with some of my friends from Cuba. During summer vacation I went back to the Fourteenth Street Beach on Sundays and also to the congregation. It was very different from the bar mitzvah club in Havana, when we used to meet at the luxurious Patronato House.

On weekends, the kids would bring a record player to dance and sets of dominoes to play. A group named the Bagels was formed; it brought back memories from Old Cuba with famous tunes such as “Guantanamera” and “Son de la Loma.”

At the beginning, all of the religious events took place in what was essentially a little nothing storefront, a place used for socializing, playing dominoes, meeting people. On the High Holy Days, congregants would go to nearby synagogues.

The rabbi was Dow Rozencwaig, a Holocaust survivor, an orthodox and affable man. He pulled the congregation into a strong community. The services were in Hebrew with a Yiddish accent. It was pure Ashkenazi orthodox with separate seating of men and women. Spanish was never used in the services. The older people spoke Spanish and Yiddish. There were snowbirds, mostly Cuban Jews and some others from Latin America—Colombians, Peruvians.

In 1965, the name of the synagogue was officially changed to the Cuban Hebrew Congregation. In 1969, I got on the board of directors of the synagogue, was president in 1992 and then in 2007.

One of my friends told me the Jewish religion in Miami is made up of three parts: 33 percent prayers, 33 percent social, 34 percent gastronomy. Many people who attend services come especially for the *kiddush* [ceremonial blessing pronounced over wine or bread on the Sabbath] afterwards.

In 1980, services were conducted with a hundred-year-old Torah from El Patronato Synagogue in Havana. The next year a gala marking the synagogue's twentieth anniversary was celebrated at the Fontainebleau Hotel.

Lots of work was done in the early 1980s; leaders of the congregation helped Cubans who came to South Florida from the port of Mariel. In 1984, an American rabbi, Barry Konovitch, replaced Rabbi Rozencwaig, who had put in twenty years and was set in his orthodox ways. The congregation wanted a more modern approach. That was an exciting time.

The following year, a new and very large synagogue was dedicated at 1701 Lenox Avenue. Teddy Kollek, the mayor of Jerusalem, visited the synagogue and spoke to the congregation.

Today most Jews live on the northeast side of Miami in Aventura, North Miami, Sunny Isles. In 2011, the fiftieth anniversary of the Cuban Hebrew Congregation was marked.

THE SAGA OF THE *ST. LOUIS*

MARCOS KERBEL: On May 13, 1939, the transatlantic liner *St. Louis* sailed from Hamburg, Germany, for Havana with almost a thousand passengers aboard, most of them German Jews. It came into the harbor of Havana on the 27th of May, and some Jews with United States visas were allowed to disembark. There were estimates that before this time 2,500 Jews had been allowed into Cuba. But now, those without visas were denied, and Cuba's president, Federico Brú, issued an order for the ship to leave the waters of Cuba.

Amid the panic and anger, the *St. Louis* sailed on to Miami. It was so close to shore that the lights of the city could be seen. Some of the passengers sent cables to President Franklin D. Roosevelt and Eleanor Roosevelt asking for help. They were never answered. There was an anti-immigration feeling in the United States back then.

The sorrowful story of the *St. Louis,* which docked with Jewish refugees in 1939, only to be turned back by the U.S. Coast Guard. Courtesy of the Jewish Museum of Florida

On June 6, 1939, a coast guard cutter led the *St. Louis* out to sea, and the ship made its way back to Europe where England, Holland, Belgium, and France took in some of the passengers. A quarter of them did not survive the Holocaust. On June 3 and 4, 1989, a fiftieth anniversary reunion of twenty-five survivors of the SS *St. Louis* was held. There were religious services in memory of those who died in the Holocaust. The idea came from Rabbi Barry Konovitch of the Cuban Hebrew Congregation in Miami Beach in honor of the survivors. One of them told me: "You know, the city looked so beautiful and glamorous that day, and we were stuck on the boat with nowhere to go because no one wanted us."

Now, a plane flew overhead pulling a "Never Again" sign, and Hitler's private yacht, the *Ostwind,* was sunk off the coast of Miami Beach and in view of the synagogue, and a marker was dropped into the water near the place where the *St. Louis* lingered in the harbor in 1939.

HELEN KAPLAN: Although I can remember fire drills such as going under the desk, collecting war stamps, and war drives, we never really knew much about what was going on with the war effort. All I knew was that the *St. Louis* was docked right off the shoreline by the synagogue, and the passengers—all of them Jewish refugees who were trying to escape the Nazis—were not allowed to disembark. We thought that was the most terrible thing President Roosevelt did. Still, when he died, everyone felt so bad about it. My history teacher actually fainted in the classroom.

15

The Cuban Impact

> New Year's Eve at the Cuban Hebrew Congregation, everyone sings national anthems from Cuba, Israel, and the United States.
>
> —Marcos Kerbel

AL SCHLAZER: In the sixties and seventies, I was the only American playing in the Cuban League. I was a pitcher. All top talent played there. It was a big deal, a big-time thing. The players came in the fall and played all the way through into the spring. Then they went back to Cuba to compete in their regular leagues.

On Sundays, a lot of the homes located near the park had people making round potatoes stuffed with meat plus other different Cuban dishes. All the players would come into the different houses while they were playing ball there. They'd buy beers, soda. But every time I walked into a house with Basha, my wife, they would think that we were from the government. And everything started disappearing off the stove.

The stands were packed—packed with Cubans. They put up money on every pitch. We wore uniforms with sponsor names on them. My first sponsor was Flagler Medical, owned by a fellow named Tony Perez. He was loaded with money, and he paid his players pretty good to play for him. We would go over to his house; he had big parties for the team. I also played for another team that was owned by a big Cuban bakery. They put up a lot of money to get their players.

There was a Cuban newspaper that covered all the games in detail with lots of pictures. They chose most valuable players and pitchers. Every year I was the MVP as the most valuable pitcher in the league.

I learned some Spanish, had a good time. It was really fun. They were super, super nice people. I hung with them all the time, played with them, went to parties.

Back in the sixties, before I moved up to Miami Dade College, the classes I taught at Riverside Elementary were filled with Cuban students. Right down the street was a little Latin restaurant that presidents visiting Miami always went to eat at. It was called in Spanish The Texas Star. It was on Twelfth Avenue and Flagler Street, not far from the Orange Bowl.

That was when they had the Cuban influx. My goodness, every kid in your class was Spanish. They spoke very little English. They were great kids. At recess I went out with them and played ball with them. I also taught English as a second language at Miami Jackson High School. They were hard-working kids. We would sing songs, do a lot of things in English.

JOHN NIVEN: When I came to the United States from Havana in 1957, we lived in the Cuban area in southwest Miami. There weren't many Jews around, but my first friend happened to be a Jewish kid. We sat next to each other in class; he was wearing a star of David.

I asked him, "Where did you get that?"

He said, "I'm Jewish," and we became friends.

Most of the Jews lived in Miami Beach. I met my wife there in a place on Alton Road where the Jewish kids got together.

MARCOS KERBEL: At midnight every New Year's Eve at the annual party of the Cuban Hebrew Congregation, everyone sings three national anthems—Cuba, Israel, and the United States.

ALAN NIVEN: I came here before Castro, in 1957, on a ferry that used to come from Havana to Miami. My first view of the city was waking up on the boat and looking at the MacArthur Causeway. There was just a little strip of land, maybe two or three buildings ten stories high. We got off the boat, my mother, my father, my sister, and me. We felt lost. We didn't know where to go.

A taxi driver gave us a ride to downtown Miami, which was a very small place with little buildings. We had been given the name of a hotel: the Everglade. But when we got there, it was full; we couldn't get in. Fortunately, the taxi driver spoke Spanish and took us to another hotel where there was room. We went down to eat, and it was like an automat. You went around with a tray. I had never seen anything like that.

We didn't have money to stay in a hotel. So the next day, my father, who was a tailor, talked to some people. And they got a hold of a little house, and we roomed there with this little old lady. It was right off the Miami River, right near downtown. We slept in the living room, all four of us.

Three or four days later, my father was working. They gave him a name, a contact, a place. Where? Miami Beach, specifically Lincoln Road—at that time you could drive through it. He worked at Austin Burke, one of the stores on Lincoln Road.

JOHN NIVEN: I can absolutely remember my first time in the United States. It was after the Bay of Pigs. We came by plane, and by the time we landed, it was nighttime. After we got settled in the Fairfax Hotel on Collins and Seventeenth Street, my dad walked me across the street to see the beach, and I looked out to a new beginning. I was in a new place and set to discover a whole new way of life. My dad was a photographer. Miami Beach became a favorite backdrop.

MARGARET GRIFFIS O'BRIEN: My mother originally came to Cuba from Spain. Her brother had left Cuba fast before things really got tight. And once he got here, he sent for her and my grandmother. It was easy then to come over from Cuba. Generally, it was people with money who made the trip.

PHILIP SMITH: There was a movie theater near my house when I was a kid. And every Saturday the sirens would go off for practice because we knew there was going to be a war with Cuba. Unlike the rest of the country, we had no bomb shelters, because it was not possible to dig down without hitting water. Basically, we just assumed we would be annihilated by Castro's nuclear weapons that he would get from Russia. We lived in a state of alertness—in a way it was like living in Israel today.

Marcos Kerbel with his father in Cuba.
Courtesy of Marcos Kerbel

FANNY KERBEL: When my father saw what was going on in Cuba, he said, "Not my child. I'm getting her out." Boys were being sent to the military, never to return again. Girls my age were being sent to the countryside to help educate the peasants and coming back pregnant. That was not what my father wanted for me.

I came to Miami from Cuba on January 8, 1961. I was twelve years old and all by myself. One of my father's brothers was here; I was going to live with him. In Cuba, you needed a special paper that authorized you to leave, but my parents weren't able to get it. So I said I was eleven and a half years old. I was scared and crying as I kissed my parents good-bye. But I always trusted them and followed directions.

Two days later, on January 10, my grandmother, along with my three-and-a-half-year-old sister, arrived in Miami. My grandmother brought twenty-two suitcases along with her. One held a set of dishes, another silver. She figured she'd take whatever she could.

THE CUBAN IMPACT

My father was a lawyer and a judge. He was born in Warsaw, came to Cuba as a little boy, and grew up to become a teacher and then a lawyer. While in law school, he worked as a tailor to pay his tuition, and there he met and became good friends with another tailor, Camilo Cienfuegos, who would become a partner of Fidel Castro and was a true revolutionary—later on, Castro would have him shot. Camilo asked my father if he would teach some kids, and my father said he would.

Years later, one of those kids happened to be the person in charge at the airport just at the time when my grandmother was leaving. He recognized my father—who had come to the airport to assist my grandmother—and he helped put her suitcases on the plane.

Once in Miami, my grandmother began looking for a place where she, my sister, and I could live and where my mother would be able to stay with us when she came here. We would walk down the streets of South Beach, but everywhere we went it was, "No children, no pets." Jews were not renting to other Jews with small children.

But one lady, at 1326 Euclid Avenue, decided to give us a chance and rented us an efficiency apartment for about $50 a month. There was a school about three blocks away, and when my mom came later, she registered me. I had gone to an American school in Cuba, so I already spoke English.

At home, I had played the piano. But here the teacher said, "There's no place for a piano in our orchestra." She made me play the cello. I took private lessons; I played on a Stradivarius, and I made it to the first chair many times.

Before Castro, we would come to Miami Beach every summer for vacation. We would stay at the Sagamore Hotel, go to Wolfie's, I would play miniature golf. So I had been to Cuban hotels. But this was different. This was America! We were part of the American society!

After a while, we moved to Flamingo Park. I would walk around and overhear the old-timers talking about how good Communism was. I thought it was horrible. We had left our country because of Communism, and here people were saying how good it was.

One Sunday, my grandma, parents, sister, and I were driving to the beach on Fourteenth Street and Ocean Drive, the gathering place for Cubans, when my grandma said, "Fanny, there's someone behind you honking his car."

I turned around and saw a young man whom I had met Friday night. Now, he kept saying "Hello, hello. Where are you going?" I told him we were going to the Fourteenth Street beach, and he said, "That's where I'm going. I'll see you there."

We spent the afternoon together, and that night he called me. "We're going to go to Les Violins Supper Club," he said. Les Violins was a Cuban nightclub on Seventeenth Street where the waiters and waitresses were in the shows. There was a $5 cover charge that included one order of French fries, one order of rum and coke, and three shows—Las Vegas style. One of them was *Fiddler on the Roof*.

That was my first date with Marcos. We came back at four in the morning. My parents were ready to call the police.

MARCOS KERBEL: I was born in 1946 and started elementary school in a non-Jewish school half a block from my house, which was located outside of Havana. It was hard at the time to bring a bus back and forth to the Jewish school. But after a year of trying, they finally got a bus, and I started going to the Jewish school in 1953–54. Those were the most productive years for the Cuban Jewish community. By 1959, the community had about fifteen thousand Jews: twelve thousand in Havana, the rest spread out.

Cuba was a very nice place when I was a child. We would go to school during the week, and on weekends we'd socialize on a wharf. In the late fifties, the luxurious Patronato, the major Jewish community center in Havana, was the place for Sunday gatherings. It was a ritual all of us loved. Gossiping, kidding around, having some fun: we did all these things. Afterward our parents allowed us to go on our own to the Wakamba, a good restaurant. And after that, as part of the routine, we would catch a movie at the Roxy Theater.

It used to be traditional: at noon, a Jewish factory would release a whistle. It was called the Shapiro bell. And at nine o'clock at night, a cannon shot would go off. As the situation deteriorated in 1958, from time to time the cannon noise would be replaced by bombs going off in Havana and in other parts of the country. Politically, things were deteriorating.

I was in the sixth grade in the public high school when the Castro regime took over. That was 1959. The government began merging classes and schools. There was fighting in the streets. Castro was against the Catholic Church, but he was not really anti-Semitic. Still, the Jews always said, "Don't get involved in politics."

Marcos Kerbel's Cuban bar mitzvah.
Courtesy of Marcos Kerbel

At the beginning, most Cubans were pro Castro; the Jewish community helped out. When the new government announced a land reform, Jews donated money and tractors. But then, around 1960, Castro began intervening and expropriating large businesses: first were the American companies, and later the smaller businesses. My parents' retail business was never confiscated. But Castro's people started putting pressure.

I didn't realize at the time that it would be very difficult to leave everything and for my parents to start again at the age of fifty without the language. By the summer of 1960, many people wanted to get out, but temporarily. They thought it wouldn't last, because they believed America wouldn't allow Cuba to go Communist.

At the Patronato on Sunday mornings, there'd be some friends who'd say "I'm leaving next week."

Some of these teenagers already had visas to go to Miami with their parents. Most of them had come to Miami on regularly scheduled airline flights through

Kingston, Jamaica, or straight through to Miami. I had these two girl cousins who announced, "We are leaving April 15." I said, "Where are you going?"

"Miami."

I knew they had no passports and could not get visas, because there was no diplomatic relationship between the United States and Cuba.

I asked, "How are you going?"

"We don't know." It was a very, very secretive operation.

The girls' father was my godfather. I went to him and said, "Look, I want to get out. I want to do the same thing the girls are doing."

He agreed.

I was fourteen then. My godfather made arrangements for me through a fellow merchant in downtown Havana who had been appointed through the Hebrew Immigrant Aid Society (HIAS) as its representative.

Six weeks later, that representative came to us with a letter containing instructions to go to Pan American Airways and pay for the ticket. I would be traveling all alone. It was very difficult, especially for my grandmother and my parents, thinking that they might have to leave a county and a way of life again, this time for the United States. For them it would be their second time around.

But we all thought it was a temporary move. It wasn't until after the Bay of Pigs on April 15 to 19, 1961, that people realized things would not go back to normal as quickly as we had thought. There would be retaliations.

The Jews who left did not do so because of anti-Semitism. It was because of the failed promises of the Kennedy administration, their failure at the Bay of Pigs to follow the air support plan that had been put in place during the Eisenhower administration.

I arrived in Havana Airport on May 10, 1961. I still remember it was Pan American Flight 422 that I got on, but I hardly remember anything about the short flight.

We landed; I went down the steps of the airplane, and there was a representative from HIAS waiting for me. He said, "Marcos, welcome to Miami. Here's your ticket. You are leaving at seven o'clock tonight for Los Angeles. Don't worry about it. We will take good care of you."

I was given a survival kit from the American Red Cross. In it was Colgate toothpaste, a bar of soap, Burma Shave, Gillette razor blades, and other stuff.

Pan Am flight 422 from Havana to Miami brought many Cubans to life in Miami and the United States, including Marcos Kerbel. Courtesy of Marcos Kerbel

I had an aunt in Miami who had arrived on a boat from Cuba with her two kids. I called her. She knew I was coming, but she didn't know when. Now, she rushed down to the airport with the kids. I couldn't stay with them, because they already had taken some children, and they were all living in one small apartment.

"Look," I said, "the luggage didn't come." I tried to use that as an excuse to stay overnight.

But actually it was the best thing that could have happened. Unlike most of the Jewish Cuban kids who stayed in homes in the vicinity of Miami, I was able to go to LA, where I lived with an orthodox Jewish family until June 1962 when I was reunited with my parents. They had immigrated to the United States on the second-to-last plane from Cuba just before the October 1962 missile crisis. Between 1960 and 1962, the majority of Cuba's Jews left.

What I did was participate in a very early part of the Pedro Pan Operation. There was a big concern among parents and grandparents that the Castro government was going to control the kids and send them away to work and study under government control. The parents realized that they had to send the children first. I was one of those kids. The parents put the lives of their kids above their own.

There was a rumor that the Pedro Pan Operation was a CIA operation. That was not true. The program was led by Monsignor Bryan Walsh of Miami in conjunction with Secretary of Health, Education and Welfare Abraham Ribicoff, the son of Jewish immigrants. Catholic Charities and HIAS played major roles. The name Pedro Pan was coined by Gene Miller, a reporter on the *Miami Herald.* The official program was called the Unaccompanied Children Program.

The immigration from 1960 to 1962 brought about fourteen thousand kids from Cuba to the United States. It was the biggest movement of unaccompanied minors ever in the Western Hemisphere. Many children wound up in temporary Miami shelters and then were set up with places to live all over the United States.

Not all the stories were happy. Some of the parents stayed behind because they were old or not well. Many children never saw their parents again. The Pedro Pan was something like a Kindertransport, the bringing of Jewish children out of places throughout Europe to England during World War II. My story had a happy ending. I was ultimately reunited with my parents in Miami, and we all were able to make lives for ourselves in the United States like so many other Cuban Jews.

DAVID WALLACK: In the late 1970s, Castro allowed anyone wanting to leave Cuba access to the docks at the port of Mariel. The largest flotilla ever launched for nonmilitary purposes set sail in practically anything that could float. Among the refugees were twenty-five thousand prisoners and mental patients. The economic, logistical, and infrastructural strain on South Florida further intensified racial tensions.

When the Mariel wars came about, there was a rush to Key West; people set up flotillas, grabbing people out of that port. They took hundreds of people every day. What Castro did was send people out of the insane asylums. South Beach—which was in desolation row—was the cheapest place the government could find to house those people.

CLARENCE DICKSON: The Mariel boatlift was a mass emigration of Cubans that brought people out of Mariel harbor in Cuba and into Miami between April and October 1980. The government set up tents for them under the I-95 Expressway. That's where the term tent city came from.

Thousands of people lived there. Some were criminals; some were insane. Others were able to turn their lives around here. They came without papers. We photographed them, fed them, fingerprinted them, gave them clothing. At one point, one of our officers heard a voice calling him. It was his grandmother who had come from Cuba. They were reunited right there in the tent city.

JOSEPH KRUTEL: People in the Mariel boatlift—there were thousands of them—were just dump loaded. Castro cleaned out his prisons, allowing anyone wanting to leave Cuba access to the docks at the port of Mariel, and Carter brought them in.

Oliver Stone came down here and filmed what was happening. That was what set Miami back. Those thugs controlled South Beach for a few years until they got cleared out, until guys like Tony Goldman came from New York and said, "I need to clean this up and take it back."

MITCHELL KAPLAN: A small fraction of the people Castro let out were from his prisons and mental hospitals. But there were some great artists in the Mariel boatlift. They were all over the place.

ANN BUSSELL: With Mariel, Cuban people who had passports from Miami were now allowed to go back and pick up relatives. But in order to get their parents or aunt or uncle out of Cuba, they needed a boat, and many of them didn't have the money for that. They would go to the banks and try to get a loan.

When they got to Mariel, they were told, "First you have to take the people who are here, and then you have to come back a second time to get your relatives." That was when they saw that the first people who got aboard had come from the prisons, jailhouses, insane asylums. Meanwhile, they had made the investments of buying or renting boats to bring their families over. What could they do? They took the prisoners and brought them to Miami. And only after that were they allowed to go back and pick up their relatives.

RED HELLER: There was a time when I didn't see one of my officers for a few days. "Where is he?" I asked one of his friends.

"He took his boat, and he's going to the Mariel dock to pick up his family."

I said, "All right, we'll carry him on sick leave."

But what happened is that when he pulled up to the Mariel dock, his family was nowhere to be seen. Instead, his boat was loaded with people he never saw before. It took him another year to get his family back.

The warehouses were on the mainland. They were the worst; they housed hundreds of thousands of people. People who worked as waiters, salespeople in department stores, sophisticated people of high culture, doctors and attorneys, decent people—many of them were dumped in the Mariel boatlift, which just dumped everybody on us. We used to stand there and watch all these boats come in from every different direction, loaded with people waving. Eventually, the people who were supposed to be picked up got out, but it was very difficult. Many had to go to Portugal, to Madrid. In many cases the Cubans who went to get their relatives never got them. Carter was president at that time.

MITCHELL KAPLAN: I was a high school English teacher during the period of the Mariel. No one knew what to do with the kids. There was no ESL, no federal funding. They could barely speak English. They had just been plopped in schools. They were all over the place. It was really, really tough, the aggregation of Mariel before they could figure out what to do with them.

THE CUBAN IMPACT

RED HELLER: My first wife was the granddaughter of a Cuban Jew who owned an apartment house in Havana. We went there on a belated honeymoon. I was a police officer, but I lasted only three days. I checked out as soon as I saw bearded guerrillas throwing people around. This was September 1959, just at the beginning.

By the time of the cocaine cowboys, I was a major assigned to the northeast district, where I had the opportunity of making multiple arrests when it came to narcotics. It was a field day for police officers. There was a lot of corruption.

Criminality had reached Miami shores with the Mariel. The criminal element that came over were people who were better off being arrested and serving time here than they'd be in Castro's prisons, where they'd be beaten to death. I remember how they would take trucks, crash them into the side of warehouses. We would capture them and take them to the station. "What are you going to do to me that Castro didn't do to me?" they'd say. "Put me in jail so I can have three meals a day and a place to sleep."

CLARENCE DICKSON: Boats full of cocaine would come down the Miami River in the middle of the night. The "river cops," who were actually Miami cops, would come aboard in uniform and initiate a confrontation with the boat crew. Then the crew and some of the cops would vacate the boat by jumping overboard. Some drowned, but these rogue officers took several bags of cocaine, put them in the back of their cars, which were police cars, and turned in the rest.

The cocaine was worth millions. The regular police didn't know that the crews had jumped overboard, that there were drugs in the cars. They saw bodies floating down the river on the Miami side, and they didn't know where they came from.

The county found the bodies. My guys took a look at the bags of cocaine that had been confiscated from the boat and turned into the property bureau. Our detective went back and looked at pictures of the cocaine and said, "Hey, there are four bags missing here." Those were the bags the rogue cops had taken home.

That was when the main investigation began. But our guys didn't know about the drowned guys floating down the river. The county was working on that. The rogue cops had jumped from the boat because they thought they would be shot. Some survived, some didn't.

The upshot was that the county and city finally talked to each other, something they normally didn't do. And we tracked down the Miami River cops. All seven of them were caught.

JOHN NIVEN: The Cubans who came in 1961 were the group that built the city. Mistakes were made. The commercial underpinning of the city gave way. But we are an incredibly beautiful city. All you have to do is go out on one of the causeways, any of them. I've lived here almost all my life, and any time I go across one of them, I still get a thrill. I say, "What a beautiful place." I tell you, I haven't found this kind of majesty in many places. And, then, I'm an urban person inspired by the sight of the skyline.

The city, by the time of Mariel, had an overwhelming Hispanic influence. And the Hispanic community saw the dynamics taking place, and they were cognizant of the fact that these were displaced people, unfortunate victims of a regime. They have since mingled into society, tremendous citizens. There are many success stories of the emergence of the Mariel population into the mainstream.

A lot of the Cuban Jews stayed together. They formed a congregation—the synagogue on Seventeenth and Michigan is still there, and a lot of Cuban Jews still go there. But in the past few years, it has faded away. Most of their children have moved to other areas. The Cuban Jewish population of Miami Beach has dwindled; the population has spread out.

ALAN NIVEN: There was some dispute among the Hispanic communities. But the Cuban Jews integrated easily into the American community. The Mariel influx may have pushed some Jews out of Miami Beach, but not the Cuban Jews. The larger Jewish community may have moved north, but the Cuban Jews have largely remained.

Compared to Havana, Miami was a quiet, conservative place. You walked out of the plane in Havana, and there was a big wide boulevard, music, laughter, vendors on the street—so much life. It was an open city going back to the pirate days. If Castro had not taken over, Havana would have turned into another Miami. The charm is still there, but it is at a standstill, as if time stood still.

At the same time, Miami Beach today is a very diverse city, very international. It doesn't fit into the conventional retirement stereotype. It has a beat. When I go anywhere on vacation, I can't wait to return.

I always tell people that Miami Beach is the city of tomorrow.

16

Mini Memoirs

MICHAEL ALLER: My father was in the stone and quarry business. He brought a great deal of Italian marble into this country in 1962. We lived in Detroit; and in November the quarry would freeze, and they couldn't quarry. So we were down in Miami Beach every year for six months. I was adopted, but I was never inquisitive enough to ask about my natural parents. I just adored my mother and father, they adored me, and the three of us were always a unit.

Our apartment was in the old Romney Hotel on Twenty-third Street, right on the ocean. It has since been torn down—there was no historic preservation in those days, but if there was, it would have been the crown of Art Deco, an absolutely magnificent old-world hotel with a bar where the men would go, and paddle fans in the lobby that looked like they were made of straw spinning around. It dated back to the thirties and was absolutely magnificent, with a gigantic pool, an ocean promenade, and the Bamboo Restaurant with great food.

My father retired very early; he was still in his sixties. He was devoted to his wife and child. His money bought me an education in a private school in Miami. Before he died, he said to me, "Always remember your mother is a queen. Do whatever she wants and love her as much as I do." He died in 1968; my mother passed away in 1990.

Sophie Tucker, the great star in the twenties, thirties, forties, and fifties and the last of the red-hot mamas, lived in the Romney. It was her home when she wasn't working. She was big-breasted, big-boned, although she wasn't that tall. When you'd see her on stage, it was always with her hair up.

My mother and Sophie were friends. They played bridge together. My mother made an outfit for Sophie, a gray crocheted dress and hat. She always said it took her fifteen years to do it because Sophie was so large.

My parents were café society; they went out a lot. Sophie did not like the tumult of people coming up to her. So my mother would say, "Sophie, why not sit with Michael." And she would say, "OK."

"Michael, don't you have to be in bed?" she'd ask me.

And I said, "I don't have to be in bed until eight o'clock."

"Well, why don't you get started now?"

Her mentor was George Jessel. I loved George, his attitude. I liked what he stood for. He was the greatest fund-raiser for the State of Israel. I traveled to Israel with him seventeen times.

I first met George in Detroit. Then I connected with him in Miami Beach, and we glued together. I was trying to get into show business at this time but only as a singer. I didn't have a voice.

"You have no talent," he said to me, "but you're a good speaker."

I said to him, "I want to be you."

MARVIN REY BAUMEL: In 1938, I came down to Miami from Brooklyn's Coney Island, where I was born and raised. Primarily it was because of my mom's health. I had just turned thirteen and had a bar mitzvah by the skin of my teeth. I knew nothing about Miami Beach except for the ads I saw close to the roofs of trolley and subway cars that showed a drawing of a man and a woman sitting on the beach under an umbrella enjoying the sun and the palm trees.

My dad had decided to give up his retail business and start anew. It was September; there was a forecast of a hurricane heading for Florida. That was going to be some welcome, we figured. As it turned out, the hurricane hit New York City.

There were no expressways those days, just roads weaving through towns and farmland. The car broke down several times. At one point, it would not go over twenty-five miles an hour. Finally, my dad pulled into a used-car lot and bought another car for something like fifty bucks.

We stopped at guesthouses and cottages along the way. It was two dollars a night for the three of us. Further south, we stopped at a cotton field where people in fields were actually picking cotton. All I knew from cotton was cotton balls. In Georgia, we passed a chain gang where prisoners were shackled, wore striped uniforms, and were supervised by a shotgun-carrying guard.

When we finally pulled into Miami Beach after days on the road, my dad had only about two hundred dollars. Our first stay was at a small hotel: the Princess Anne on Ocean Drive. The owner was a friend of a friend. It was a complete change of everything to be there. It was hot but really pleasant. I remember being fascinated by the swaying palm trees.

My father opened a handbag concession in a jewelry store on Washington Avenue. That provided an income—I don't know how. For my part, I did what any kid would do—go to school and spend the summer lying on the beach.

I can remember one summer day walking with my brother and passing the Roney Plaza on Twenty-third Street. It was the first large luxury hotel on the beach. We continued walking. It's hard to believe now, but then there was nothing but sand dunes. I remember my brother and I cracking up because some idiot was building a hotel on Thirty-seventh Street. Who would come up so far for a hotel on the wrong side of the street!

I fell in love with everything Latin: the music, the food, the girls. I wanted to be Cuban. In high school, I learned to read and write Spanish. At age fifteen I spoke it fluently.

I couldn't afford to buy a set of bongos, so I took two Quaker Oats containers, turned them upside down, and tied them together with strings. Those were my first bongos. Kids in school called me Bongo. One day my dad surprised me with a pair.

Those were the days of the ten-inch wax records. Whatever spending money I had, I would spend on them. I didn't have anything to play my records on, so I went to somebody's house to listen.

My brother played the violin and got all the attention with his classical music. That may be why I turned to Latin music. On good days, you could hear music from Cuba as if it were here in Miami. I was swept away. I had a friend from a Jewish family who had just come from Cuba. A lot of Jewish families could not get into the States so they went to the Antilles, to Cuba, maybe Puerto Rico, places such as that.

In the early forties, when I was in high school, a lot of the musicians were being drafted, so I got the chance to play bongos with a band. When I got out of the service, I ultimately wound up back in Miami and for kicks jammed with two guitar players and a singer/maraca player.

One day I saw a classified ad looking for "strings" for a weekend. I said, "We're strings"; maybe not the kind they were looking for. We auditioned at the Latin Room of the Pan American Hotel in Miami right off Flagler and northeast Second Avenue. The manager liked us and hired us for the weekend.

"What's your name?" he asked.

"Marvin Baumel."

"Naahh, I can't use that. You're a Latin band."

"Let me think."

"Naaah, you can't think. I gotta call the *Herald*. The deadline is an hour from now."

I thought fast. I had a recording by Machito called "El Rey del Mambo." I said, "Rey . . . Rey Mambo."

Few people really knew much about mambo then. It was just breaking in this country. I thought, *Rey Mambo*. What the hell? I could use it for a weekend. Little did I know I would end up using the name for fifteen years. That was 1947. And my wife wasn't too happy with "Mrs. Mambo."

I had this job over the summer. The hotel was sort of crumbling; it was on its last legs. We played in the lounge, The Latin Room, and played behind the bar. There was no dancing. We didn't wear the rumba shirts or sashes. We just had Cuban shirt jackets, which were ideal for the hot climate. It was in this climate that Rey Mambo was born.

Eventually, I worked with my quartet at the posh Ciro's Supper Club in Miami Beach. I remember Esther Williams dancing to our music, smiling. She was gorgeous. There were alternating bands at Ciro's. We were the so-called rumba band. Louis Armstrong came there with his jazz band. Walter Winchell came in one night and enjoyed what we were doing so much that he gave us a nice mention in his column: "Rey Mambo's rumba magic."

I performed with my band in Copa City. That premier nightclub had the biggest names in show business, everybody from Tony Bennett to the June Taylor Dancers. In the fifties, Miami Beach was really in the forefront of the Latin music rage. People who supported Latin music, who loved it, were the Jewish people. Jewish tourists who danced at New York's Palladium and vacationed in Miami Beach had to have their Latin music—and Chinese food.

During the fifties you could walk up and down Collins Avenue, and every hotel would have a Latin band. It really hit big. But the Fontainebleau was the premier one from its inception. There was always a Latin band playing in the Boom Boom Room downstairs. I did some off-nights there. My wife, whom I met when I was in Daytona Beach and still in the army, sang with my band.

When you worked a gig then, it was usually nine to twelve. During the season you worked six nights a week, with Mondays off. I opened a lot of the hotels; one was the Seville, and I was there for three years. I opened the Thunderbird motel, the Aztec, the Sahara. They were brand-new and very fancy.

Working so many years with Latins, I kidded around with a Cuban accent, which nobody did. At a function called The Footlighters, any big-name entertainers who were working in town would show up. The audience was almost exclusively local business professionals.

I was at this luncheon at the Seville Hotel where I was the bandleader. Somebody didn't show up. There was a vacant seat on the dais, and I was asked to sit there to fill it up. Professional entertainers such as Phil Foster, Sammy Davis Jr., Dick Shawn, Johnny Mathis were there. I told the emcee, "Don't call on me to talk."

The emcee called on me. He introduced me as a former senator from Cuba.

I just started talking. Everybody was cracking up. Alan Gale was a very popular entertainer then who was present. He wanted to bring back vaudeville, opened a theater, and hired me for two weeks. I broke up the band and decided to do stand-up comedy.

Also there at that luncheon was an agent who ended up being my agent for twenty-five years. My first engagement as a corporate humorist was in Miami Beach in 1966 at the Fontainebleau for the Florida Association of Insurance Agents.

"Do no more than fifteen minutes," my agent said. "Do something that has to do with insurance."

Latin dancers, 1960s

I was so nervous. I couldn't do more than twelve minutes of material. I had them introduce me as the former president of the Cuban Insurance Agency . . . "The CIA." They were hysterical, and I got a standing ovation. That launched my career as a corporate humorist. For almost four decades, I traveled all over the country, Canada, and Europe. I spoke to more than a million people and was the subject of a feature story on the front page of *The Wall Street Journal.* It was then that Rey Baumel, "The Genuine Authentic Fake!™," was born.

And it happened in Miami.

KIMBERLY FALCONER: Growing up as a fifth-generation Floridian in the city of Stuart, I was taught how to run a boat before I learned how to ride a tricycle. I grew up on the water. When I graduated from college and the choice was either Miami or New York, I opted for Miami. It was more attractive with endless sun and water. I also thought of it as an emerging city.

I moved to Miami about twenty years ago and did marketing and public relations for the marketing agency that handled the Florida Keys and Key West

Tourist Development Council and later other things in the world of marketing. When I finally had enough of the corporate world, I knew I wanted to do something with the water, the sea. It took me several years to figure that out.

Vacationing in Hawaii, where my friend had an ATV touring business, I noticed that Zodiac RIB Boats—rigid inflatable boats—were used for whale watching and things like that. They are very practical, secure, and nimble, but for some reason they are not seen widely in tours in the mainland United States, although they are used by the coast guard and the Drug Enforcement Agency.

Although I had never seen them in Miami, I had handled boats similar to the Zodiac RIB. Now, I thought, *why couldn't I get one of those boats and do something in Miami, some kind of business on the water?* I did a lot of research on Miami history and culture and put the idea together: a tour on the water based on what I found interesting. Miami history and true stories are stranger than fiction. And there is endless fascination with them on the part of curious tourists.

Before we went out with customers for the first time, we tested the tour with friends, family, and some concierges—people in the industry. There were all kinds of kinks we had to get out of the way before we opened for business. Finally, after three or four months of touring, we started selling a tour. This way we got feedback and refined the process. At first, the tour ran for two and a half hours. That was too long. We finally settled on two hours as being just right.

My first week in the business was the last week of September 2008. I had used my background in public relations to come up with the name: Ocean Force Adventures. I wanted something that sounded strong but was also attributable to what I was doing. What we do is not just a boat ride, not just a sightseeing tour. It is an experience with an adventurous aspect.

Most of the tour is within Biscayne Bay, but we also spend time out on the ocean, and we get to visit Stiltsville, which can only be reached by water. Its history dates back to the 1930s, when the first shack on stilts was built above the water by "Crawfish" Eddie Walker. More buildings followed, and Stiltsville became a place of mystery. Stories spread about illegal activities such as gambling and drinking liquor, which was banned during Prohibition. The wooden houses, shacks on stilts, are one of the highlights of the tour. Some people have heard about Stiltsville and come on the tour especially to see it. Others have never heard about it and are charmed by the sight of the colorful structures. Stiltsville has served as the setting for novels, movies, and TV shows such as *Miami Vice*. It has a special pull for all who witness it—houses on stilts sticking out of the water. That's real Miami!

Other sights we talk about and view include Port Miami; celebrity homes on Star Island and Fisher Island; downtown Miami; the Venetian Islands and the historic Miami River; filming locations for *Miami Vice*, *Scarface*, *CSI Miami*; Biscayne National Park and Cape Florida Lighthouse; Key Biscayne and the site of President Nixon's Winter White House. There is also always a variety of marine life including stingrays, sharks, manatees, and dolphins.

Especially memorable in my years with Ocean Force Adventures have been dolphin sightings. There is something about seeing these incredible creatures, free and enjoying their surroundings, that never fails to impress me and to excite our passengers. We take great pains not to intrude on their world. Sometimes the dolphins are playful and put on a show. Other times they are coy and do not want to be bothered by enthusiastic people on a boat with cameras at the ready. We respect the dolphins, no matter what they want to do.

Biscayne Bay boasts some of the most remarkable landmarks, natural and historical locations, in the world. The speed and the agility of the Zodiac RIB enable us to explore the majority of them during our two-hour tours. This tour is just perfect for adding a good dose of sun, fun, and saltwater adventure to anyone's Miami vacation mix.

Tourism is the life blood of Miami and Miami Beach, but so many take it all in without ever taking to the water, which, for me, is the best way to discover, appreciate, and learn about what the "City of Tomorrow" has to offer.

ROBERSON DE FRANC: I was born in Haiti, lived in the town of Port au Prince. I lost my mom when I was sixteen. My dad was in jail at the time. I had two sisters and one brother. I was the oldest. There was no one to help us, so I had to work to keep us going. If you don't have a job, life is very complicated.

In 2011, I came here on Air France all alone. I had never been on a plane before. My dad was living in New York by then, but I chose not to live where it is so cold. Instead, I came to Miami. After three months, I got a job as a houseman in the Conrad, a hotel near Brickell. They paid me $9 an hour. Now I work at Brickell for $7.50 an hour, but I get tips and benefits. I've been to Little Haiti. They say a lot of bad people live there. There are a lot of good people, too, but if you say you live in Little Haiti, they think you are bad.

I miss Haiti. Even though the politics are not that good, it's my country, and my family is there, so I go back and forth. It's very dangerous to come by boat, but people do it.

Haiti is beautiful, but I am very glad to be here. I was so excited to become an American citizen. My daughter is coming here soon. If you are under eighteen, you're automatically an American citizen, and she is fifteen.

I have two jobs, and life is difficult. I have to send money to my family in Haiti. But if you have a family, you help each other. I have no troubles with people. I go to a Baptist church. Here the Americans, the Cubans, the Haitians—we all get along.

ROBERTO JUAREZ: I went to the San Francisco Art Institute, then moved on to do graduate school at UCLA in film and video. That was the big thing at the time. I worked in New York City as an artist but had problems keeping a studio—it was really expensive. Then someone suggested South Beach.

This was 1988, 1989. I flew down, and immediately I fell in love with Miami. Standing there, in the warm water, watching the moonrise, it was "Moon over Miami." A cliché, but it was true. I stayed at my studio on Washington Avenue between Sixth and Seventh Streets for a long time. I made a lot of great paintings there. It was the light, the air, the people that got into me. It was a place of peacefulness and contrasts and beauty. It changed my life.

New Yorkers would come down and tell me, "You don't stay in Miami." But I did. I knew there was a larger Miami, but I didn't have a car. Just the fact that I could walk to have breakfast and lunch and that it was inexpensive, just to see the cultural mixing, was really exciting.

Miami Beach was a very different place then. My idea of Miami was to wear flip-flops and skimpy clothes, to watch people on the streets, to have lunch, go to the beach, go to the studio and work. I always got up early and went to my store to paint.

At first I stayed at a very large hotel that was right on the water at Ocean Drive and Sixth Street. There were mostly elderly Jewish people there. It was almost like a retirement home, but there was a niceness about it, too. I know some called it "God's Waiting Room," but at the same time, there were so many vibrant and fantastic people there.

They had beautiful stories, lots of experiences to share. There was a man who made paper hats that were as great as any folk art sculptures I have ever seen. There was a woman who painted; she had real talent. My studio was an old store. I had two cats. In order to get them into my hotel room, I had to go through the hotel lobby where all the elderly people were sitting with the kitties under my sweater.

There were all kinds of combinations on the street back then. There were black transsexual prostitutes walking the streets, looking for ways to make money. There were elegant boutiques; there were hustlers; drug dealers. At certain points it got really dangerous. There were a lot of drugs, things going on in the streets. So I made sure I was in my room before it was too late.

Next door to me was Dr. Kahn, who had a health foods business. He was almost like a community center. He took care of people. He and his son, Jordan, who was a musician, welcomed me from the first day I saw the store.

Eventually, I bought a Volkswagen that was like a Herbie Love Bug. It was a very beach- looking car. There was a little parking area behind my store where I made a little garden. But the store was so large that eventually I remodeled the space in the back and lived there.

Alongside my store was a bar called Jessie's Doll House. Some pretty serious drinkers hung out there. It had a whole collection of ragged dolls set in little places on the walls. Some of the dolls with whom we sat drinking were pretty ragged, too.

One was named Frances Smith. She was a go-go dancer/stripper from the Pussycat Lounge up the street who had seen better days. But somehow every day she put together an outfit that was unbelievable. It was one of the treats of the day to see Frances walking down the street in one of her ensembles. She piled up her hair with wigs and falls. Fake eyelashes, heavy makeup, high heels. Oh, my God, she was so amazing.

Once she asked me for five dollars. I told her I would pay her five dollars if she would model for me. She did, and after that I started using her as a model. She also appeared in videos I did of local people dancing in front of my paintings. Eventually those paintings made their way to a major gallery in Coral Gables.

Not all Latinos are the same. I am Mexican and Puerto Rican. I have noticed some discrimination because of my background. I recall lying on the beach one day when a haughty kind of blond Latin lady looked at me and said in Spanish: "There is a burned Indian," but in a nasty way. That was atypical. The majority of the relationships I had with people of all nationalities in Miami were pretty fantastic.

Being there was a break for me from the bleakness of New York City in the eighties. AIDS was in Miami, but in New York it was really bad. There was a point where I stopped going to memorials. I would only draw and paint what I saw and felt. I lost five people in one year.

At that time, there was the only gay bar, the Sea Gull. Now there are many gay bars. In the seventies, it must have been a really hot place. It had lost a lot of its glamour, but it still was a place you could go to and be welcome and dance and meet people. It was a center. Every night there was some kind of different event. One night it could be drag queens, the leather festival; the next, old guys. That was all part of what made it easy for me to be there. It was a place I could go to and have a community.

I lived through a golden decade. It created opportunities that could never have happened in New York. But when it was over, it was over. I got the Rome Prize and went to Rome and couldn't go back to Miami to live.

But recently I came down to Miami to finish up things for my commissioned piece for the new Children's Courthouse in downtown Miami. It is a huge piece, a set of murals that it took me seven years to complete. We put it up, and it was magic: it was Miami.

I don't live in Miami anymore, but I don't forget it.

HELEN KAPLAN: My family came from the Lower East Side in Manhattan. My father had an uncle who was probably the first Jew who lived in Miami Beach. He had an apartment building that had the oldest synagogue in South Beach. My brother was bar mitzvahed there. I had a sister who was ten years older than me. I was the baby in the family.

On the Lower East Side everything was dismal, dark, and either Jewish or Italian. My dad had owned a cleaning/tailoring store with a big presser in the back. We lived a street kind of life on Forsyth Street.

Then my father came down for a vacation, and he saw the life in Florida. My mother had terrible problems with the cold. So he looked around, and it was literally sand in his shoes. He couldn't stop thinking about moving to Florida. We came by bus; it was a big schlep.

My father had some money, I guess. He bought two buildings, one on Euclid Avenue, which he sold, and one at 811 Jefferson Avenue, which he built—and is still standing there. It's called the Jewel Apartments, and that was where I grew up. We were near Flamingo Park, where I learned to play tennis and roller-skate. That was our whole life, and what was so amazing to my sister was that we could go outside any time without wearing a coat—she was more impressed with everything than I was.

We lived in an apartment my father rented that was in a wooden building on Sixth and Michigan. It was all pink and white with two big bedrooms, a big living room, and a porch. Then he bought an apartment building that is still standing there called the Enjoy Apartments. One of my uncles wanted his son to live in Florida, and my father had the money to put down a deposit on an apartment house. We all lived in this twelve-unit building where each apartment was individual and everything faced the outside.

There definitely was a Jewish presence. My mother was semi-kosher. She was one of those intellectual people, would read a lot. She asked me to take out books in Yiddish from the library. We lived on South Beach. The Art Deco buildings were brand-new then. My girlfriend's father built the Park Central, which was redone recently along with a couple of other buildings that are still there. The water was on one side, and all the small hotels, no more than four stories high, were on the other. We had a bike, and as we got older, one of my friends got a car for her birthday. But we would walk everywhere. We would meet at Flamingo Park and go to school together—Central Beach Elementary School on Washington Avenue; Ida Fisher, junior high and high school combined. It was all Jewish except for one girl, Ruthie Jenkins, who was my friend for a long time until she moved to Atlanta.

The elementary school had three hundred kids, and it would swell up when the snowbirds came. They called us stuck-up because we didn't bother getting to know them too well because in a short while, they would leave. It was such a close-knit community. I had a very happy childhood.

Wolfie's on Twenty-third Street is where all the kids met. They had all the Jewish food like chicken soup and *knaidlach*. We never had a lot of money, so we would order three pieces of bread and one sandwich.

My father became successful with a cleaning store on Forty-first Street, which was more affluent. He prospered in Miami; my mother's health improved. It was a good move for them.

My brother had a good education—he went on to graduate Phi Beta Kappa from the University of Florida. I went there for two years as well. I met my husband in the fifties when he was going to law school.

Mitchell and I started Books & Books in the same place in Coral Gables that it is right now. Of course, it was just a little space, nothing like what it is today. Still, it was the site where Mitchell brought culture to Miami.

JOE KAPLAN: I was in the air force during the Korean War. While I was serving, my parents moved from Chicago to Miami, so when I was discharged, I enrolled in the University of Miami. While I was in law school, Helen and I got married. In October of 1954, I graduated from the law school at the University of Miami and started my own firm specializing in labor law. There were no other labor lawyers around then; I was the first.

Originally, I worked for a woman lawyer. When she left, I took over her practice and became the lawyer of Cesar Chavez and the only union-representing lawyer in the state of Florida. Cesar organized the farm workers' union. He was a kind and wonderful man; he lived in our home, became part of our family. Every morning, he would swim in our pool while our daughter, who loved him dearly, would sit at the edge of the pool and engage him in conversation. When she got older, she moved to New York and represented the farm workers.

Cesar was a quiet, small man of Mexican descent; very thin, nice looking. He also was a powerful speaker who wanted to organize the whole state—the grape workers, the orange pickers, all the farm workers. He was a vegan and taught our daughter how to be one—which she is to this day.

More than sixty years ago, I organized a big drive for the farm and hotel workers in Florida. The thing that stands out in my memory is how the farm owners attracted workers from the Caribbean whom they brought over. But they were not citizens; they had very few rights, and the pay was terrible. I became their champion.

The major labor dispute I was involved in was the hotel workers' strike at the Fontainebleau in the 1960s. We closed it down for weeks until the strike was settled. The hotel workers' union was led by a bunch of mainly Jewish people who left the labor movement later on and went in different directions. At that time, the union was taken over by Hispanics.

My work with them eased off in the late seventies because public sector unions had begun to form: police, firemen, teachers. Florida was not as developed in this regard as New York or California.

I served as a municipal judge in Miami Beach. The last few years, I represented the Police and Fire Union workers. Then the city opened the ranks to anyone who wanted to go to the Police Academy. They asked me, "Joe, are you sure you want to become a cop?" I did. So I went to the Police Academy for six weeks and became a cop who went around with a partner in a patrol car. There were a lot of drugs at the time.

Helen and I bought two houses, one on Palm Island, the other on Hibiscus. One is connected to the other. We lived through the hurricanes, most of the time by staying indoors. Once we went to the Fontainebleau. It was much worse there; all the windows broke.

MITCHELL KAPLAN: I was born in 1955 at Jackson Memorial Hospital. My first year I lived on Coral Way where my parents shared a duplex with my father's parents. But very quickly after that, we moved to Fifteenth Street off West Avenue close by a condo complex called the Morton Towers and the YMHA. But most of those early years I lived with my parents on Hibiscus Island.

I guess a way of viewing that time is that it was a tale of two cities: South Beach, which was basically middle- to lower-middle class; and North Beach, which was much more homogenous and middle- to upper-middle class. All told, Miami Beach was not a tony place. Housing was cheap. People were living on their Social Security, and the median age was sixty-eight. Now, put me into that: a kid who was growing up during a time of upheaval and living basically in a retirement community. It was a place I wanted to leave as soon as possible.

Even though I lived on a residential island, all the schools I went through were on South Beach. I was middle class, but the schools I attended were filled with an incredible diversity of kids: blacks, Cubans, sons and daughters of seasonal workers, cab drivers. When I was in middle school, a lot of the kids were African

Americans who were bused over from the mainland. One of the guys on the school board, a guy named Jack Gordon, knew there would be rumblings about the busing and asked my father to assume the role of PTA president so he could help smooth the way. As a result my father, who was a very liberal guy and a union lawyer, now became the first male PTA president, and I got razzed a lot.

Miami Beach was 180 degrees different from what it is today. It was a town that was not happening, a small shtetl-type village where there was one murder a year. When I was a young kid, I would sleep over in my grandparents' house on Eighth and Jefferson for the weekend. I would take the bus and play at Flamingo Park, which was great. But it was a city that was falling apart.

Starting in the early 1960s, Miami Beach was in complete decline. The forties and the fifties were the heydays. Then it became passé. It was no longer a tourist attraction. Lincoln Road Mall closed down, because they were battling to save Miami Beach by turning it into a pedestrian mall. The hotels, even the Fontainebleau and the Eden Roc, were in a state of decline. There were still some remnants of the old Miami Beach, but by the late sixties, it was really run-down. With Mariel in the early eighties, it became even worse. The reason is that the cheapest housing was in Miami Beach. There were crack houses south of Fifth Street.

Some of the city fathers had the idea they would turn South Beach into another Venice. They would build canals from the bay to the ocean. My father was battling with them, because they had put a building moratorium in place that meant no construction, no renovation. It lasted for ten years, during which time a lot of people felt their property was going to be condemned, and the city would buy it for the Venice project. So they did nothing, and the property became the cheapest around, a traditional economic ghetto. Meanwhile, you had my grandmother living on Eighth and Jefferson, and she wouldn't leave.

It was a strange mix, and I went to school in the middle of it. The city fathers allowed certain things to happen that were horrific, such as tearing down the Roney Plaza on the beach. It was as beautiful as the Biltmore in Coral Gables. Yet they allowed it to be torn down and replaced with a nondescript building. There was no preservation on the beach.

The integration of schools was the mid-sixties and seventies. From my view, it was a very harmonious integration, although it was a one-way integration—

they never sent any white kids to black schools. It also seemed a hand-selected integration to me. They wanted to make it work. And it did work for a very long time.

Now it seems a good thing that I was in a high school with black kids. I would have preferred a repeat of what happened in Shaker Heights, Ohio, in the forties and fifties, where they actually had families moving into integrated neighborhoods. To an impressionable kid like me who came from a politically involved family and was a bit of a rebel, I was very in tune to what was happening in the world in the sixties and seventies. There was not much of an antiwar movement here, and I wanted to connect with other young people from around the world where things were happening. Nothing was happening in Miami.

Except that in 1972, both the Democratic and Republican Conventions took place in Miami Beach, McGovern and Nixon, "St. George and The Godfather," as Norman Mailer said. It became the stuff of literature when Hunter Thompson wrote *Fear and Loathing on the Campaign Trail.* It was the last gasp of everything that happened before. We were trying to stop Nixon's limo from leaving the Fontainebleau Hotel. Tear gas was being dropped from helicopters. Vietnam veterans against the war were there. In Flamingo Park, the SDS was on one side, Abbie Hoffman on the other. The SCLC with Ralph Abernathy was there, as was a fringe group called the zippies. All they wanted to do was take LSD and all that stuff. People were swimming naked in Flamingo Park. Jane Fonda came through the park. It was a really, really vibrant, interesting period of time. I was a sixteen-year-old kid, very radicalized. I didn't know what I was doing.

The years I went to Miami Beach High, from 1969 to 1972, were very tumultuous.

After Fidel took over, a lot of Cuban refugees came to Miami. In fact, my period of going through school was matched by what was happening in Cuba. What happened was, forces came together in the mid-eighties that changed not only Miami Beach, but Miami itself. *Time* magazine came out with an article: "Miami: Paradise Lost?" Every other year there was a big riot. All of Miami was collapsing.

JOSEPH KRUTEL: No one is better able to give you the backstories because I was there, privy to my father and his friends who were high profile. My godfather was Jack Cooper, one of the partners of the Biscayne Kennel Club, which was across from Joe's Stone Crab. It was a pari-mutuel, a racetrack for greyhounds. Later on it became an ROTC training facility; now it's a development site.

My father came down from Brooklyn in 1944. His father was from someplace in Odessa, Russia; they lived in Flatbush and then moved to Miami Beach, where I was born and raised. I went to Miami Beach High School, as did my father and his sister. My aunt was voted queen of her class when she graduated; my father was voted best looking when he graduated two or three years later.

There was this Sunday morning breakfast "the boys" would have at Wolfie's on Twenty-second and Collins. It was owned by Wolfie Cohen, a big-time restaurateur of the period, and it was a cool place with large photographs of Clark Gable and Humphrey Bogart on the walls. My mom and dad had met there. Kids would hang out there. But the breakfast was for my dad and his buddies. Because of my father, I would be the one child who was always around. I must have been eight, nine years old. Every Sunday morning around nine o'clock they would meet in one of the candy-apple "pleather" back booths. Rosie, a big, fat black lady, was their own private waitress. She wasn't the only black server; the place was race neutral, gender neutral, with men as well as women waiting on tables. But that table was Rosie's and the boys'. The place could be otherwise packed, but no one else could sit there. You'd walk into the restaurant, ask for that table, and you'd be told: "No. Don't even ask."

"What do you mean? Nobody's sitting there."

It was off-limits.

There was always the best breakfast—French toast made with challah, the bread basket filled with coffee crumble, black raisin pumpernickel bread, onion rolls, and their famous mini prune danishes—you know, things Jews are famous for.

My godfather, Jack Cooper, had a house on the water on North Bay Road. That was the boys' clubhouse. You'd see the Cadillacs parked outside—Eldorados, dark colors, black or navy, sometimes white. The property was maybe half an acre, with two tennis courts in the back. Eddie Dibbs, a Jewish kid from Brooklyn, came out to play/practice tennis there all the time. He became a big name and ranked as high as the number five player in the world.

Nobody lived in the house, and no one outside of the boys was allowed at the house. But it was an actual home with bedrooms upstairs, beautifully furnished, art on the walls, major stuff. During the week, maids would come to clean, replenish the refrigerator with fresh food, drinks, candy bars, anything they liked. It was the boys' own country club, because even with all their money and power, they couldn't belong to the country clubs.

When La Gorce almost went broke in the nineties, it was Jewish money that kept that country club going. Nevertheless it was no blacks, no Jews at a point in time in the fifties.

Quite a few judges used to come to the house: Jason Berkman and Bernie Frank, to name a couple. The top, top bookmaker, Hymie Lazar, would be there, along with Alfie Mart. "Hey, I gotta talk to you," Hymie would say to one of the guys, and they'd go off and talk. Meyer Lansky was there, too. Like the others, he'd sit around, smoke his cigar, and play cards. They played cards a lot. Mostly gin rummy and/or bet on games.

But I was the only kid around and was like the adopted son. If you saw the movie *Goodfellas*, you'll remember Henry when he first starts out, he makes the coffee and so on, the kid who always hung around.

I'm talking about the late-1970s. Today, the house is no longer there; they knocked it down and replaced it with a mansion. Now Matt Damon and other stars live on the same North Bay Road. But at the time . . .

My father was Jewish, my mother was Cuban. I lived on Fifty-first Street off Alton Road, very close to Carl Fisher Park. I was born in Mt. Sinai Hospital, raised on Miami Beach, went to Miami Beach High School.

The whole neighborhood was basically Jewish. My mother was from Havana originally, but when Batista came to power, she and the rest of her family fled to New York. They lived on Riverside Drive, but she and her stepsister went to boarding school in Plattsburgh, New York. It was very cold, and she was a warm-weather person.

My father was a plumbing contractor whose company was called Standard Plumbing; he had a fleet of more than fifty trucks that did the work on Miami Beach. The building is still there, only now it's the Armani Exchange. His company did all the work for Ben Novack, the original owner of the Fontainebleau Hotel. It was built by Ben Turchin of Turchin Construction, who built most of the hotels on Miami Beach; he was also one of the guys. The two big things back then were gambling and the track.

Jesse of Joe's Stone Crab was a friend of my father. Joe was the grandfather of JoAnne Weiss. She was married to Irwin Sawitz; their child, Stephen, is now the heir apparent and runs the place with the help of his mom.

We used to go to Joe's and pick up from the back of the restaurant, as did the cops. My godfather would pay for everything. You'd get there in your car, call out your order, and a guy named Calvin, who ran the kitchen with an assistant named Lloyd, would take care of you and the cops.

North Bay Road, homes, Alton Road, and the golf course were on that end of town. Now it has a long, long name, The Miami Beach something. I don't care what the hell they call it. To me it will always be called the Bayshore Golf Course. That's where all the fellas played.

They had big tournaments. Jackie Gleason, who was a friend of my father's, played at Bayshore. All *The Honeymooners* were shot here on Miami Beach; my father would watch the tapings. The way they did it, you'd think it was Brooklyn. But it was Miami Beach. My father was a big-time pool player; Jackie was a very good pool player/hustler.

There was this little Jewish guy—I think his name was Abe Rutschaisky, although he was known as Abe Rich. He had a tiny shop called Star Cues, where he used to make his famous two-piece cue called the Sneaky Pete. My father, my godfather Jack Cooper, all the big pool sharks and hustlers would go there and have their cues custom-made by Abe. Now I look at my cues, and they still are perfect two-piece cues.

As a kid, I saw Abe all the time. I was the kid they took all over, to the shop where the cues were made, to the pool halls, wherever my father went to see his cronies. But I wasn't allowed to go to the racetracks.

Among the restaurants they loved to attend was the Famous, an old Rumanian type of place with skirt steaks, flanken, and chopped liver with schmaltz. There were always seltzer bottles on the table, and my brother and I would always have seltzer fights. The waiters would rush over, see us, and back off in a second.

There was a lot of money around, a fusion of money, a lot of it from Tony Goldman who said, "I need to clean this up and take it back." This was the Riviera; this was where it was. The days of the Fontainebleau, Frank Sinatra and Dean Martin, the Rat Pack. These guys were the biggest of the biggest. I saw them all as a child, although I wasn't old enough to grasp what was going on.

The Fontainebleau was the Fontainebleau. It had the Poodle Lounge. Jerry Lewis would perform there. Lenny Bruce, Alan King, Larry King, who was a big-time gambler. My father was friends with all of them. I met them all. They'd be in town, they'd take a cabana there.

I was like the Eloise of the Fontainebleau; my family always had a cabana at the hotel.

The real hangouts were Wolfie's, the Famous, the Roney Pub owned by Walter Kaplan, who also owned the Embers, which was the epicenter of Miami Beach nightlife. My father was very close with Walter. There was a famous, good-looking Italian maître d', Mario de Lucci. He was always dressed in a tuxedo, knew everyone and what everyone would drink. You'd sit down, boom—there's a whiskey sour. He was THE guy for whoever came to town, whether it was Dino or whoever. If Mario didn't know you, you had no table.

The Embers was a fancy place, speakeasy-type. You had to be dressed to the nines to get in. It was known for the ribs, chicken. It had this big open pit in the front window with embers glowing, on the corner of Collins and Twenty-second Street across the street from Wolfie's. Now it's the Miami Beach Library.

I had always hung out with my father—who was very strong, a big guy physically, had a presence. My father never let me and my brother sleep out. So the first time for me was when I went away to college—Tulane University. When I came back in 1991, things had changed a lot. It was a difficult time for me. I wanted to stand on my own feet. Ultimately, I kind of evolved from under his wing.

He was super tight with Jimmy Hoffa, because of all the construction work and the unions. He was very close to a guy named Cal Kovens, who was a very big developer and a friend of George Steinbrenner. The Yankees used to train in Fort Lauderdale for spring training, and I was a huge Yankees fan. My father used to arrange for me to go to the games, get on the field, you know. At the time, you don't think this is anything special.

My father was a great guy; he was very giving and caring. But he was a typical Jewish street kid from Brooklyn. You know—you hustle; you do what you gotta do. No handouts, no inheritances. My mom was born into an aristocratic world. Her father was a well-educated man who worked for Batista. We had nannies who spoke Spanish. She was a great mother; she took care of the house and my father, all his relatives.

January 17, 2014, was the ninth anniversary of my father's death at the age of sixty-six. By that time, the whole thing of the breakfasts, the house with the tennis courts—some, like Judge Bernie Frank, were very good players—the way you got dressed to go to a game—all of that had died. Now I'm involved in commercial real estate, mostly around Lincoln Road and the Wynwood and Design Center.

I think Miami still has a lot of room to grow. Look at the weather today and what's happening up north. How did it all end? I think that as it became corporate America—that's when it started to end.

What I know growing up here, though, is that it was Jewish; it was always Jewish and it still is Jewish. Italians and Jews are very close; they have the same kind of values, family; there are a lot of similarities.

My childhood best friend went on to become a major Hollywood film director, Brett Ratner (he is also a Cuban Jew born and raised on Miami Beach). I'm also consulting/producing on a new HBO TV series called *Ballers* starring Dwayne "The Rock" Johnson. The costar is Rob Corddry with his character named Joe Krutel.

But I loved the Miami Beach of my day. I was the king here. I lived in Miami Beach like I was Frank Sinatra. There was never a club, never a wait. I guess it was just this aura that my father and his friends had created, a kind of thing that I just inherited without doing anything.

SUE LEVENBERG: I first came to Florida in December 1948 with my fiancé. We stayed in a little cottage on the sand in Hollywood, drove around in a black Buick convertible, and visited Miami Beach, which I thought was dazzling. I had never seen such a glitzy place.

The next year we honeymooned in Miami Beach at the Sherry Frontenac on Sixtieth Street and Collins Avenue. I think it's an assisted-living building now, but back then it was one of THE hotels. The Delano on Seventeenth and Collins was also a honeymoon place built in the Miami-modern style. Both were lively and also very glamorous, more so than anything we'd seen in the Catskills. Most of the people around were honeymooners like us, from New York.

We continued to live in New York for the next eighteen years. It was only when my father-in-law passed away that we moved to Florida. He and my husband had owned a screen-printing on textiles business on Bleecker Street in New York. It closed after he died, and so we came to Florida with three of our four children—

the oldest remained in New York, where she was going to school. It was a major move. I came down with two teenagers and a boy of nine. We bought a franchise from a hot dog emporium called Lum's on Collins and Sixteenth Street. I was about thirty-nine or forty, and this was the first time I had worked.

Unfortunately for us, US 1 was being built around that time. The roads were completely torn up, and business was hurt very badly. So after about a year and a half, we got another business, a famous juice bar called Lee's. It had been on Washington Avenue for many years, but now it had been moved to Collins, right up from Wolfie's. An open store, it had all kinds of juices, piña coladas, hot dogs, and tropical drinks.

At first we lived in South Miami, below Coral Gables, in a ranch house with a pool. Then we moved to Bay Harbor Islands. One night we were having dinner at a local restaurant called Inside with Ralph Daniels, the man who operated the place, and I said to him, "Ralph, this place is my dream. Someday I'd love to own a little restaurant like this."

"It's for sale," he said. "How would you like to buy it?"

"I would love it."

Within two weeks, I owned it.

We bought Inside from Maida Heatter, daughter of the famous news commentator Gabriel Heatter. It was a forty-eight-seat bistro with brick walls on a street lined with lovely, elegant shops, and it served American cuisine with the best hamburgers you could imagine. At the same time, we continued to own the juice bar.

Maida was a very elegant lady and also a famous dessert chef. Although I was a good cook, I had never made the desserts Maida was known for. But she told me, "You'll come to my home, and I'll teach you how to make them."

She taught me how to bake. Among my favorites was a chocolate mousse, very Bavarian. She knew how to arrange things in a very charming yet practical way, and she had a beautiful home.

I didn't change a thing. The staff, the menu: everything stayed the same. During the day, we had hamburgers that were named for dear friends of Maida's. We had lovely waitress service and clients who came from far and wide. My place was at the cashier's desk, where I greeted people.

We ran Inside for ten years, and it was wonderful. At the same time, we kept the juice bar running for a few years, but ultimately we sold it. There was a tremendous

South American trade for it until things got very bad in South America. But by then, we were tired of it and wanted to concentrate on Inside. And we did, with the press, both local and Miami Beach, and with the photographs that I took. It was very popular; everybody knew about it.

During this time, my first husband passed away. A while later, one of my customers said, "I'd like to introduce you to someone."

That someone turned out to be my second husband, who was the sales manager at Harry Hollywood, the Cadillac dealership across the street from Inside. We romanced, we wed, and were married for nearly thirty years until he died.

I had twenty-eight years with one husband and nearly thirty years with another husband. I had the black Buick convertible for my first car, and a red Eldorado convertible for my latest one.

Oh, and yes, I own a sixteen-year-old Jaguar convertible, which will hit fifty thousand miles any minute. An XK8.

DIEGO LOWENSTEIN: The Lowenstein story goes back to the mid-1960s when my grandfather left Argentina and started to invest in South Florida. Originally, he was in the meat business in Germany. Fortunately, he was able to get out before the Holocaust and settle in Argentina.

He was a very capable man and built a very significant business there, but in the mid-sixties, he decided to move on to Florida and diversify. By this time, my father was already involved in business with him. They had some real estate holdings in Argentina, but they were not significant. Times were tough with the military dictatorship, although the family did very well in real estate in spite of that.

But they always loved Florida, had vacationed there many times. And so in the mid-sixties, they decided to move the business to Miami and to diversify.

Early on, they began acquiring properties. In 1966, they purchased the White House Hotel in South Beach. They sold it in 1973. In 1967, they acquired the Copacabana Hotel and sold it in 1970. The following year, our family purchased the 352-room DiLido Beach Hotel, the famed Miami Beach property that had been designed by Morris Lapidus in 1953. Through a $200 million dollar renovation, they completely restored that landmark hotel, turning it into the Ritz-Carlton South Beach in 1997. They strove to maintain the Art Moderne style of the early fifties, so that it would fit in with the Ocean Drive–Collins Avenue historic district.

Diego Lowenstein, a relaxed and smiling CEO of Lionstone Development. Courtesy of Diego Lowenstein. Courtesy of the Ritz-Carlton Hotel

The Ritz-Carlton opened for business New Year's Eve 2003. To me, it is the only real and true luxury hotel property in South Beach, a very special asset. We take great care to hold dear all its special attributes, among them the gorgeous lobby.

And it has stayed true to the original design, speaking to the fact that it is a Morris Lapidus building. It doesn't read big, but it is actually one of the larger South Beach properties: 375 rooms. Along with the Fontainebleau, Eden Roc, Deauville, and Seville, the Ritz-Carlton is one of the hotels that made Miami in the fifties. It is registered and cannot be demolished; our Ritz-Carlton is one of the best performing Ritz-Carltons in the world.

I was born in 1968 and started working in the family business when I was a little boy. I learned the ropes and served my time working on the deep fryer, cleaning kitchens, working behind front desks, in the accounting department.

After graduating from college in 1990, I joined the family business full-time. I lived in Europe and Argentina and then relocated to Miami with my wife and children in 1999. We've done some wonderful things.

We are Latino Jewish. There are a lot of us in the Miami area. That is a connection for us. My big business connection is my closeness with my father. Sometimes it takes two words with him, and we both will understand.

We developed the Epic in Brickell in 2000. In terms of design, financing, site, restaurant, and spa, it is my own brand from scratch. We tore down the Dupont, the building that was there but was not historically designated. It was an eyesore, one that everybody was so happy to see come down. The Epic is one of the most significant transactions we have done in the twenty-first century.

Getting into the real estate business here was a little bit of diversifying out of a country, out of a sector, out of an operating business. That's the way the family saw it, a good way to balance out the family portfolio. Over time, all these hotels were run by the family as individual hotels, unbranded hotels for many, many years through the seventies, through the eighties. My father was very active. We had a team of executives who were active. We primarily focused on Latin America, doing a lot of business with Argentina, Brazil, Colombia, Venezuela, Central America—tourist properties. Together they added up to six hundred rooms. At the same time, they continued to dabble with commercial properties, developing more shopping centers.

View from the Ritz-Carlton. Courtesy of the Ritz-Carlton Hotel

I always say that my grandfather and father were visionaries, because they bought real estate, but even more so, because in the really tough times in Miami, they decided not to sell. A lot of people left the market when it was a disaster, when there was crime, when you couldn't get a tourist to come here.

But they stayed with it, held on to their assets. I think that is the most significant part of our family story. Buying right, buying great real estate was part of it. But holding on was the most important thing.

Real estate is about location. And here, we're all about the water and waterfront. That's key to us. Look at the geography, look at the climate. If we only could figure out how to deal with the hurricanes, this would be total paradise.

LUISITA PACHECO: My ancestors are from Spain. They came to New Mexico where my great-great-great grandfather fell in love with an Indian princess. He married her, and they migrated to Colorado. My great-grandmother lived on a reservation—she was Navajo. On my father's side, my grandfather was Jicarilla Apache. Nine generations of my family are from Colorado.

I was born in Denver. When I was fourteen years old, José Greco's troupe came to town. I told my mother I wanted to audition for his company. She asked how I was going to do that, because I didn't know how to dance Spanish dance. I told her I was going to fake it.

José Greco was kind. He let me audition. Of course, I was terrible. "Well, you are very talented and you are a very beautiful girl, but you have no technique," he said.

He told me I needed to go to Sevilla, and I needed to learn to speak Spanish. I came home and told my mother that, even if I had to swim across the ocean, I was going to go to Sevilla and become a Spanish dancer. My parents did not come from a wealthy background. They sold their life insurance policies, and the following month my mother took me to Spain.

It was 1959. My mother put me in a convent and arranged my lessons in Spanish and dance. I danced every day for hours and learned how to be the best! My castanets had grooves in them—that's how hard I practiced.

No one spoke English, but in four months' time I was speaking Spanish. The Spaniards I met called me la gringa—the American. But I became more Spanish than the Spaniards as I lived in the convent and learned about their foods and customs.

One day, I was practicing in the studio when a gypsy woman came in and said she wanted to read my palm. I told her to go read the other girls' palms because I was in the middle of finishing my dance.

After she had read each one's, she came back to me and said, "Tú eres la última"—"You are the last one." She had to read my palm, she told me, or it would be bad luck. The reading said I was going to cross water and see the world. I asked if I was going to be a famous Spanish dancer. She said I was going to make money and become famous, and a man was going to fall in love with me, marry me, and become a very important part of my life. He was going to become famous, she said. But I was fifteen years old and didn't want to hear about any man. I just wanted to be famous.

After a year, my parents said it was time to come home. Once I got back, I explained to my mother that I needed to go on tour with someone. I had been in Sevilla dancing, and I wanted to continue my career. She agreed, and so starting in New York and for the next twelve years, I traveled around the world living out of a suitcase.

My mother was with me when I was dancing with a Spanish group in Miami, and we went for a boat ride and saw the houses of the movie stars. "You know what? I'm going to live in Miami in one of those big houses," I said to my mother.

That was the first time I came to Miami. The second time was forty-two years ago in August of 1969. That was when I met Ferdie. We went out to a nightclub and talked until four in the morning. It was love at first sight, Ferdie said. But that was not the case for me; I had to be romanced.

The next day at one o'clock he picked me up in a green Cadillac convertible. He liked Cadillacs, he told me. It did make an impression.

He said, "We're going to the movies," and drove me to the theater. *Midnight Cowboy* was playing. "I have office hours now, but you can watch the movie."

After the movie ended, I waited outside the theater for a little while until Ferdie drove up and took me home. It was our very first date.

I was with the troupe back then, heading to Puerto Rico. My parents were there, and Ferdie met them. Then I went back to my apartment in New York. During Christmastime, Ferdie came to New York, and we spent some time together.

On the plane back to Miami, Ferdie picked up a copy of the *New York Post* and saw a picture of me beside a headline that said, "On again off again romance for Shecky Greene—on again."

I had been dating the comic Shecky Greene. He wanted to marry me. After the plane landed in Miami, Ferdie called me up and asked me to marry him. I had known him for about a year; our romance was really a lot of letters. People don't do that nowadays.

We looked at several houses before we picked the one in Bay Point, an area that was developed in the 1950s. We have been living there for forty-two years as of 2014. Both of us wanted a place where we could plant roots. What I said would happen the first time I came to Miami did happen. I got to live in a big house.

As a young married couple we would go to the big hotels such as the Eden Roc, Fontainebleau, and watch Sammy Davis Jr., Frank Sinatra: all the big-time stars. Big shows. Sammy was my favorite. He tap-danced, sang, played the drums. He did everything. He was a real showstopper. You don't see that today.

When I married Ferdie, I told him I was not going to stop dancing. Instead, I started a school of dancing in Miami, where I taught not only flamenco but also classical, regional Spanish dance. Most of my dancers were Cuban. It was the seventies, and we had a real show. A lot of my students from that time have their own schools in the Miami area.

Miami is such an international city with so many cultures and languages. You are living in the United States, but it's like another country.

HAROLD ROSEN: I grew up in Watertown, New York, where there were very few Jews. I was bar mitzvahed in the Knights of Columbus. My mother made ten to fifteen cakes and invited the Yids from all over the area.

My whole family was in junk. But there were a lot of paper mills in the area. When I got out of high school, I could make great paper; I knew nothing else. You know what the weather is like in Watertown. It was always freezing; there are weeks when you can't get out. So I listened to records. I loved *Yiddishkeit*, the music, the language.

I joined the navy the day after I graduated from high school. While I was in college, someone told us that you could get into law school in Miami if you had two years of college. There must have been twenty of us who signed up for it, but only two of us went down to Miami: a big Irishman, Dick Mulgrew, and myself. This was after the war. I would go on the GI Bill all the way through college and law school, buy a house . . . it was the greatest thing.

I came down in 1948, all by myself, and by car—a blue Mercury convertible. I got to Miami in August, and immediately, I knew I would live and die here. The heat was wonderful. I lived on the beach for the first six months of college, and then I moved to the dormitory at the University of Miami. One of the first things I did was get a pick-up truck and begin buying batteries at gas stations. I bought them for fifty cents apiece and sold them for $1.50. I knew the junk business.

In 1950, I got called back to the navy for the Korean War for two years. They wouldn't let me finish school, and I only had six months to go. And this goddamn dean said, "Well, Rosen, if you're stationed near a law school, I'll send you your marks."

I'll never forget that. His name was Rascal. He wouldn't let me finish. I went to Washington. Senator Claude Pepper was there, and he was the greatest. He took me around to the Navy Department.

After I graduated from law school, I became a commissioner. I joined every organization there was, because I knew no one. I joined the Elks. I joined the Junior Chamber of Commerce. I joined the Lions—every club. And I wasn't just a card-carrying member. I used to go to the old people in the hospital so I could make an appearance on the floor of the meeting the next time. I wasn't a great speaker; I was a great schmoozer. And I always made a living, buying and selling.

Early on, I learned there are feral cats around Miami. They were brought in a long time ago to take care of the rats. A lot of people don't like them. They start to own you. In Miami, this vet group gets them, spays them, and brings them back to where they came from. There's this girl, Lynn Bernstein, who takes care of the cats in Miami. But when they have problems, they always call me. They have a big cat committee in Dade County.

I represented the tow-truck companies for twenty-five years. Everybody hates the tow-truck companies. But I got along well with them. All of a sudden we had two companies on the Beach that were very close to each other. I got them the raises that they needed, and I took care of them even after I was mayor.

I became mayor in 1973 after being on the City Commission—which is like the City Council—since 1970. There had been an opening, and a friend of mine, Leonard

Weinstein, put my name in for the job as commissioner. It was unanimous. Did I expect to become the mayor? Never. It was all a mistake. I got lucky.

There were still all these old Jews who lived in the hotels on rent control who used to send me letters that said, "Don't start your car." But once we got rid of rent control, people who owned buildings started to fix them up. This was the late seventies; Miami Beach was coming around.

We closed Lincoln Road under my administration. It was a question of whether we should do it. We had a mayor named Chuck Hall, who was the epitome of a mayor—six foot two, always fashionably dressed; he drove around in a Rolls-Royce convertible.

We had the 1972 convention here. These protesters were marching around, and he was with them. I said, "How can you walk around with the black flag of anarchy above your head?"

Mayor Hall died in office. I was playing cards at the Elks Club on a Saturday morning when his driver called me up. "The mayor is dead," he said.

Under our organization's ordinances, the vice mayor does not automatically become mayor. But I took the votes because I was vice mayor. It was a tie. I became mayor. Fat little Jew with white hair following Chuck Hall. It was unbelievable. But I did a better job.

I was mayor for three years. I loved it. I had a limo, a driver. It was an ego trip. I had always been an enlisted man until now. Now it was, "Yes, sir, Mr. Mayor."

But I had kids in college and was so busy as mayor that my law business went down the drain. I had to make some money. So when my term ended, I got out.

I tried a lot of drug cases. The Cubans weren't bad.

Then came the Haitians.

"How many kids you got?"

"Three."

"How would you like two?"

Another guy calls: "You know, water is deep; cement is cheap."

I got out of that business. These were rough hombres.

PHILIP SMITH: My parents came to Miami from New York, because that was where the work was. That was in 1950. I was born in 1952. My father was a decorator throughout the Caribbean and Florida, worked for Carlos Prío Socarrás, president of Cuba from 1948 until he was deposed by a military coup led by Batista in 1952. My father did his Miami Beach place. A high-society interior decorator, he worked out of a store on Lincoln Road and Jefferson Avenue doing interior design for Walt Disney, Dean Martin, President Paul Magloire of Haiti, among others.

When my father was chosen to decorate the presidential palace of Haiti to coincide with Vice President Nixon's state visit, the job was put on the highest priority by the Haitian government. They needed to do up the public rooms in two to three weeks. They hired an Eastern Airlines plane, removed all the seats, turning it into a cargo plane. Officers from the Haitian military came to my father's office on Lincoln Road to pick up supplies. My mother opened all the windows on the second floor and started throwing bolts of silk and brocade fabric out the window to the waiting officers below. There was no time to walk up and down the stairs. They also put pedal sewing machines on the plane, because they were afraid they wouldn't have enough electricity.

The Nixons come. My father does this incredible job, and they give a state dinner in his honor and tell him because he did such a great job, they want him to stay on and do all the other rooms in the palace.

He says, "No, I have to go back to be with my wife and son." But they won't let him. The Tonton Macoutes show up with machine guns and surround my father. They imprison him until he finishes the entire palace. He tried to escape twice. Finally, after six months of house detention with no communication with my mother, he was freed and given a glass paperweight with a photograph of the president. That was payment for the entire job.

Shortly after this incident, my father found an abandoned pineapple processing plant in what is now the Design District and renovated it to create his next design studio. Just as in Lincoln Road, my father was a visionary in terms of selecting locations for design destinations.

My parents originally lived in Keystone Point, which is off Biscayne around 140th Street. My father's attorney, along with other people, would come at night and have a party at the Keystone Point house. The attorney was a bachelor. His liquor bill was phenomenal; he couldn't get any sleep.

Then my father swapped houses with him, and we ended up in this big house in South Miami west of Coral Gables. It had a Japanese garden. The property was magical, like paradise. Miami was not as built up as it is today. There were fewer people, fewer buildings, fewer cars, fewer roads, and more animals. It was normal to see snakes, rabbits, and birds in the yard, even in the house. We had an unusual house that was open to the elements, so all sorts of wildlife were also part of the house. Sadly, with all the development, many of the animals have disappeared. We rarely used air-conditioning, so all the windows and doors were open to the trade winds. We had ceiling fans. I'm one of the few people in Miami Beach who does not like air-conditioning.

This was 1955, 1956. Flights to Nassau were $15. We would fly down for the day. My parents would buy liquor, duty-free, for their entertaining and carry back the bottles in straw bags. My mother gambled with Meyer Lansky. My father was working with the ex-president of Cuba, Carlos Prío, and Julio Lobo, the sugar baron. They were treated very well.

My father was one of the first people in the Design District. He bought an old pineapple plantation. His office was the processing plant for the pineapples. He opened up a decorating studio there that soon began attracting other people. It was a small clique of decorators and showrooms, still a bit dicey at night. But then he started something called Design Derby, a yearly event at Hialeah Race Track, where decorators would come and take over and create showrooms for their work. It was a big social event.

Living in Miami at that time you felt like you were living in exile, but not because of a dictatorship. You felt you were exiled from American culture. On the national weather screen on TV they didn't have a little dot for Miami. They didn't tell you the weather there, because it didn't matter. It was a forgotten place.

During the summer, they closed the hotels, but in an effort to keep the staff, they paid them $6 a night. We used to move into the hotels for the summer. There was the pool; there was air-conditioning. We stayed at the Carolina, the Deauville. There was no traffic. The stores were closed.

I went to private school until eighth grade, because my mother was so concerned about the quality of the public schools down here. But I wanted to be a regular kid, so from the eighth grade on, I went to public school, and I survived. This was 1966. The school was integrated, but there was a minority of black kids; they stuck together. Then in middle school they started something called the Inter Cultural Council, which I was elected to. I was the only white guy. This was before the Latin population existed in Miami.

One day in 1968, out of the blue, my father discovered he could talk to the dead and heal the sick. This was at a time when there were no CAT scans, MRIs, or heart transplants. If you were really sick with cancer or heart disease, basically you went home to die. These are the people my father healed. He never took money for his work. He considered it a gift.

Here I was, growing up in Miami during the sixties, with a father who was a psychic healer. It was very difficult for him to deal with doctors and hospitals that wanted to put him in jail for healing the patients they left for dead. People would come into his office in the Design District. He'd look at them and say, "You know, you're on the verge of going blind."

They'd say, "What are you talking about?"

As he started healing people, he ended up destroying his business. Instead of going to the doctor, they would go to my father. He would heal them at no charge. Our house became like Lourdes; people would come in the middle of the night.

In the 1920s, when he was in his twenties, he worked for Charlie Chaplin in Hollywood, building sets. He would write down his dreams, and the next day he would see what he had dreamed about. For example, he would see a train wreck in the desert and a fire and children screaming. The next day, he'd wake up and see the headline story in a newspaper was about a train wreck in the Nevada desert where thirteen children were killed.

When he cured anybody, he would have that person write him a letter saying, "This is what the doctor said. This is where I am now. I am free of cancer"—or whatever disease he had been suffering from. Or, "My baby whom I brought to you was deaf. Now he is hearing normally."

My father, somehow, was able to send energy. If someone came in with a bag of medicine, he'd put it on the table, hold a pendulum over it, and figure out what medicine the person really needed. He would take that medicine and put it on a semi-board with magnets and energetically send him the medicine. The person would taste it in his mouth and in that way get the medicine without any side effects.

Here's this kid who just wants to get high, hang out, have fun, and he has to deal with a supernatural father. When I was growing up, *I Dream of Jeannie* and *The Addams Family* were reality shows. I just wanted a normal father who mowed the lawn and fell asleep in front of the TV. Instead, I got this guy who talked to dead people—and in the end, lucky me.

When this thing happened to him, it was like he was becoming an emergency room physician. Today healers have office hours, but when I was a kid, people were knocking on the door at three and four in the morning. It was scary, weird. As a result, day-to-day small interactions got lost in the shuffle.

While he was healing people at no charge, my father was being chased by the authorities, including the police and the FDA. In many ways he was an outlaw—a spiritual outlaw. He was doing work that no one, not even doctors, could do. Back then, there were no MRIs or CAT scans. So when the doctor sent you home with congestive heart failure or liver cancer, that was it. There were no other options. He helped a lot of people who were getting ready to die.

There's a big difference between my father and most of today's healers. A lot of the healing done today is nonspecific, where he would do very specific medical healing. He would diagnose a tumor and get rid of that tumor.

My father and his work existed outside of time. When you go to the doctor and you're given antibiotics, they say it'll take ten days for you to get better. My father's healings weren't governed by our reality, so they were instantaneous. Boom! You were healed. You might take some time to accept this gift, but as far as he was concerned, his work was done.

My father was seen as a Communist, a devil worshipper, and just plain crazy. We easily could have been arrested or institutionalized. So I transformed myself into this very normal-acting person who never aroused suspicion from anyone. I had to do these Academy Award performances just to get through the school day. I still do a lot to blend in and come off as a regular guy.

My father taught me a great deal of what he was doing in the hopes that I would carry on his work. He left documentation behind, because, as he said to me, "I know people will think I'm crazy. I'm not. This is something that happened to me for whatever reason."

Working with people and curing many, my father taped everything—his phone calls, healings, and lectures. He left behind more than five thousand pages of spirit dictation, along with rooms full of various documents.

My work on my memoir about my father, my life in Miami, and so many other things began in 2000. It was written from his documentation and from what I saw. I completed *Walking Through Walls* at the end of 2007, and at first, I was very, very unhappy with the book. It just wasn't clicking. I felt I was not doing my father and mother the justice and honor they deserved.

But, then, the book really came together. So, of course, I gave myself a little pat on the back. It was MY book, right? Because I was the person who sat down and wrote the book, who could possibly take credit for this?

About two weeks before I handed in the manuscript, I came across yet another folder of his papers. I was concerned that it contained something crucial and I'd have to make changes in the book. I thought, *Oh, boy, I hope there is not some earth-shattering material in here that I left out. I don't have time to do any more rewrites; I need to get this in to the publisher.*

I read a few of the messages in the folder. So far so good. I had already covered this material. Then I came across a message to my father from one of the spirits dated 1971 telling him to "organize all his papers and material because Philip is going to write a book on you." That was nearly thirty years before the book was even an idea in my little brain.

A week after I found that message, I discovered a bag of unmarked audiotapes. I picked one, like picking a number out of a hat, and popped it into my car's cassette player. On it, my father is having a psychic reading with an Englishwoman. She says, "Your son is going to write a documentary on your work. Make sure you have everything ready for him."

I thought, *Wow, Mr. Smarty-pants, you thought this was your idea, but you had nothing to do with it.*

I was just the secretary. If I had known ahead of time that this was in the stars, I would have been a lot less anxious about writing the book.

I wanted the book to be airtight. Otherwise, people might say I made up this stuff, and I didn't want to discredit my father's work. I was fanatical about putting only those things in the book that could be validated. Now, when I go back and read his papers, there's a whole other level of profundity that escaped me the first time.

The entire experience, like Miami, has a hold on me. It's a very special place—the light, the breeze, the approach of a rainstorm, the scent of night-blooming jasmine. I hope there will still be a natural Miami left now that we've entered another construction boom. People forget that every apartment that gets built means more water use, more cars on the road, and more emissions. I'm not quite sure how much more this paradise can take. People are incredibly fortunate to live in this paradise. There is no place like it in the world.

JOHN TURCHIN: We lived through the full gamut, saw the three eras from Miami of the 1960s to the end of the century. But my era, the time I came in, was the eighties, when the resurgence started. It was the time of *Miami Vice*. The models came down; the Marielitos were two blocks away. We wore the silk suits, hosted the parties, lived the story of *Scarface*, carried a gun and lots of money. I was personally knowledgeable for what happened from then to what we have today. We created it.

In 1982, along with some partners, I began trying to put it together. It took four years before we finally opened Club Nu, a nightclub on the site of the old Embers restaurant on Twenty-second Street. It was famous for its salad dressing, its ribs and duck. I still have the beautiful crystal chandelier hanging in my house.

But now we were at Club Nu with a twenty-four-hour liquor license—the only one in Miami Beach—and a two-thousand-person legal occupancy. Once a month we'd bring a junket down to South Beach. People from *Interview*, *The Village Voice*, *Taxi*. It was all-expenses-paid for the avant-garde: the boxing crowd, the models, the drug dealers—everybody was here. It was totally wild but a safe place for them to have fun. The police were on the payroll. They made me hire two off-duty officers; we paid them in cash.

We worked with the record companies. We'd get through three or four promotions a night, starting with the five-star restaurant at nine o'clock. They'd be gone by eleven, twelve o'clock. Eleven o'clock the club would expand. The next group would come in from eleven until three, the group after that between three and five, and the next wave at five to six in the morning. Five thousand people would come in in a night from the Keys to Miami Beach.

The record clubs would give us any act they wanted to break in and see how it would work in the dance clubs. We were a disco, had the Bee Gees release albums. But we also had a live stage. Liza Minnelli played in the club. We had Gloria Estefan, Mick Jagger. When any act came into town, we'd feed them, give them a safe place to party. Rod Stewart would fly in, and we'd have a room with twenty-five girls in it for him.

We went through phases. We had the whole reggae movement; the rap stuff; the whole urban movement in the entertainment world.

The whole drug movement had come in from Jamaica and Colombia in the seventies. When I was growing up and going to Miami Beach High School, you could go to the marina, and there'd be these mother ships cruising up the coast. Anybody with a boat could rush up and buy what they wanted, cash and carry. Kids I went to school with did that. They wore Rolex watches; you could tell by the kind of Rolex they were wearing where they were in the smuggling industry. The powerboat racing came from the drug industry. The challenge was who could build the fastest boat to go the farthest with the biggest haul.

John Turchin at work. Courtesy of John Turchin

There was cocaine, Quaaludes in the thousands. The money came into south Florida—all cash. The stories about cocaine cowboys were all true. The amount of cash being infused here was more than anywhere else in the country, and it filtered into the economy. In Club Nu, a drug dealer would come in, spend $10,000, $20,000. We had thirty-five cocktail waitresses, twenty-two bartenders; they walked out with $1,000, $2,000 in tips a night. What did they do? The next day they went to the stores, bought things such as clothes, cars—all cash. The Marielitos were two blocks away, and they robbed and killed. The drug dealers made south Florida.

We were in the club business from 1986 to 1996. Then the city condemned our property. They used eminent domain and put the ballet and the library on our property. We were the only club that ever got bought out by the city. I sold my sound system to Chris Paciello, who had a club named Liquid, and I got out of the business.

It was the late 1990s. The Delano opened. It took Ian Schrager to put the name back on and make a cool hip hotel in Miami Beach for the beautiful people.

When the Beatles came in, we got front row seats at the Deauville, because we were connected. My sister met the Beatles there; she brought Ringo home for dinner and ended up on the cover of *Life* magazine with the Beatles.

We were in another real estate downturn at that point, and my brother said, "Let's open a nightclub." The big mega clubs were not here yet. So we built the major dinner club, a five-star restaurant that seated 150 people. My maître d', Dino Piola, is still there.

I had studied clubs around the country at that time, looking at nightclubs, and I noticed that they would go through a pattern of closing down after a year or so, go out of business, change their name, and open again with the same management. I thought, *instead of going in and out of business every year, let me repeat the place*. And I had a great run of reincarnating the place every six months. I'd buy a great restaurant, resurrect it, change the name, have a grand opening, and they'd all come again.

In the building world we fall into a recession every ten years. The city fathers in the eighties, Mayor Alex Daoud and the others, were part of the renaissance of Miami Beach. The city commissioners, the builders were still around. My father was a councilman. There were payoffs, corruption, no different from today.

The last wave of the eighties was the cheap hotel room. But also it was the time, and the beautiful women came back. People follow beautiful women. Miami has probably the most beautiful women in the world, and they're all here.

ROBERT ZUCKERMAN: My parents divorced when I was an infant and both remarried. So from age four, I had a stepdad. We lived in New York, then Connecticut. Then in 1970, when I was about fifteen, I decided I wanted to visit my biological father, Mathew Michael Zuckerman, who was living in Miami Beach. I knew about him. He had written to me on my thirteenth birthday about my bar mitzvah and the meaning of my Hebrew name.

I was very much into tennis at the time; I was a tennis fanatic. In late 1970, I flew to Miami on Eastern Airlines with two buddies to play in the Orange Bowl Junior Tennis Tournament in Flamingo Park. I had never been to Miami before. My friends and I ended up staying at a place on Ocean Drive. We paid $9 a night for a room in a senior hotel. Today that setup would easily cost about $500 a night. The old bubbies were sitting out in front, rocking on chairs. We were just three young kids in white tennis clothes.

I am six foot four. I can remember walking down below Fifth Street, and this old lady stopped me, looked up at me, and went, "So nice and tall." That became a kind of refrain of my friends, which we still use to this day. We found a place for breakfast, paid $1.25 for a full breakfast that included eggs and grits and potatoes, the whole works.

I had arranged to meet my biological father and his wife in front of the William Penn Hotel on Washington Avenue. I think it was a historic place, but it's not there any longer.

My buddies and I were standing there in our tennis clothes. My father came over to us and shook our hands. He was a big man, six foot six, an urbane orthodox guy; he wore a yarmulke—a skullcap—and tzitzit—fringes—and had big glasses. He was also a practicing dentist in South Beach.

We went to an Italian restaurant and talked over many things. The decision was made for me to come back to Miami the following school year, my junior year. Also, he would get me a tennis coach.

I returned to Miami in 1971 and lived in my father's house at 3456 Prairie Avenue, below Forty-first Street. It was a very quiet area. They used to say you could shoot a cannon up Washington Avenue and no one would hear you. The shul my father attended was just a few blocks from his house. He was a dignitary there, had a lot of respect from the congregants, had been very involved in it since he moved into the neighborhood in the 1950s. I went to shul with him every Saturday and of, course, on the Jewish High Holidays. It was a little bit awkward for me, because I had been raised extremely reform, went to temple maybe once or twice a year.

I was a big teenager who smoked pot. At one point, I had gotten a pot seed and planted it in a Dixie cup in my room. When my father wondered about it, I told him it was a watermelon seed.

My major experience in Miami Beach was being there for that junior year in high school. It is a memory I treasure. On the one hand, there was some bitterness and anger, but there was also the need to make a connection.

I sat in my father's office one day and asked him why he had not contacted me all those years. Because my mother had remarried, he said, he didn't want to cause any additional tension. I later found out the divorce had been very painful for him.

Seeing my dad davening with tefillin, watching him as he prayed every day as he stood by the window, was very moving and memorable. I had not really been exposed to religion until then and decided to delve into it.

I actually started going to what they called Mesivta, which was the all-boys orthodox high school on Alton Road and Nineteenth Street. I was tutored by a rabbi, learned how to read Hebrew, wore tzitzit, put on tefillin every day. I did the whole nine yards.

Interestingly enough, however, there was another kid at Mesivta, Aaron Leventhal, who was not really religious at heart. During lunch break, we would put our yarmulkes in our pockets and sneak off to Burger King on Forty-first Street for cheeseburgers.

My dad liked photography. That probably played some role in my getting into that field. He had an old Nikon that he would take with him on his trips to Israel, Africa, different vacation sites. He especially liked taking pictures of animals. We would sit in his Florida room, he'd take out this old-time projector, and pull down the screen. Then, for the next hour and a half, whoever was there would be subjected to watching hundreds of slides.

I went to Wolfie's, Pumpernick's, Rascal House. Those places were not kosher, but they served Jewish-style food. I would hang out there and also go to the more kosher places. I spent a lot of time at the Fontainebleau pool, where my dad had a cabana.

Our love grew over time, although my father's financial support for me was minimal. He loved Israel, went there four, five times a year. In 1974, he bought me a plane ticket to Israel. Even though I had to make my way alone, I had a great time and stayed there hitchhiking around the center and north for six weeks.

I moved my mother and sister down here in 1997. After my father's wife, Sarah "Cookie" Feder Zuckerman, died in 1998, I became very close to my father, and we spent more time together.

Although I was a resident of Miami, the bulk of my work was as a photographer in the movie industry in Los Angeles, although I would always come back because of my family. In Los Angeles, you see the sun set over the ocean in the west. But in Miami, you see the sun rise over the ocean in the east. There are sunrise weddings on the beach because of the light.

People are taken by Miami's pastel colors and its architecture. And they think about Biscayne Boulevard, downtown Miami, Art Deco. But west of those areas is a vast stretch of land where these incredible old buildings go back to the 1920s. Very often when I have to drive from one corner of Miami to another, which is a great distance, I prefer to take the local streets in order to experience the varied and beautiful architecture, the texture and light of Miami. Sometimes I pull over and photograph the buildings. I try to capture the way they look with the light on them at different times of the day. The light, the water, the different neighborhoods and areas: a paradise for photography.

Since 2003, I've been dealing with a rare, untreatable, and progressive genetic disease. Currently, it has me paraplegic and wheelchair-bound. I've retired from the movie business and live full-time in Miami in order to be by my mother and two sisters, all of whom have health issues. I am a Dean's Distinguished Fellow at FIU (Florida International University) College of Architecture + The Arts, as well as an active community partner with Miami Dade County Public Schools. I love empowering young people and feel this is an honor and duty, to make the world better for those who follow. But in truth, those I teach are also my teachers.

DAVID WALLACK: When I had my care facility, The Eastern Sun at 900 Ocean Drive, and I lived there, I used to swim a mile a day in the ocean. I'd swim out to the boat markers where the boats are not allowed to come inside of, and I'd head to First Street and back. That was my swim. One day I walked out on the beach to go swimming and envisioned a great horse race, sort of like the Miami Grand Prix but with horses. This was in the early 1980s. I envisioned it with bleachers on the west side up the beach from Seventh Street to Twelfth Street and yachts lining the ocean to the east.

I met someone who was into Arabian horses, and he told me about endurance racing, which is a twenty-six-mile horse race dominated by Arabians. This endurance racing is done all over the world. I envisioned it like a car race but with horses on the beach. There were none of the big condos back then at First Street and Ocean Drive. The dog track had been knocked down years before, and it was all cleared and sitting empty. It was a perfect place for all the stables and the trailers. I called it The Arabian Horse Desert Classic. I bought a beautiful Arabian black stallion named Centurion. Next thing you know, we were riding horses on the beach for CNN to promote what we were now planning—the biggest off-track purse horse event in the world. I hired a big special event coordinator, and you might say, we were off to the races. I began advertising it in the international Arabian horse magazine.

We heard that Queen Noor of Jordan was interested in putting her horses in, and it was starting to take on a life in international equestrian circles. Everyone loved it! Remember, Miami Beach was quite quiet in those days.

I brought it before the Miami Beach City Commission. They voted "Yes"! Then to the Dade County Commission and again unanimously, "Yes"! It was going gung ho. But there was this big, big, powerful guy, Alec Courtelis. He was the biggest breeder of Arabian horses in America, and Courtelis was also the most powerful Republican fund-raiser in all of Florida. His political friendships went all the way to the president of the United States.

The hitch was that in order to give away any prize or prize money for winning a race, Florida law deemed it gambling, and we needed a vote of the Florida state cabinet in Tallahassee for a special permit to do so. At that time, the Florida cabinet that would vote on the permit was four Democrats and three Republicans.

We had the Democratic majority votes. The governor of Florida was Martinez, and George Bush Sr. was the president of the United States. Alec Courtelis was the president's largest fund-raiser. He slept in the White House when he visited the president in Washington, D.C.

Courtelis has been working for years on developing Arabian horse racing pari-mutuel on tracks like thoroughbreds, and they were already racing Arabians on tracks in Tampa and Baltimore. His goal was to promote the sale of Arabian racehorses and, as such, create a higher-priced market for them aside from show horses and pleasure-riding Arabians.

And here I am, ready to do the biggest money prize Arabian horse event off the track, and I didn't cut him in on the deal, or get his blessing, which I knew would never be given.

I, along with my partner and the City of Miami Beach lobbyist, went to Tallahassee for the vote. We had delayed the vote until all the political work had been lobbied properly. We were assured of all four Democratic votes, which would give us our permit. The Florida attorney general even visited Ocean Drive to review the plans for the event. And with nothing going on in Miami Beach, they towed his car away on Ocean Drive. Can you believe that? Even back then . . . no mercy! But he was a Democrat and would still support us! So, now, it was ready to vote upon in Tallahassee. And so . . . they voted. The very first person to vote was Democrat Betty Campbell, commissioner of education. Right off, she shocked and rocked everyone in the room . . . none more than me, by voting a total surprise "No." That killed it instantly. Then, all the other Democrats who supported it all the way, looking totally befuddled and not believing what just happened, knew they had lost and so they all then voted "No." I walked out of there into a bar right across the street in total disbelief and had them line up ten kamikazes and threw them down, one by one. I was so drunk that the airline would not allow me to board my flight. I was sick for three days.

Years later, I found out how it happened. Alec Courtelis called in President George Bush, who called Governor Martinez (who later was made the drug czar in Washington), and they made a deal with Betty Campbell to turn her vote. The president of the United States killed the race! As a political science major at the University of Miami, I must say it was a great lesson in what real political power is.

Everyone loves Miami Beach. Courtesy of Frommer Archives

And that was the end of the Arabian Horse Desert Classic. It was going to be three days of great racing and the first mega-event for Miami Beach. But, like a mirage in the Mojave, the Arabian Horse Desert Classic vanished. To this day, some old politicos say to me, "Remember the horses on the beach?" Boy, do I. And, to this day, I have never drunk another kamikaze.

EPILOGUE

GEORGE NEARY: It happened because of the movies. If you want to see a hotel where Fred and Ginger would be staying if they were around right now, go to The National on Collins Avenue in South Beach. The movies popularized the Art Deco theme. Think of *Grand Hotel*, Busby Berkeley—that's where people from all over the world saw Art Deco. From there, they were inspired to take that particular vision into their own cities.

Today, if you want to show that you arrived, what do you do? You have Frank Gehry do a building for you. Michael Tilson Thomas is the artistic director of the New World Symphony, and Frank was his babysitter. They grew up together; Frank did that building to Michael's specifications as a favor. It's not Bilbao, but it is an unusual building designed for Michael's needs for his orchestra.

There are districts like the Upper East Side in New York all over the country. But in Miami, they are unique. You had this group of people determined to save Miami Beach, and that's how it was saved.

SUE BRUSTMAN: The new museum in Miami is the Pérez Art Museum. It is spectacular, interesting in the way Bilbao is; the floors feel like a boardwalk, the trees hang down from above. It has a huge expansive view of the ships coming in on the waterways. It has chairs on the steps. The architect is Herzog & de Meuron, an architectural firm that is one of the most famous in the world.

ROBERTO JUAREZ: The Pérez Museum, my God, it is gorgeous, the setting and the art and the adventure of it all.

DIANE WOOLFE CAMBER: Miami has attracted a lot of adventurers and visionaries. And now it has evolved into a more international destination. When people speak Spanish to me, I always think how I love all of that.

When I was about to move into my house, people told me, "You don't want to live in Miami Beach; it's not the Miami Beach you remember."

But I love my house; my father built it. I love the Beach. I know Miami Beach will have a renaissance.

Boca and Palm Beach are lovely, but there's no *there* there. It's all these wealthy people getting some culture while they enjoy the winter season, but it's very insular. In Miami, you can get it all.

JIM LAWRENCE: Two things helped Miami: an artistic community and movies such as *Miami Vice* that were set here lent it glamour, and made Miami hot. And the Historical Preservation Board. Many great buildings were lost, but others were saved. Now you have to go through a lot to get a building put up.

CLAIRE WARREN: The things you remember:

The eccentric tie guy Silver Dollar Jake in a Cadillac convertible with a parrot sitting on a ledge in back of his car, throwing out silver dollars. He made a living selling silk ties.

Standing on the corner of Lincoln Road and Washington and looking up all the way to Forty-first Street.

Rocky Pomerantz, our mailman, who became a policeman and then police chief. His beat was from Washington to Collins. He married my best friend, Ruth Mason.

Being a bobby-soxer and seeing Frank Sinatra and Sammy Davis Jr. perform at the Eden Roc before they were the Rat Pack. Frank was awesome. Sammy's performances were breathtaking.

JEFF LEHMAN: For the past six, seven years, we're full in the summer. People hit the clubs, watch the celebs, get a feel for the area for half the price. We call the summer "festival season." There's a swimsuit festival, a water sports festival, something every month.

The metropolitan area of Miami is the tail that wags the south Florida dog; in terms of Miami, it's Miami Beach. It used to be a honeymoon destination. Today it's a wedding destination.

Miami Beach is not just the story of immigrants who came from other countries but immigrants who come from other cities. There's the modeling, the acting, the hotels, the clubs, the energy of the city. Any city that attracts young people the way Miami Beach does will grow. There's a mystique to the place. People are curious. They ask, "How does it work?"

MARC SOYKA: Miami is a city that didn't follow the trend of warehouses and lofts and all these things. We have banks from South America. We have ten to fifteen million people visiting us. We have fresh air, because we don't have any industry. It's one of the three, four cities in America that's truly international, where so many different languages are spoken. There are more Latins here from countries all over South America, tourists all over the place.

South Beach is what is called the Upper East Side, because it's as east as Miami gets. Also it has all these different neighborhoods, all with different characters: Coconut Grove, Coral Gables, like in Manhattan. We have a midtown, too, that started just a few years ago. Tony Goldman got in there and changed it all. It's in the process of being the SoHo of Miami.

Brickell is one of the most beautiful and exciting downtowns in America. They're building like crazy and developing. There's room for another eight million people in the city of Miami.

MICHAEL ALLER: I am what I am, a seventy-four-year-old member of the gay community; I have seen the gay life come up in Miami. Years ago, in the fifties and sixties, it was very quiet. Then things started to change: gays felt comfortable here. They could wear a bathing suit. They could hang out on a gay beach. They could do their thing in Miami, which is a place for everyone to live and let live.

PHILIP SMITH: There used to be huge areas of Miami that were considered disposable areas, but everything is valuable now. I'm driving in and see something being built, and I think, *Where did they find that parking lot?* It's Whole Foods.

JOHN TURCHIN: Where it used to be drug money coming into Miami, today it's legitimate. You have people from all over bringing their money here, buying real estate here. Their home governments can't take their money.

Apartment units in downtown Miami are being bought by people from around the world. They're in a safe economy, a safe place. They don't have to appreciate in value. They just have to be there. That's what's fueling our economy.

The Brazilians, the Argentinians, the Venezuelans—they're in force in downtown Miami. We're developing a tower downtown designed by Zaha Hadid, the most famous female architect in the world. We're getting $1,200 a foot and bringing in a whole new class of international architects. The Chinese are coming here. They've become big basketball fans since the Miami Heat started winning.

We're building across from the Miami Heat. Sixty floors, narrow, on the ocean. Miami has world-class architects coming to put their signatures on them. The trend is higher density on smaller land. Build taller, narrow, now. It's all economics.

JOHN NIVEN: I always tell people Miami Beach is the city of tomorrow. The problems that we tackle here in the school system, the entire nation will tackle in the foreseeable future. The problems we see in the health care, the country will soon see. When the drug trade was at its peak here, the country felt its effects later on. That's what makes great cities. Such struggles propel great cities to greater heights. Shanghai, New York: they get their impetus from people wanting to be there.

It doesn't take much to fall in love with Miami Beach. All you have to do is be on one of the causeways and look ahead.

ALAN NIVEN: I'm pretty lucky to have come here. I met my wife here. My mother worked in a garment factory for a Jewish owner. My father was a tailor. They pushed my sister and me to become professionals. I became a doctor; she is a teacher. We have progressed here.

But I think this city has slowed down in that it was not prepared for what has happened. Traffic has gotten out of hand. Highways are hard to drive on. There's been such an influx of people, we aren't prepared to handle it.

DIEGO LOWENSTEIN: We are very optimistic about Miami; we are looking for more opportunities, looking to buy more real estate, more hotels, more commercial spaces. In real estate you buy right: the right location, the right kind of development.

Sometimes a Latin has a different perspective than a homegrown American, because he or she can see the importance of Miami. It's possibly more significant to a Latin than to a New Yorker, because Miami is truly the gateway to Latin America.

RED HELLER: During the crisis, a lot of people put us down. We had too much inventory, they said. But meanwhile, we're number one in the United States from a real estate perspective. Why? Because of the Latins. The Latins are believers in Miami. That's why you'll see Miami grow.

I think in twenty to thirty years, nobody will recognize this city. It plays the same role as Hong Kong plays with China, as Singapore plays with Southeast Asia. It's a gateway; it has so many feeder markets for businessmen as well as vacationgoers. In times of capital flight, people are comfortable investing in Miami where their hard-earned money is protected and can appreciate. I don't think there's a single Latin American country that doesn't have a very strong, direct presence in Miami.

Whether it is trade with family members who live here or who have a large extended family in their countries, there's always something going on. That's why airport traffic is growing the way it has been, why there are so many new housing developments and hotel products.

When any of the Latin American countries are down, Miami benefits, because people want to come here. When their countries are up, Miami benefits, because Americans want to visit them. We are in a great position from that standpoint compared to Los Angeles.

From the seventies through the recessionary times, Miami suffered, because northeasterners would not come down. But over recent years, Latins have discovered it. There's also a strong Europeans presence here. The market has become much more diverse. And that means it's a healthier market, not dependent on one destination. It's also become a market that is not seasonal. Latins are coming at a particular time, Europeans at another, Americans at still another. We've lost the seasonality, and that's great for the hotel business. We have stable occupancy throughout the year.

I think Miami is magical for what it gives you. To be surrounded by water, the ocean and the Intracoastal Waterway, is something people feel good about. The geography is so beautiful; the diversity of people is great. I have friends from all over the world; it's like having a nutrient to be exposed to people from so many different countries. The food has become much, much better. Before, it was okay. Now we have great chefs, world-class restaurants. We have the sports. Finally, we have the culture: the New World Symphony, the performing arts center, the new museum, the new science museum that's opening, Art Basel.

GEORGE NEARY: Basel in Switzerland had been around for more than forty years. When word got out that there was interest in having a second place, a lot of Miami collectors said, "Why not check out Miami Beach?" The hotel is across the street from the convention center, and the setting of the outside is perfect. Basel is a huge success, just another layer of culture and art added onto the fabric of the Miami Beach experience.

SUE BRUSTMAN: Our firm was founded in 1985. It specializes in culinary; we were one of the first of several PR firms in the United States to focus on culinary. People thought I was crazy. "What are you going to say about restaurants?"

I said, "Just wait." I saw it; I just saw it. I'm very good at trendspotting. I saw these owners and chefs were building communities. They were taking the ingredients and putting together beautiful soufflés that would eventually become part and parcel of the identity of communities. Everybody has a story to tell, and in restaurants they tell stories and back causes, welcome interesting people. You can talk about recipes, you can talk about local foods, ingredients. There is so much richness to such conversations as opposed to talking about a building, a hotel, which can be interesting for a year and that's it.

EPILOGUE

MICHAEL ALLER: We have 158 different ethnic and cultural backgrounds in Miami Beach. If you stroll up and down Lincoln Road—there are more than fifty sidewalk cafés—and inhale the aromas of different foods from Cuba, Mexico, Italy, Germany . . . Your taste buds will salivate from all types of restaurants. We have Emeril's Restaurant (Emeril Lagasse) at the Loews Miami Beach, Evolutions with David Bouley, the great chef at the Ritz-Carlton. We have David's Cafe, Cuban cuisine on Meridian . . . whatever tempts you.

SUE BRUSTMAN: What Barbara Capitman and Tony Goldman and so many others did was to keep the pedestrian scope of Miami Beach. In a time when developers have so much money and politicians are so greedy, that is a very hard thing to do. Just imagine if all of a sudden there would be skyscrapers in the middle of South Beach.

Coconut Grove is another pedestrian-sized place. That's what made it so open to the arts. You could walk around: see what was happening across the way, down the block.

It used to be that downtown Miami closed on the weekends. It was dark and not very attractive to the local residents. Now all the hotels have upbeat restaurants. It's so much more exciting.

When you live in Miami, you get very lazy about how far you want to drive. If it's more than five miles from my house, I don't want to go. Wynwood, South Beach, Coconut Grove, Coral Gables are all within a few miles, a twenty-, twenty-five-minute drive.

So many things are happening simultaneously. The Design District wasn't a bad area during business hours, but it was so isolated you wouldn't want to walk down there at night. In the area of Biscayne Boulevard that we used to call hookers' row, there was a lot of prostitution and bookmakers and drug dealers. Now you can walk down to the performing arts center, which we waited decades to get, and you'll see all the restaurants and rentals and condominiums that are brimming with interesting people.

JOHN TURCHIN: My father built the Four Ambassadors when it seemed gambling would be approved. This was in the sixties; they planned to include a casino. The hotel was torn down. Miami doesn't need gambling. We're a world-class city, an international city.

IRA GILLER: It's a time good for us and for Miami as well. It's exciting. We are going through a cycle unlike the one in the seventies when we were resting on our laurels and expecting people to come to Miami Beach when they were going to Vegas and the Caribbean. We are much more proactive as a community in promoting this place as the place to be. It's different today than it was ten years ago. It will be different ten years from now than it is today. But it still has the vibrancy and excitement that draw people from all over the world. The traffic that we see here in January, for example, is tremendous, and yet it's part of the economic engine. Our year-round population used to be thirty, forty thousand. Today it's one hundred thousand.

LISA COLE: The city of Miami is growing much faster than we were prepared for. We wished for and wanted to be a big city. But I don't know what direction Miami is going in. I watched SoBe grow up; I remember when the Cuban refugees lived there. I lived close to Little Havana: watched it grow; saw all the towers and cranes. Now it's a little Manhattan. We have the Miami International Book Fair, the Miami Beach Boat Show. A big festival used to be a couple of thousand people. Now it could be twenty thousand.

The first wave of Cubans arrived when Castro took over in 1959 through the early sixties. They were professionals and business people who came here with virtually nothing. By the time of the Mariel boatlift, we had become Hispanic already. There were many criminals, and Miami Beach was caught off guard. The African American culture was offended when attention was diverted to the Hispanics. There were huge cultural shifts going on. A lot of people from Miami Beach moved north. They wanted more of a suburban feeling.

You know the saying, "Be careful what you wish for."

Miami is changing and growing. From First to Fifth Streets in Miami Beach used to be a gross area. That has changed. You have Ocean Drive, Lincoln Road: beautiful lofts, condos. It used to be a seasonal place, not year-round, a little bit of land for hotels, condos. But you've got the ocean, the bay. You're away from SoBe, but you can come home to quiet and peace. Where we are, the mid-Forties and

Fifties, is spreading to Sixty-third Street, which used to be a pocket of low-income, fading-away buildings, run-down hotels. Now it's a little Argentina, a little Brazil. New neighborhoods. Middle-income people moving in.

Surfside has always been a good place to live. They have a height ordinance so they can't build so high. Then there's Bal Harbour/Bar Harbour. Over the bridge is Sunny Isles—163rd to 190th. It used to be themed kitchy motels. Now it's massive buildings.

CHARLIE CINNAMON: In my heyday, Miami was a colorful, magical, glorious place. There was the club scene in the fifties and sixties—very different from now. But I am still doing my work. I represent all the Broadway shows that come in; I am still full-time working.

Miami has always had a changing face. What you see today will not be the same thing you will see a couple of years from now. It is never the same.

MARTIN JEAN: I always had an interest in architecture, so one of the first things we did when we came here was take a tour of the region with the Miami Design Preservation League. The Art Deco in Miami is tropical Art Deco evoking water themes, lighthouses, buildings with a beacon on a lighthouse.

Miami Beach is an all-historic district now. SoBe encompasses Sixth to Twenty-third Street. South of Fifth is the next area.

I run the seven miles down Ocean Drive every morning, and the buildings seem to smile down on me. What a great way to start the day.

> They say you don't go to Miami Beach because it's heaven. Heaven is where you go to die. You go to Miami Beach because it's paradise.
>
> —Marc Soyka

Acknowledgments

This is our sixth interactive oral history as a husband-and-wife team. And like the others, with a nod to Tennessee Williams, we have relied on the kindness of strangers. Only in this case, they have become friends, giving of their time and memories, photos and contacts, tolerating the repeated calls and follow-up interviews. The result—*It Happened in Miami*—appears just in time for the one hundredth anniversary of Miami Beach.

Every one of the participants through these pages provided us with stories, insights, and perceptions. Some took a special interest in our project: Jo Ann Arnowitz, Deborah Briggs, Marcos Kerbel, George Neary, Dave Rogers, and Philip Smith—you acted as coaches and trailblazers, and we are in your debt.

To the team at Taylor Trade Publishing, a loud shout-out for being there for us throughout the long, sometimes frustrating, but ultimately rewarding adventure that working in oral history always provides.

Special thanks to the gentlemanly and steady man at the top: Rick Rinehart, and to Karie Simpson, Kalen Landow, and Janice Braunstein for being there for us.

Myrna Katz Frommer and Harvey Frommer
Lyme, New Hampshire
January 2015

INDEX

Abbott, Patsy, 113
ACLFs. *See* adult congregate living facilities
Adrienne Arsht Center for the Performing Arts: Fifelski at, xiii, 117–18; Moss on, 119
adult congregate living facilities (ACLFs), 7–8
Albee, Edward, 18, 112
Ali, Muhammad, xvi, 84, 101–11, *103*, *107*
Aller, Michael, xi, 171–72; on Art Deco preservation, 4; during early days, 75–76; on gay community, 23, 217; on Lapidus, 60, 63; on Lincoln Road, 42; on postwar glamour, 51–52; quote by, 60; on restaurants, 221
Alpert, Helen, 113
Anchor Hotel, 73
anti-Semitism, 150–53
Arabian horse racing, 212–14
Armani Exchange, 31, 188
Armstrong, Louis, 174
Arnaz, Desi, 68
Arnowitz, Jo Ann, *145*; Jewish Museum of Florida and, xi, 145, 147–50
art and artists, 34, 77, 127–29; in Coconut Grove, 114–15, 221; Lincoln Road and, 44, 48
Art Basel, ix, 129, 220
Art Deco, 64; buildings, x, 68, 215; Jean and, xiv, 223; preservation of, 3–15, 17, 21, 22; revival of, 137–38; as term, 11
Art Deco District: acclaim of, 20; as historic district, 3; preservation of, xvi; renovation of, xii
Art Deco Preservation League, 3, 12
Art Deco Weekend, 22
Art Moderne, 11, 193
Art Nouveau, 14
Ayers, Georgiana: community activism and, xi; segregation and, 84, 86–89, 93–94

Bacall, Lauren, 125
Baldwin, James, 124

Balfour building, 11
Bal Harbour, 44, 45, 50, 83, 122, 152, 223
Ballers, xv, 191
banana boats, 76
Barry University: Bramson at, xi; Kerbel, M., at, xv; teachers at, xii
Bass, Johanna, 130
Bass, John, 130
Bass Museum: Camber at, xii, 65, 130; Cubina at, xii, 130–31; Lawrence at, xv, 129–30; "Precious Legacy" exhibit at, 130
Baumel, Marvin Rey, 172–76; during early days, 73; at Fontainebleau, 175; Latin music and, xi, 173–75; segregation and, 85
Bay of Pigs, 159, 164
Bayshore Golf Course, 74, 189
BBar Lounge, 140
Beatles, 80, 208
Berle, Milton, 57, 86
Bessie's Bistro, 149
Betsy Hotel, 5, *136*, *140*; Briggs and, xii, 139, 141–44; Cohen, S., at, 4–6; Lehman and, xv, 135–44; Plutzik, J., and, xvi, 139, 141–44; Ponder and, xvi, 139–40
Biltmore Hotel, 130
The Birdcage, 33
Biscayne Kennel Club, 186
black entertainers, 84–86, 93
Blackstone Hotel, 72, 74, 78
Bond, Ward, 78
Bongos, 26
bookmaking, 97–98
Books & Books, 23; Kaplan, H., at, xiv, 183; Kaplan, M., at, xiv, 121–22; in *Miami Herald*, 46
Boom Boom Room, 54, 175
Bramson, Seth H.: at Barry University, xi; segregation and, 81–83
Brayer, Howard, xi
Brazilian Explosion, 26
Brickell Bridge, 76
Briggs, Deborah, xii, 139, 141–44
Broad, Shepard, xii, 75
Brownsville, 86
Brú, Federico, 154
Brustman, Sue, 221; on art, 127–28; on Art Deco Weekend, 22; gay community, 20; on Goldman, T., 23–24; Greater Miami Convention & Visitors Bureau and, 20; on models, 20, 21; on Pérez Art Museum, 215; public relations and, xii, 16–17, 220
Buffman, Zev, 114
Burdine's, 81–82
Bush, George, Sr., 213
businessman, Loomis as, xv
Bussell, Ann Broad: on anti-Semitism, 151–52; Cubans and, 168; during early days, 74–75; on Lansky, 98–99; on smuggling, 97; as teacher, xii

Camber, Diane Woolfe, 216; on anti-Semitism, 150–51; on Art Deco preservation, 4, 10–12; at Bass Museum, xii, 65, 130; on bookmaking, 97; during early days, 67–69, 73; on opera in Coral Gables, 112; segregation and, 88
Cameo theater, 4
Campbell, Betty, 213
Campbell, Naomi, 21
Capitman, Andrew, 17

INDEX

Capitman, Barbara: Art Deco preservation and, 3–4, 8, 10–11, 13–15, 17, 22; movie theaters and, 77
Capitol Theater, 70
Capone, Al, 30
Carey, William, 138
Carlyle Hotel, 33
Carter, Jimmy, 167, 168
Casa Casuarina, 30
Castro, Fidel, x, 161–63, 166–67, 186, 222
Catalina Hotel, 53
celebrities: at Coconut Grove Arts Festival, 115; at Mango's Tropical Café, 26, 40; at Miami Book Fair International, 123–25; at News Café, 32; at the Strand, 17; sunglasses, designer, and, 134. *See also* entertainers; models
Century building, 11
Chaplin, Charlie, 69, 203
Chavez, Cesar, 183
chefs, xii, 23
Chinese people, 218
Cienfuegos, Camilo, 161
Cinnamon, Charlie, 223; on Art Deco preservation, 4; Coconut Grove and, 112–15; on postwar glamour, 49–50; public relations and, xii
Ciro's Supper Club, 174
Clover Club, 85
Club Nu, 206–8
Coconut Grove, 112–15; art and artists in, 114–15, 221; Goldman, T., and, 2; segregation in, 78
Coconut Grove Arts Festival, 115
Coconut Grove Association, 114
Coconut Grove Playhouse, 113–15
Cohen, Sarah, 4–6
Cohen, Wolfie, 187
Cole, Lisa, 222–23; on Ali, 109; Fontainebleau Hotel and, xii, 57, 59, 61–62, 97; public relations and, xii
Colony Hotel, 31
Colony Theater, 48
community activism, Ayers and, xi
Condé Nast, 20
Cookie World, 57
Cooper, Jack, 186–87, 189
Coral Gables: during early days, 67–68, 77; opera in, 112
Coral Gables High School, 78
Coral Gables Museum, xv, 129–30
Coronado Hotel, 151
Courtelis, Alec, 212–13
Courtney, Marlo: on Art Deco preservation, 12; Goldman, T., and, 1–2; Miami Beach Planning Board and, xii; on models, 22; Soyka and, 1–2; at Tony Goldman Properties, xii; Wynwood and, xii, 128–29
CPAs, xiv, xv
Crawford, Joan, 53
Crescent building, 11
The Crew, 100
crime, 59, 96, 169
cruise ships, ix
Cruz, Miguel, 26
Cuban Hebrew Congregation, 153–54, 157, 158
Cubans, 6, 157–70, 186; Jewish community, xv, 152–54, 158, 161–64, 166, 169–70, 173; "Little Havana" and, x; Mariel boatlift

and, 59, 123, 167–70, 222; postwar glamour and, 55; prejudice against, 89
Cubina, Silvia Karman, xii, 130–31
Cunanan, Andrew, 32

D'amico, Antonio, 30
dancing: lessons and contests, 51, 54; Pacheco, L., and, xvi, 196–98
Dandridge, Dorothy, 85
Daniels, Al, 82
Daniels, Ralph, 192
Danis, Susan T., xiii, 118
Daoud, Alex, 21, 208
Davis, Sammy, Jr., 7; during early days, 80; at Fontainebleau Hotel, 7, 52, 55, 85; segregation and, 85
Deauville Hotel, 208; anti-Semitism and, 150; entertainers at, 53, 99; Landsberg and, 99; postwar glamour and, 50, 53, 59
Debicki, Elizabeth, 134
Deitch, Jeffrey, 128
Delano Hotel, 34, 137, 144, 191, 208
Denny's, 56
Dermer, David, 35
Design Derby, 202
Desilets, Deborah, 63
Dessommes, Roberto: on models, 30; News Café and, xiii, 30–33; quote by, 27
Dibbs, Eddie, 187
Dickson, Clarence, *85*, *90*, *92*; Cubans and, 167, 169–70; in *Miami Herald*, 92; police department and, xiii, 89–96; quote by, 81; segregation and, 85, 89–96
di Filippi, Arturo, 116, 118
Diplomat, 49, 50
Disney Sport Attractions, xvii
Dixon, L. Murray, 140
Domege, Eric, xiii, 131–34
Dorsey, Dana, 81
drag queen shows, 33
Dray, Claude, 139
drugs, 59, 83–84, 95–96, 98, 169, 207–8
Dundee, Angelo, 102, 104–6, 108–11
Dundee, Chris, 101–2, 104, 109, 111
Dynamo Art CocoWalk, xiii

early days, 67–80, *68*
Eastern Sun care facility, 6–8, *7*, 10, 212
Easton, Helga, 113
Eden Roc, 34; decline of, 185; entertainers at, 58, 99, 198, 216; gambling at, 97; Landsberg and, 99; Lapidus and, 58; postwar glamour and, 50, 55–56, 58
Ellis, Jimmy, 104
Embers, 99, 190, 206
Emmet, Sully, 104
Empress Hotel, 113–14
Engel, George, 114
Enjoy Apartments, 182
entertainers, 22; black, 84–86, 93; at Deauville Hotel, 53, 99; departure of, 7–8; at Eden Roc, 58, 99, 198, 216; at Fontainebleau Hotel, 51–53, 58, 189–90, 198; in Overtown, 84–86; postwar glamour and, 50
Epic Hotel, ix, 195
Essex House, 11

Fairfax Hotel, 159
Falconer, Kimberly, xiii, 176–78
the Famous, 189, 190
Farmer, Gary, 16–17, 19

INDEX

Federated Department Stores, 82
Field, Irving, x
Fifelski, Alice Arslanian, xiii, 117–18
Fifth Street Gym, 101–11
First Street jetty, 8, 24
Fischer, Carl, 47
FIU. *See* Florida International University
Flamingo Park, 71–72, 74, 161, 182, 186
Fleisher, Moe, 105
Fleur de Lis room, 52
Florida Grand Opera: Danis and, xiii, 118; Moss and, xvi, 115–19, 121; Tebar and, xvii, 119–21
Florida International University (FIU): Kerbel, M., at, xv; Schlazer, B., and, xvii; Wolfsonian Museum and, 14, 127–28; Zuckerman and, xviii, 211
Florida Limited, 73
Fontainebleau Hotel, 34, 37, 144; Baumel at, 175; Cole and, xii, 57, 59, 61–62, 97; Cuban Hebrew Congregation at, 154; decline of, 185; during early days, 79–80; entertainers at, 51–53, 58, 189–90, 198; Lapidus and, 58, 61–65; McSwane at, xv, 53, 57; in *Miami Herald*, 55; Novak, B., and, 54, 56, 58, 61–62, 188; postwar glamour and, 50–59; prostitution at, 98; segregation and, 84–86; Sheldon, L., at, xvii, 54–57, 59, 85; workers' strike at, 183–84
Footlighters, 80, 175
Foster, Jodie, 33
Four Ambassadors, 221–22
Four Seasons, ix
Franc, Roberson de, xiii, 178–79
France, Roy, 137
Freeman, Alden, 30
Gale, Alan, 175
Gale, Jackie, 55
gambling, 97–99, 221–22
Garcia, Lilia, xiii; on Coconut Grove, 115; on Lincoln Road, 44
Gardner, Ava, 55
Garland, Judy, 52, 55–56
gay community, 20–23, 217
Gehry, Frank, 215
Gigi Room, 55
Giller, Ben, 149
Giller, Honey, 79–80
Giller, Ira, *8*, *9*, *52*, 222; on Art Deco preservation, 8–9, 14; during early days, 67, 79–80; Jewish Museum of Florida and, xiii, 145, 147–49; on Lapidus, 60, 62–63, 65; on Lincoln Road, 43; on postwar glamour, 49–50, 58–59; quote by, 145
Giller, Norman, *9*
Gleason, Jackie, 51, *52*, 54, 80, 104, 189
Godfrey, Arthur, 152
Goldberg, Bart, 10
Goldfinger, 53
Goldman, Joey, 128
Goldman, Tony, xii, 34, 128, 167, 189; Art Deco preservation and, 8–9, 12, 21; Brustman on, 23–24; Coconut Grove and, 2; Courtney and, 1–2; quote by, 1; Soyka and, 1–2, 27–28, 217
La Gorce, 151, 188
GQ: Farmer and, 16; Smith, P., and, xvii, 22, 62
graffiti street museum, 128
Grand Hotel, 215
gray money, 98

Greater Miami Convention & Visitors Bureau: Brustman and, 20; Neary and, xvi
Greater Miami Opera, 116, 118
Greco, José, 196
Greene, Shecky, 50, 198
Gross, Harry, 99
Gross, Jack, 99
Grove Playhouse, 69
Gusman Theater, 69

Hadid, Zaha, 218
Hall, Chuck, 200
Hampton House Motel, 86
Harlem Theater, 86
Heatter, Maida, 192
Hebrew Immigrant Aid Society, 151, 164
Helen Mar building, 19
Heller, Irving "Red," 219–20; on Ali, 107–8; Cubans and, 168–69; during early days, 78–79; police department and, xiii–xiv; South Florida Shomrim Society and, xiv
Henderson, June, xiv, 37–41
Herman, Robert, 118
Herzog & de Meuron, 215
Hibiscus Island, 72, 184
Hibiscus Tea Room, 82
Hilton, xii
Historic Preservation Board, 138
Hoberman, Richard, 11
Hoffa, Jimmy, 190
Hoffman, Abbie, 186
Hohauser, Henry, 50, 147
Holocaust, 120, 153, 155, 193
Hotel Leslie, 14
hotels, 4
The Hotel (originally Tiffany), 12
Hotel Victor, 68
Housing and Urban Development (HUD), 11
Humphrey, Hubert, 80
Hunter/CGAF Galleries, xiii
hurricanes, 117, 147
Huxtable, Ada Louise, 65

incorporation, of Miami, 82
Ingram, Robert, 94
Inside restaurant, xv, 192–93
insurance, Rogers and, xvi, 4, 104–5
integration, 82, 185–86
Interview magazine, 17
Israel Discount Bank, xv

James, LeBron, 140
jazz, 85–86, 142
Jean, Martin: Art Deco and, xiv, 223; MDPL and, xiv, 223; on Versace mansion, 30–32
Jessel, George, 75–76, 172
Jessie's Doll House, 180
Jewel Apartments, 182
Jewish community, 145–56; anti-Semitism and, 150–53; Cubans, xv, 152–54, 158, 161–64, 166, 169–70, 173; in hotels, 4; Lansky and, 98–99; New York Jews, x; prejudices against, 78; *St. Louis* and, 154–56, *155*; World War II and, 74–75, 166
Jewish Museum of Florida, 98, *146*, *150*; Arnowitz and, xi, 145, 147–50; Brayer and, xi; Giller, I., and, xiii, 145, 147–49; "Mosaic: Jewish Life in Florida 1763 to the Present" exhibit, 147
Jim Crow, 81

INDEX

Joe's Stone Crab, 8, 18, 23, 37, *146*; Bacall at, 125; history of, 145, 189

Joey's, 128, 129

Johnson, Jack, *11*; on Art Deco preservation, 11–12; on Casa Casuarina, 30; Miami Beach Community Development Corporation and, xiv, 11; Miami Beach Planning Board and, xiv

Juarez, Roberto: as artist, xiv, 179–81; on Lincoln Road, 45, 48; on Pérez Art Museum, 216

Kaplan, Helen, 181–83; at Books & Books, xiv, 183; during early days, 74; on postwar glamour, 51; segregation and, 85; on *St. Louis*, 156; at University of Florida, xiv

Kaplan, Joe, xiv, 183–84

Kaplan, Mitchell, *46*, *122*, *127*, 184–86; at Books & Books, xiv, 121–22; Cubans and, 167–68; on Lincoln Road, 46; Miami Book Fair International and, xiv, 121–27

Kaplan, Walter, 190

Keillor, Garrison, 125

Kenilworth Hotel, 153

Kennedy, Joe, 98

Kennedy, John F., 53, 164

Kerbel, Fanny, xiv, 160–62

Kerbel, Marcos, *160*, *163*; at Barry University, xv; as CPA, xv; as Cuban, 158, 162–66; at FIU, xv; quote by, 157; on *St. Louis*, 154–56

King, Martin Luther, Jr., 88, 95, 142

Kiwanis Club, 60

Klein, Calvin, 22, 30, 32

Kollek, Teddy, 154

Konovitch, Barry, 154, 155

Krause family, 137

Krupa, Gene, 98

Krutel, Joseph, 186–91; on Ali and Fifth Street Gym, 105–6; *Ballers* and, xv, 191; Cubans and, 167; on postwar glamour, 57–58

Ku Klux Klan, 88, 91, 151

labor union lawyer, Kaplan, J., as, xiv, 183–84

Landsberg, Morris, 99

Lansky, Meyer, 98–100, 188, 202

Lapidus, Morris, 193; Aller on, 60, 63; Eden Roc and, 58; Fontainebleau Hotel and, 58, 61–65; Giller, I., on, 60, 62–63, 65; Lincoln Road and, 42–43; *Morris Lapidus: An Architecture of Joy*, 63; Smith, P., on, 60–66

Latin music, *176*; Baumel and, xi, 173–75

Lawrence, Jim, 216; at Bass Museum, xv, 129–30; at Coral Gables Museum, xv, 129–30; during early days, 73–74, 76–77; on postwar glamour, 56–57; quote by, 67; segregation and, 88

Le Corbusier, x

Lee's juice bar, xv, 192

Lehman, Jeff, 216–17; on Art Deco preservation, 14; Betsy Hotel and, xv, 135–44; Miami Beach Visitor and Convention Authority and, xv; at National Hotel, xv, 137–39, 143, 144; Palms Hotel and, xv, 137, 139, 143, 144; on postwar glamour, 51, 59

Levenberg, Sue, xv, 191–93

Lewis, Jerry, 8, 58, 190

Lincoln Road, 42–48

Lincoln Road Arts Center, 44
Lincoln Road Mall, 43, 185
Lionstone Development, xv
Liston, Sonny, 105, 108–9
"Little Havana," x
Loomis, Neil: on Art Deco preservation, 4–6; as businessman, xv
Lowenstein, Diego, xv, *64*, 193–96, *194*, 219
Lucci, Mario de, 190
Lyric Theater, 86

Magloire, Paul, 201
Mailer, Norman, 125, 126, 186
Mandarin Inn, ix
Mandel, Alan, xvi; on anti-Semitism, 151–53; during early days, 76; on Lincoln Road, 43–44
Mango Gang, 23
Mango's Tropical Café, *38*, *39*, *40*; celebrities at, 26, 40; Henderson and, xiv, 37–41; music at, 26, 36, 39–41; Wallack and, xiv, xviii, 24–26, 34–41
Mansion, 77
Mariel boatlift, 59, 123, 167–70, 222
Martin, Charles, 86
Martin, Dean, 7, 50–53, 57, 189
mayors: Daoud as, 21, 208; Dermer as, 35; Hall as, 200; Rosen, H., as, xvii, 199–200
McFadden, Bernarr, 150
McSwane, Floyd Mac, xv, 53, 57
MDPL. *See* Miami Design Preservation League
Merrick, George, 68, 130
Mescheloff, Moses, 147, 149–50
metal scrap drive, 74
Meyer, Hank, 16
Miami Beach: in 1950s, *51*; everyone loves, *214*
Miami Beach Chamber of Commerce, xiv, 14
Miami Beach Community Development Corporation, xiv, 11
Miami Beach Flamingos, 72
Miami Beach High School, 79, 82, 186–88, 207
Miami Beach Planning Board, xii, xiv
Miami Beach Visitor and Convention Authority, xv
Miami Book Fair International, xiv, 121–27, *125*
Miami Children's Courthouse, xiv, 181
Miami City Ballet, 15, 117, 123
Miami Dade College, xvii, 158
Miami-Dade system: teachers in, xii; Warren and, xviii
Miami Department of Parks & Recreation, xvii
Miami Design Preservation League (MDPL), xvi; buildings saved from demolition by, 14; formation of, 3; Hoberman at, 11; Jean and, xiv, 223; work with, 137
Miami Film Festival, 123
Miami Herald, 17; Books & Books in, 46; Dickson in, 92; Fontainebleau Hotel in, 55; Home Section of, 50
Miami International Airport, xiv
Miami Vice, 22, 178, 216
mid-century modern (MiMo), x, 43, 50
Miller, Gene, 166

INDEX

Miller, Maxwell Victor, 68
Miller, Robert, 45
MiMo. *See* mid-century modern
Miracle Theater, 77
mixed use/entertainment (MXE) zoning, 24–25
models, 20–22, 29–30
Modernism, 43, 64
Monroe, Marilyn, 53
Moore Space, xii
Morgan Theater, 86
Morris Lapidus: An Architecture of Joy (Lapidus), 63
"Mosaic: Jewish Life in Florida 1763 to the Present" exhibit, 147
Moss, Justin: on Adrienne Arsht Center for the Performing Arts, 119; Florida Grand Opera and, xvi, 115–19, 121; on Lincoln Road, 44–45
motels, 49
movie theaters, 77
The Museum of the Streets, 24
music: jazz, 85–86, 142; Latin, xi, 173–75, *176*; at Mango's Tropical Café, 26, 36, 39–41; rock, 59
Muss, Steve, 57, 62
MXE (mixed use/entertainment) zoning, 24–25
Myerson, Bess, 149

Nabucco, 120–21
National Hotel, 215; Lehman at, xv, 137–39, 143, 144
National Society of Art Deco, 15
Nation of Islam, 110
Nautilus Hotel, 73
Neary, George T., xvi, 215, 220; on Art Deco preservation, 3, 8, 12, 14–15, 22; during early days, 75; on gay community, 22–23; Greater Miami Convention & Visitors Bureau and, xvi
Netherland Hotel, *13*
News Café, 12, *29*; celebrities at, 32; Dessommes and, xiii, 30–33; opening of, 21; Soyka and, xvii, 28–29, 32, 36–37, 47; Versace and, 31–32
The Newsstand, 122
New World Center concert hall, 48
New World Symphony, 15, 117, 215, 220
New Yorker building, 12
The New Yorker, 46
New York Jews, x
The New York Times, 46
Niven, Alan, xvi, 158–59, 170, 218–19
Niven, John, xvi, 158–59, 170, 218
Niven, Mary, xvi, 44, 89
Nixon, Richard, 186, 201
Norimar, Erica, 26
North Beach Elementary, 151
Novak, Ben, 54, 56, 58, 61–62, 188
Novak, Charles, 61

O'Brien, Margaret Griffis, xiii; Cubans and, 159; during early days, 75, 77
Ocean Drive, 27–33
Ocean Drive Association, xii, 24, 34–35
Ocean Drive Improvement Association, 35
Ocean Force Adventures, xiii, 177–78
Ollie's, 104–5
Onassis, Jackie Kennedy, 134

O'Neill, Terry, 58
opera, 112. *See also* Florida Grand Opera; Greater Miami Opera
Orange Bowl Parade, 55
Ostwind (yacht), 155
Overtown, 81, 93, 95; entertainers in, 84–86

PACE program, 141, 142
Pacheco, Ferdie: Ali and, xvi, 101–4, *103*, 106–11, *107*; quote by, 101; segregation and, 83–84, 86
Pacheco, Luisita, 196–98; on Ali and Fifth Street Gym, 101–2, 105–6, 110–11; as dancer, xvi, 196–98; segregation and, 84
Pacheco Gallery, xvi
Padrón, Eduardo, 122, *127*
The Palace, 33
Palm Beach Symphony, xvii, 120
Palms Hotel, xv, 137, 139, 143, 144
Pan American Airways, 67, 164, *165*
Pan American Hotel, 174
Park Central Hotel, 12, 27, 182
Parkway Theater, 69
Parra, Miguel, 39
Pathé's "March of Time," 152
Pavarotti, Luciano, *116*, 118
Pedro Pan Operation, 166
Perez, Tony, 157
Pérez Art Museum, xvii, 215–16
PG Family Foundation, xii
photographer, Zuckerman as, xviii, 100, 210–11
Pierce, Edward, 55
Piola, Dino, 208
Plutzik, Hyam, 141
Plutzik, Jonathan, xvi, 139, 141–44
Plutzik Reading Series, 141
police department: Dickson and, xiii, 89–96; four-car convoys, 8; Heller and, xiii–xiv; "river cops," 169–70; segregation and, 88–96
political conventions, 53, 186, 200
Ponder, Ed, xvi, 139–40
Poodle Lounge, 58, 190
Port of Miami, ix
postwar glamour, 49–59
"Precious Legacy" exhibit, 130
Presley, Elvis, 53, 55
Princess Anne Hotel, 173
project houses, 75
prostitution, 59, 93, 98, 221
public relations: Brustman and, xii, 16–17, 220; Cinnamon and, xii; Cole and, xii
Pulitzer, Lilly, 19

Rat Pack, 57, 59, 80, 189
Reader's Digest, 99
Renaissance Hotel, 6
Resnick, Abe, 12
restaurants, xii, 9, 220–21
restaurateur: Levenberg as, xv, 192–93; Soyka as, xvii
Revere Hotel, 31
Reynolds, Debbie, 55–56
Ribicoff, Abraham, 166
Rice, Anne, 124
Richard Department Store, 88
riots, 88, 93
Ritz-Carlton, 138, 144, 193–94, *195*
"river cops," 169–70

rock music, 59
Rodriguez, Douglas, 23
Rogers, Dave: on Ali and Fifth Street Gym, 101–2, 104–5, 111; on Art Deco preservation, 4; during early days, 71; insurance and, xvi, 4, 104–5; on postwar glamour, 53–54; segregation and, 86
Romney Hotel, 171
La Ronde Room, 52–55, 59, 61
Roney Plaza, 10, 173, 185
Roney Pub, 190
Roosevelt, Eleanor, 154
Roosevelt, Franklin D., *70*, 154, 156
Rosen, Bernie: on Ali and Fifth Street Gym, 101–2, 104, 108–10; during early days, 69–71; WTVJ and, xvi–xvii, 70–71
Rosen, Harold, 198–200; on Art Deco preservation, 4, 13; on Lansky, 99; as mayor, xvii, 199–200; quote by, 3
Roth, Christian, xiii, xvii, 131–34
Royal Palms Hotel, 76
Rozencwaig, Dow, 153–54
rumba, x, 174
Ruth, Babe, 72

Sagamore Hotel, 138, 161
S and G Syndicate, 98
Sans Souci, 51, 98
Savitz, Lenny, 53
Saxony, 98
Schlazer, Al: Cubans and, 157–58; Disney Sport Attractions and, xvii; at Miami Dade College, xvii, 158
Schlazer, Basha: on anti-Semitism, 152; during early days, 71–73, 78; FIU and, xvii; at Miami Department of Parks & Recreation, xvii; segregation and, 84
Schrager, Ian, 144, 208
Schulberg, Budd, 106–7
Sea Gull, 181
Segafredo, 47
segregation, 78, 81–96
Seville Hotel, 53, 54, 175
Shavers, Ernie, 110
Sheldon, Bert, 54
Sheldon, Laney: at Fontainebleau Hotel, xvii, 54–57, 59, 85; on postwar glamour, 53–57, 59; quote by, 49
Shore Club Hotel, 34
Silver Dollar Jake, 216
Sinatra, Frank, 85; during early days, 80; at Fontainebleau, 7, 51–55, 57–58, 189, 198
Singer, Isaac, 123, 126
skyscrapers, ix
Smith, Esther, 50
Smith, Frances, 180
Smith, Lew, 50
Smith, Philip, *18*, 200–206, 218; on anti-Semitism, 152; as artist, xvii, 17–18; Coconut Grove and, 112; Cubans and, 159; *GQ* and, xvii, 22, 62; on Lapidus, 60–66; on Lincoln Road, 42–48; on postwar glamour, 50; quotes by, 42, 112; the Strand and, 17–19; *Walking Through Walls*, xvii, 204
smuggling, 97, 207
South Beach: development of, xii; national acclaim of, 20; population of, 17; renovation of, 6, 23–24, 136; revival of, x, 18

South Beach Elementary School, 75
South Florida Arts Center, 44
South Florida Shomrim Society, xiv
Soyka, Marc, *28*, 217; Courtney and, 1–2; Goldman, T., and, 1–2, 27–28, 217; on Lincoln Road, 47–48; on models, 29; News Café and, xvii, 28–29, 32, 36–37, 47; quote by, 223; as restaurateur, xvii
Soyka Restaurant, xvii
Spacey, Kevin, 33
Spanish language, x, 89, 173
Sterling Building, 46
Stiltsville, 177–78
St. Louis (ship), 154–56, *155*
Stone, Oliver, 167
the Strand, 17–19, 23
Straus, Roger, 126
Street Art Show, 114
Sullivan, Ed, 51
sunglasses, designer, *132*; celebrities and, 134; Domege and, xiii, 131–34; Roth and, xiii, xvii, 131–34
Sunny Isles, 49, 71, 100, 154, 223
surf shops, 8
Surfside, 223
Surrey Hotel, 54
Sutherland, Joan, *116*, 118

teachers, xii
Tebar, Ramón, xvii, 119–21
Tenth Street Auditorium, 4
Theodore, 46
Thomas, Danny, 55
Thomas, Michael Tilson, 215
Thompson, Hunter S., 124–25, 186
Thunderbird, 49, 175
Time magazine, 123, 186
Tony Goldman Properties, xii
Tony Rome, 55
tourism, xi, xvi
tropical modernism, 43
Tropics Hotel, 105
Tucker, Sophie, 171–72
Turchin, John, xvii, *13*, *45*, 188, 206–9, *207*; on Art Deco preservation, 13–14; on Four Ambassadors, 221–22; on Lansky, 99; on Lincoln Road, 45–46
twilight, *19*

"Unexpected Opera in Unexpected Places" series, 119
University of Florida, xiv
University of Miami, 69, 75, 130, 199
Upstairs at Greene Street, 2
USO, 53, 73, 74, 75

Van Dyke building, 43, 47–48
Vanity Fair, 20
vaudeville shows, 4, 77
Versace, Gianni, 30–32, 40
Versace mansion, 19, 30–32
Viceroy Icon complex, ix
Viceroy Tower, xiii
Vidal, Gore, 125–26
Village Tavern, 68
Les Violins, 162

Walking Through Walls (Smith, P.), xvii, 204
Wallack, David, *6*, 212–14; on Art Deco preservation, 6–8, 10; during early days,

72; Eastern Sun care facility and, 6–8, *7*, 10, 212; Mango's Tropical Café and, xiv, xviii, 24–26, 34–41; on models and gay community, 21; quote by, 16
Walsh, Bryan, 166
Warhol, Andy, 132
Warren, Claire, 216; during early days, 73, 75; on gambling, 97–98; Miami-Dade system and, xviii; quote by, 97
Washington Avenue, *20*
Wayne, John, 78
Weber, Bruce, 22
Weiss, Jenny, 145
Weiss, Joe, 145
Wet Paint Café, 23
White Milk Dairy, 87
Wild Things, 26
Williams, Esther, 174
Williams, Robin, 33
Williams, Tennessee, 112–13
Wilson, Joseph, 141
Winchell, Walter, 174
Winfrey, Oprah, 124
Wolfie's, 99, 104, 161, 182, 187, 190
Wolfson, Mickey, 14
Wolfsonian Museum, 14, 127–28
Women's Wear Daily, 132
World War II, 73–75, 130, 166
Wright, Frank Lloyd, 63
WTVJ, xvi–xvii, 70–71
Wynwood: Courtney and, xii, 128–29; revival of, 12, 24, 128
Wynwood Kitchen and Bar, 129
Wynwood Walls, 128, 129

Yevtushenko, Yevgeny, 124

Zerivitz, Marcia Jo, 147–48
Ziff Ballet Opera House, 119
Zuckerman, Robert, *100*, 209–11; FIU and, xviii, 211; as photographer, xviii, 100, 210–11

About the Authors

Myrna Katz Frommer and **Harvey Frommer** are a wife-and-husband team who successfully bridge the worlds of popular culture and traditional scholarship. Celebrated oral and cultural historians, this is their sixth full-fledged oral history. The Frommers are also professors in the Master of Arts in Liberal Studies program at Dartmouth College as well as prolific travel writers.

Their articles on national and international destinations and Jewish communities around the world have appeared in myriad outlets including *The New York Times*, *Newsday*, *New York Daily News*, *Los Angeles Times*, *Haaretz*, *The Forward*, *Golf Digest*, *International Herald Tribune*, *USA Today*, and *The Washington Post*.

The Frommers are currently working on another oral history—*It Happened in Israel*. Harvey Frommer is also a noted sports journalist. The author of forty-two books on sports, his latest is *When It Was Just a Game: Remembering the First Super Bowl*.